1978

Emotionally Disturbed and Deviant Children

New Views and Approaches

WILLIAM C. RHODES
University of Michigan

JAMES L. PAUL
*University of North Carolina
at Chapel Hill*

Prentice-Hall Inc., Englewood Cliffs, New Jersey 07632

Library of Congress Cataloging in Publication Data

RHODES, WILLIAM C (date)
    Emotionally disturbed and deviant children.

    (Prentice-Hall series in special education)
    Includes bibliographies and index.
    1. Mentally ill children.   2. Deviant behavior.
    I. Paul, James L., joint author.   II. Title.
RJ499.R45   362.7'82   77-17630
ISBN 0-13-274662-X

Prentice-Hall Series in Special Education
William M. Cruickshank, Editor

Printed in the United States of America
10   9   8   7   6   5   4   3   2   1

PRENTICE-HALL INTERNATIONAL, INC., *London*
PRENTICE-HALL OF AUSTRALIA PTY. LIMITED, *Sydney*
PRENTICE-HALL OF CANADA, LTD., *Toronto*
PRENTICE-HALL OF INDIA PRIVATE LIMITED, *New Delhi*
PRENTICE-HALL OF JAPAN, INC., *Tokyo*
PRENTICE-HALL OF SOUTHEAST ASIA PTE. LTD., *Singapore*
WHITEHALL BOOKS LIMITED, *Wellington, New Zealand*

Contents

iii

Preface

A few short years ago, perhaps less than a decade, the term "emotional disturbance" seemed to communicate a very clear and specific human condition. There were some details lacking in our understanding, but those were merely a matter for further investigation. We would soon fill in the missing pieces, and the whole area would be tied up very neatly.

Like many areas of knowledge, that clarity has disappeared in the last few years. There has been an explosion of ideas, viewpoints, and nuances. What used to be a special province of a limited number of professionals and disciplines is the property not only of innumerable disciplines, but has now become an area of public forum and public debate. Alongside the older, simplistic public image of "going crazy" are very sophisticated notions such as "behavior disorder," "deviance," and "developmental disability." Popular magazines carry articles on "the mental illness myth," "primal therapy," "behavior modification," "megavitamin therapy," and so on.

It seemed important, therefore, to try to bring together, in an organized fashion, some of the more current systematic views of the area whose broader implications now seem more fully communicated in the sociological concept of "deviance."

It is the predication of the authors that the area of public concern transmitted through the concepts "emotional disturbance" and "deviance" will grow and increase in public centrality. The inward-turning of the 1970s seems to have moved the nation into exploration of the territory of human states and human conditions of equal relevance with outer space exploration.

The "scientific" explanations of the condition, the methods of approach to the condition, and the systems of services for the condition, will become even more politicized than they now are. Those who make any claim to knowledge or authority in this area, or whom the public sees as having any responsibility in the area, will have to be very sophisticated about the issues and know very clearly in their own minds where they stand and what they believe.

It is for this group that the following views and approaches have been assembled and presented. It is hoped that the material that follows will be useful for that purpose.

A Special Note to Our Readers

We regret that our language has no neuter pronoun. We have used "his" frequently in this book. To have used "his or her" in every case would have created an awkward style. An attempt has been made by the various authors and the copyeditor to reduce the number of "he's" following "the student," "the teacher," "the individual," and "man." We have not been completely successful in arriving at a unisex style. We hope that this does not detract from the content.

PART ONE

Introduction

CHAPTER ONE

Education of Emotionally Disturbed and Deviant Children:

EMERGING PERSPECTIVES

Education is gradually embracing the concept of the wholeness of persons. Current attention to the rights of learners is providing balance and perspective to the concern for knowledge about education that predominated during the sixties. In the past decade rigorous application of analytic concepts, increased support for educational research, and productive alliances between the fields of education and psychology, resulted in a primary focus upon the substantive knowledge base of education.

Ten years ago, rights and individual liberties, especially those having to do with freedom lost or compromised by institutional oppression, demeanment, or denial of resources, were being proclaimed in the streets. Today these issues have been moved into the judicial system. The rights to education, to due process, to least restrictive alternatives, to privacy, and to treatment are notable examples of the major litigation that is reforming the legal foundations of the education and treatment of the handicapped. The judicial system, a new meeting ground for consumers and providers of services, is hardening the basis for accountability. Action for the handicapped in the seventies has included significant litigation, new laws, consumer advocacy, public education, and an expanded public awareness and sensitivity to the problems of the handicapped. Improved standards for institutions and community facilities are being enforced; additional resources are being developed, new knowledge is being generated and utilized by service providers, and community alternatives are being developed.

The sixties began to focus attention on more personal exercise of rights and on the self-validating authority of individual experience. The drug and hippie movements, for example, focused on decontrolling the boundaries of perception, awareness, and total experience. This aspect of the counter-establishment movement was more concerned with being, with freedom, with the affective domain, and with personal encounter than with organizational and social structures, information, or academic instruction. This rebellious spirit of the sixties is now finding institutional expression and new metaphors such as mainstreaming.

Both the methodological and philosophical aspects of education have been affected by changing tides of perception of the mission of the educational mainstream. Concerns of the traditional and counter-traditional perspectives have in some instances been brought together, providing a balancing perspective for each. Examples include the development of public educational alternatives and the concern with the goals and methods of behavioral control. The goals of the educational process are beginning to consider the experience of the learner, particularly the affective domain of that experience, and provide opportunity to integrate mental and physical activity as well as to develop specific skills. There are several manifestations of the personal experience theme—for example, humanistic education, values clarification, affective education, and educational variants of Gestalt psychology.

There has been an inclination to polarize and identify with either a scientific or humanistic approach and to view them as mutually exclusive. There are several *apparent* dichotomies such as affective-cognitive and humanistic-behavioral. That there are major differences in assumptions and in point of view there can be no doubt. Both general orientations, however, represent something essential to education. One approach relates to the science of the educational process and the molecular dimension of learning. The other relates to the goals of education and the *human* nature of learners.

No single view represents a summative truth of education. A conciliation of the viewpoints must involve a deepening understanding of ourselves and our science of education. Caricaturing various positions cannot replace a rigorous pursuit of a more credible philosophy of education which leads us toward a human science of education.

The tension between the scientific and the humanistic perspectives has had some utility. It has helped identify what now comprise major themes and issues in education and major problems in schooling against which demands for change have been leveled. These themes include, for example, the human and legal rights of students, the problems of labeling, the stigma of segregated educational settings, and the cultural bias of much of the educational data base for decision making.

There is a concurrent reconsideration of the phenomenon of deviance and institutionalized responses to children who are different. Social reform, which in earlier times freed the handicapped from jails and chains, is now freeing them from institutional exile. The handicapped are coming back into sight as well as into mind. They are claiming and securing social space in neighborhoods and occupational space in the productive work force. Better understanding and appreciation of needs for privacy, individuality of experience, personal aspirations, and the capacity for caring and despair are replacing images of the spiritually maimed half-person. The right of the handicapped to life lived freely is also being established in the codes, regulations, and budgets of human service systems. As evidenced by the Education of All Handicapped Children Act (PL 94-142), passed in November, 1975, the educational system is being profoundly affected by these changing social values.

Much of the concern for accountability in the education of handicapped children has appropriately been addressed to special education. To understand the theories, practices, and professional issues involved in educating these children, it is necessary to consider the professional, technical, and philosophical context provided by special education. Relevant characteristics of special education briefly discussed here are: the role of social values, the knowledge base, and the bureaucracy of special education.

There are many different views of special education. It is a body of knowledge, a set of procedures, a philosophy of education, a service system for handicapped children, and an alternative to regular education programs. Some view it as the only source of a free public education for the handicapped. From this perspective it is seen as the major hope for an education for socially, intellectually, emotionally, and physically vulnerable children who cannot profit from the usual educational curriculum or successfully adapt to the typical classroom environment. In the view of others and in demonstrable fact in some instances, special education has become a manifestation of inequity in education. It has often served as a repository for the cumulative mistakes of the educational system and the collective failures of educators and educational science. From this perspective it becomes the primary instrument of an educational bureaucracy for maintaining power in the middle class to rule over the poor and ethnic minorities.

In this sense special education has become a focal point of cultural conflict, mediating between the institutional and segregation-oriented view of deviance and disability on the one hand and the individual rights of learners and of persons on the other.

There is no single agreed-upon boundary within which to frame a definition of special education. There is also no single standard against which to assess its efficacy. It has many different meanings, each with some basis in perceived or empirical fact. Whether it is viewed in philosophical, organizational, bureaucratic, or programmatic terms, special education cannot extricate itself from prevailing social norms. No matter how extensive the knowledge base or how systematic the procedures by which that knowledge was formulated, special education is a manifestation of what society honors and an instrument for social policy relative to handicapped children and youth.

Special education is organized to serve the handicapped. The definition of a handicap, however, and the system of expectations in which an inability or a disability is a disadvantage and, thus, a handicap must include the concept of social values. How a person (or a difference) is regarded is a matter of social rules and preferences. The apparent decision to provide a free public education for all children is a matter of social policy having to do with the politico-legal balance of rights and privileges.

As has been indicated, traditional concepts, values, and practices are being challenged and important changes are occurring. Special classes, once considered an educational haven for handicapped children, are now seen as hazardous to psychoeducational and social development for some handicapped children. Labels for handicapped children were once thought useful in making decisions about placement and programming. Now labels are viewed as further handicapping children as a result of the negative social stigma and undesirable self-fulfilling prophesy they engender. Many consider clinical labels useless in educational planning. Educational decisions were once made solely by educators— assisted, when needed, by allied professionals who understood the ways children learn and the developmental needs of children. Now parents are involved in policy decisions governing programs. Educational wisdom, at one time considered to be the best guide to educational placement, must now attend to due process procedures designed to protect the rights of the child. Institutions, no longer seen as places of sanctuary for the handicapped who would be otherwise exploited in the community, are viewed by many as undesirable residences that deny to the socially and psychologically disenfranchised the right to live in their own communities. Education was formerly viewed more as a professional, technical, and humanistic matter than a legal one. Now issues such as the bias of testing and placement are ending up in court. Education is no longer for only the "educable" child; all children have a right to an education. The view was generally accepted that schools were good educative places which consistently considered the best interests of children. Now many children are seen as victims of institutional arrangements and practices that work against their interests.

Special education, then, whatever its specific meaning, manifests a system of values implemented and maintained by a complex set of decisions. Some decisions are socially conscious and legally based; others are only implied and subtle, but not necessarily less significant or less powerful. The philosophy, the goals, the methods and procedures, the organization, the population served, and virtually all decisions will ultimately be examined within this context of social values.

In addition to its social instrumental functions, special education is also an activity with a more or less definitive knowledge base. What we know, how well (by canons of science) we know it, and how accurately we apply that knowledge is a source of difficulty. There are very basic philosophy of science questions, especially epistemological, involved in understanding the knowledge base and the claims to knowledge.

There are "bodies of knowledge," with varying degrees of empirical support, that relate to special education; child development and behavior management are examples. These different areas are not fully, critically, or evenly applied in the understanding or practice of special education. One reason for this situation is that a unifying philosophy of education that adequately provides even a descriptive or heuristic framework within which an integration could be accomplished has not been articulated, or at least not accepted. A philosophy of special education, while embracing important concerns unique to the population it seeks to serve, must be anchored in a broader philosophical context of education.

Part of the knowledge problem relates to the status of theory. In developing at least a quasi science of special education, theory, as it relates to organizing explanations of population differences, brings with it its own set of problems. Several theories of variance, for example, each with its own data and its own following of "believing scientists," claim special authority. Both the scientific problems of theory and the political problems of control and authority in explaining behavioral variance are mammoth. The ethical questions of what is right and the social questions of what is proper are in this context frequently submerged in questions of what is empirically defensible.

In addition to the problems of value and knowledge, a major source of difficulty for special education has to do with its organizational and bureaucratic nature as a service delivery system. The form of bureaucracy in which it is couched frequently results in a loss, or at a minimum a compromise, of client-directed accountability. The bureaucratization of special education is a process with many negative byproducts such as labeling and institutionalization.

Special education has the enormous potential for providing services for handicapped children who would otherwise be denied services. It also has equal potential for depriving the handicapped child of educational opportunities and, further, of directly contributing to his handicap.

Apathy toward the constructive potential missions of special education and placid acceptance of its negative potentials will directly contribute to creation of a damaging system for children. There are many complex aspects of the destructive potential, which now has a deep history. The destructive potential cannot be totally harnassed and controlled by law. Solutions on one front alone will not be adequate. Quick solutions will not turn around problems so long in the making.

There are several major ingredients to effective change of the current situation. One must be the full commitment of all involved to the task. Mediocrity in special education is the culture in which institutional and professional malpractice have grown and flourished. Another ingredient for positive change is trained and retrained professionals who incorporate into their thinking and professional style a more complete understanding of the dynamics and change of educational systems and instructional technologies. Advocates for change must find a means of surviving in the educational system while maintaining a personal perspective on children and their interests.

Technical and professional competencies must be considered in specifying the necessary portfolio of an effective special educator who will make a difference in the kinds of services children receive. Additionally, who the professional is and the commitment and values brought to the task must also be examined. Neither technical competency nor personal commitment is alone sufficient to work effectively on the renewal and reform of educational systems.

The education of emotionally disturbed children, as a professional area, is now recognized as part of the field of special education. This field has, however, had a very short history of assuming professional responsibility for children identified as emotionally disturbed. The Council for Children with Behavior Disorders, for example, was formed in 1962. In 1970, only 21.5 percent of the states had special education programs for these children. In 1961, when the National Institute of Mental Health funded several experimental programs, the idea that teachers could teach emotionally disturbed children was considered somewhat radical. It was not until November, 1975, with the passage of the Education for All Handicapped Children Act (PL 94–142), that all children, including the emotionally disturbed, were included in the legal mandate as well as the professional purview of educators.

In this short history, the conceptual and knowledge base for understanding emotional disturbance has not always been sufficient to provide guidance in developing educational policies and programs. Special educators have had to provide service based on the best understanding they could obtain. Emotional disturbance is one of the most complex problems to understand and treat in the growth and development of children, and the phenomenon can be described or explained from various perspectives.

Some educational services have been developed primarily on the basis of one understanding of the problem, excluding other perspectives. Other services have incorporated different points of view into a more eclectic understanding of the problem. Professional training programs in special education reflect these different single perspective or eclectic orientations to disturbance.

Nuances of theory or of philosophical perspective have been combined to produce so many different rationales for special educational services that agreement or even understanding between services is sometimes difficult. This is a particularly difficult situation for parents, for laypersons on school boards, and for other professional educators who do not have a background in special education. Defining emotional disturbance, developing appropriate mechanisms for identifying these children, and developing and implementing appropriate educational policies and procedures, such as those related to mainstreaming, are very difficult when there is such diversity in perspectives for understanding the problem.

Difficulties for professional special educators are equally great. What is the most effective and efficient intervention? Which understanding of the problem will provide a basis for sound educational program development?

The communication gap between different disciplines is familiar. The issue here, however, is not limited to language, conceptual schema, body of knowledge, and view of interventions. These are several ways to divide or classify the alternative conceptions of disturbance. The classification developed by Rhodes and Tracy in *A Study of Child Variance*, Vol. 1 (1973) grew out of the most extensive recent review of the concepts and available knowledge relevant to special education. That classification included the following theories: behavioral, sociological, biophysical, psychodynamic, ecological and counter-theory.

Different conceptions of the phenomenon of disturbance have had particular strength and utility in different areas. The behavioral conception, for example, has been especially productive in developing specific interventions to modify or change deviant behavior. The sociological view, on the other hand, has been useful in describing the social nature of the problem and in providing a framework within which to begin conceptualizing the role of the deviant member in the social system and environments of the school.

Insufficient knowledge about the complex problem of emotional disturbance and the lack of a common view and language to describe it, juxtaposed with the legislative mandate to provide educational services for these children, provide a situation in which several things may occur, and in some instances have already occurred. In the necessity to intervene without a clear understanding of the problem, there is the tendency to oversimplify and to accept less than adequate solutions. Narrowly conceived criteria, such as efficiency, or vague criteria are more likely to be accepted. Fragments of theory are likely to be brought together superficially and used to rationalize programs in ways that do not do justice to any of the theories from which the ideas were taken. There is likely to be more attention given to intervention methodologies than to the nature of the problem and the quality and ethical prerogatives of intervention.

In the present writing, the authors accept the following assumptions: First, different perspectives are available to explain the phenomenon of disturbance; second, each perspective has its own knowledge base and represents a sound view of the problem relative to certain purposes or utilities; third, while each special educator cannot be provided with intensive training in each perspective, he/she needs to be aware of alternative views of the problem; fourth, those not trained specifically in the education of emotionally disturbed children need to be aware of the breadth of alternative valid perspectives on the problem of disturbance; fifth, there are major issues to which professional special educators and other educators and laypersons need to be sensitized that arise from the existence of competing frames of reference and from the premise that the phenomenon can and should be understood and altered. These issues include philosophy of science questions, philosophy of deviance, the nature and impact of the delivery system on the understanding and treatment of the problem, and the ethics of intervention.

While many problems have been targeted for change or solution, the actual reform of educational systems in which those problems are manifested has not occurred at a significant level. New social technologies are, however, being generated to respond to some of the philosophical and organizational problems of providing an appropriate education for handicapped children. The fact that many handicapped children were inadequately or inappropriately served coupled with political support of appropriate services for all children led to new thinking about the needs and rights of these children. Concurrently, technological innovations, such as mainstreaming, advocacy, and deinstitutionalization, were designed to remedy some of these problems.

Mainstreaming, an attempt to serve children in the least restrictive educational setting, is a change in the traditional philosophy of educating handicapped children in public schools. As described by Pappanikou and Paul (1977), mainstreaming emotionally disturbed children is primarily a problem of mainstreaming the educational system. The focus of mainstreaming is on providing an appropriate education for handicapped children as assured by the right to education legislation (PL 94-142). In order to accomplish this it is necessary to mainstream the policies, procedures, and organizational patterns of the educational system and the attitudes and skills of teachers, administrators, and professional support personnel. A philosophically sound view of mainstreaming supports educational placement in the least restrictive appropriate setting, not the wholesale abandonment of all special classes. Its focus is upon accountability and careful educational planning and placement, requiring the best available professional wisdom.

Advocacy is a departure from our historical faith in institutions. Advocacy inside the system (Paul, Neufeld, and Pelosi, 1977) is an internal accountability mechanism that recognizes the problem of large organizations to be effectively and efficiently responsive to the needs of individuals. Advocacy inside the system is workable if, but usually only if, it is articulated with advocacy resources outside the system. Advocates outside the system are persons who have no vested interest in the organization, have nothing to lose by raising questions, are not dependent on the organization for salary, are able to take the perspective of the child in understanding problems, and can make the interest of the child the primary focus.

Deinstitutionalization is a change in the concepts of institutional service delivery. It (Paul et al, 1977) is a shift in the pattern of institutional care that attempts to reduce institutional dependency and increase community based programming for the handicapped. Group homes and therapeutic camping programs for the seriously emotionally disturbed, as alternatives to psychiatric hospitals, are examples.

The full meaning of these changes in our familiar philosophies and practices related to deviance is yet to be determined. Some see them as tears in the surface of a system that, if examined honestly, expose the weakness and decadence of all that supported the traditionally attractive surface. Others view them as points of entry to begin examining specific weakness in the system so that the total human service delivery system might be ultimately reformed to become sensitive and responsive to the needs of the handicapped.

Technological developments in education have increased at a rate that has exceeded the maturation of educational philosophy. This has resulted in our failure to incorporate and integrate into any meaningful and comprehensive image the development of a purposeful system of education for all children.

The efficient delivery and utilization of research products and the effective collaboration of training organizations and service delivery systems, for example, are among the more important deficiencies in the organizational professional and technical domains of education.

New organizational patterns for providing efficient and specific assistance to organizations and staff are emerging. Technical assistance systems with varying organizational formats and serving different client groups have been developed. Many different content areas are involved ranging from curriculum for the retarded to program planning and evaluation methodologies. Technical assistance is an organizational concept independent of a particular content area. Most technical assistance is a cyclical process proceeding from an assessment of needs to intervention designed to meet that need to an evaluation relative to its impact. It can be an important organizational medium for making information and skills more efficiently and effectively available. Becoming a positive force for children will require that special educators provide and use technical assistance effectively.

The future of the field of special education rests upon the emerging philosophies of education and in the ability of educators to provide leadership in rational change of the educational system.

Professionals in special education must be able to participate and be prepared for a number of probable futures. They must also have the skills to creatively fashion a preferred future. The focus on technical competencies must be balanced by personal affective resources and strength of character. In recent years we have come to better appreciate the importance of the personal values and character as well as the technical skills of professionals who work with handicapped persons.

Hobbs, past president of the American Psychological Association, noted that a teacher counselor working with emotionally disturbed children must be "... A decent adult; educated, well trained, able to give and receive affection, to live relaxed, and to be firm; a person with private resources for the nourishment and refreshment of his own life; not an itinerant worker but a professional through and through; a person with a sense of the significance of time, of the usefulness of today and the promise of tomorrow; a person with hope, quiet and confidence, and joy; one who has committed himself to children.... "

Porterfield, in his foreword to the *Standards for Community Agencies*, captured the essence of the reformation of professional caretaking when he observed: "The lesson has come to me with maturity that we are not our brother's keeper. We are more properly our brother's brother."

In our book we review the major recent theoretical views of disturbance. This review provides a broad understanding of the nature of the problem. It also provides an understanding of the context from which more familiar fragments of theory and practice, have been taken.

Seven major perspectives on disturbance and the general rationales for interventions suggested by each are presented. These perspectives include the behavioral, ecological, sociological, psychoneurological,* counter-theoretical, psychohistorical, and existential. There are, of course, other very important perspectives, such as the psychodynamic, for understanding deviance. The authors selected views for this writing, however, that have, for the most part, been substantially articulated within the educational system. Additionally, the views selected have influenced professional special educators principally within the last decade and represent significant thinking about the future of understanding and educating children who are different. There is no attempt to synthesize or otherwise integrate the different perspectives. We accept the view that there are many different syntheses that are valid for different uses or purposes.

A second portion of the book is concerned with issues with which theoreticians, researchers, and practitioners must deal

*Used interchangeably with the biophysical and neurosensory.

related to understanding, describing, and intervening to change the disturbed or the disturbance. These involve philosophical problems related to knowledge, to the phenomenology of deviance, and to the ethics of intervention.

The problem of knowledge is basic to considering alternative conceptions of deviance and the evidence available relative to any particular view. The chapter on philosophy of science includes a discussion of language, concepts, and assumptions that govern the development of scientific knowledge. A major part of the problem in developing a more stable and useful knowledge base in this area has to do with the nature of the questions raised and the methods of inquiry available and considered appropriate. A limiting philosophy of science will result in a limited understanding of the problem being studied. Likewise, a superficial understanding or casual attitude toward these issues will contribute to the knowledge problem, not to its solution.

The philosophical issues related to the nature of deviance are also basic. Involved are questions of man's nature and the meaning of deviance. There are many technical questions to be answered in understanding the nature of deviance and professionally intervening to alter that deviance. There are other questions, however, that require answers that cannot be reduced to technical terms. This domain has to do with existential questions. Who is man? What is his uniqueness and individuality? This balances the technical perspective of deviance with questions related to value and meaning. It is important to address this domain of understanding deviance. It is absolutely essential to understand the difference between the domains (technical and the existential or phenomenological).

The organizational and conceptual problems of service systems, whether they be classrooms or clinics, must also be addressed. The primary focus here is on the problem of the bureaucratization of services. Large organizations, and big institutions in particular, that provide services to deviant children have become direct objects of concern and study. Institutional norms that undermine individuality, self-serving organizational interests, impersonal and, in some instances, abusive environments, inflexible attitudes, and resistance to change are examples of institutionalized and bureaucratized services. The bureaucratized service delivery system that defines, identifies, and "treats" the deviant member is not independent of the deviance phenomenon. The ecological and sociological perspectives, in particular, provide bases for examining the interaction of the identifying system with the deviance it defines. There are moral as well as phenomenological issues involved. There are also organizational issues related to efficiency and effectiveness of services, management, staff training, and program development.

The problems of a bureaucratized service delivery system on one hand and the problems of theory, knowledge, and practices on the other have led some to pursue alternatives to formal and to traditional views of deviance and intervention. The counter-theoretical and counter-institutional perspective emerged out of both a dissatisfaction with traditional, more formal views of the problem and a disenchantment with the service delivery system as a viable medium for quality care and treatment.

There are many terms or labels used interchangeably to identify the children discussed in this text. These include, for example, emotionally disturbed, emotionally handicapped, troubled, and behavior disordered. There is no completely neutral term that cuts across all points of view. While these terms may appear in different contexts in this writing, the authors have attempted to focus on deviance as a generic social concept rather than on terms that are more likely to be associated with a single theoretical perspective.

References

HOBBS, N. Helping disturbed children: Psychological and ecological strategies. *American Psychologist*, 21, 12, December, 1966, 1105-1115.

PAPPANIKOU, A. J., & PAUL, J. L. (Eds.) *Mainstreaming emotionally disturbed children*. Syracuse, N.Y.: Syracuse University Press, 1977.

PAUL, J. L., NEUFELD, G. R., & PELOSI, J. W. *Child Advocacy Inside the System*, Syracuse, N.Y.: Syracuse University Press, 1977.

PAUL, J. L., STEDMAN, D., & NEUFELD, G. R. (Eds.) *Deinstitutionalization: Implications for policy and program development*. Syracuse, N.Y.: Syracuse University Press, 1977.

PORTERFIELD, J. D. *Standards for community agencies*. Joint Commission on Accreditation of Hospitals, 1973.

RHODES, W. C., & TRACY, M. *A study of child variance*, Volume 1. Ann Arbor: University of Michigan, 1973.

CHAPTER TWO

A Psychohistorical View

A Polyglot Nation

The history of the bureaucratization of care and education in this nation parallels much of the history of the larger revolutionary experiment in creating a single people out of polyglot groups. In a sense, the energy pool of human resources for a totally new country was made up of either extruded populations or voluntary refugees from other nations. In either case, by sociological definitions, they were social deviants.

This was a pluralistic society that attempted to meld diverse elements into a unified whole through a government-supervised melting pot. The state has created caregiving and educational bureaus to accomplish this transformation. These institutions seem to have, in their early days, concentrated their primary energies upon melting the strangers to our shores into the existing culture. The bureau-centered institutions flourished as long as the

17

melting pot ideal flourished. Now, with the turn of history in this country toward natural pluralism, we may be seeing the decline of these specialized institutions in their bureaucratic form. The next stage in the history of caregiving is unclear at this point. However, what is clear is that there is a national reaction to the central bureau-structured form of such enculturating functions as social welfare, education and justice, and corrections. Directly related is a growing reaction against uniform monitoring of cultural choices and behavioral life styles.

Choosing the Pattern

Ruth Benedict (1961) studied patterns of culture and concluded that each culture chooses certain human styles, traits, and behaviors it wishes to develop and throws away others. The ones it chooses are developed almost exclusive of the others.

The same human characteristics chosen as ideal by one culture can be declared abnormal by another. Therefore both abnormalcy and the ideal are culturally relative. Foucault (1973), in writing about madness and insanity, presents a similar thesis except that he sees an active process of trait rejections and repressions that is directly related to historical changes in the social animus of a culture.

Migrant Flooding

In talking about the rise and possible decline of the bureaucratic arrangement of caregiving in this country we will employ this sociological-anthropological framework to discuss and explore the phenomenon. We can look at the evolution and growth of our current national child classification system of variance and those bureaus charged with administering this system as related to our own historical choice and rejection of human traits, qualities, and characteristics. This, in turn, can be correlated with critical change forces washing over the nation in various periods of social stress in our history.

The crucial historical period for the birth of these specialized bureaus seems to be from the middle of the nineteenth century to the end of the first quarter of the twentieth century. Thereafter, during the second and third quarter of the twentieth century, they entered a period of unprecedented growth and accumulation of power in the domestic scene. The period of early bureaucratization of education and caregiving was directly correlated with the high tide of migration floods pouring into this nation. This influx began prior to the Civil War and ended with the restrictive immigration laws, which came shortly after the turn of the century and shut off the flood about the time of World War I. The rapid growth and consolidation period of the care systems correlated both with the Great Depression and the aftermath of World War II.

Institutionalizing the Pattern

When we talk about "bureaucratization" of caretaking, we are referring to a specific organizational form for changing national resources into human services. *Webster's Third New International Dictionary*, unabridged, defines that form of organization as follows: "systematic administration characterized by specialization of functions, objective qualifications for office, action according to fixed rules and a hierarchy of authority." The child care bureaus that we are referring to are the federal, state, and local services operated by the executive branch of government, and authorized and funded through the legislative branch for the care of children, with particular, earmarked responsibility for detecting and treating human variance. Its hierarchy of authority runs from the federal, to the state, to the county, and other local jurisdictional levels. The types of human variation it oversees is construed by law to be the result of physical, psychological, or social causes. As a result the educational and child care processes exercised in our society in relation to human variance, as defined by law, are a government function.

During the first hundred years of our nation's history, strangers and strangeness were adequately handled through decentralized community measures imported from the countries of origin of the early settlers. Each town, particularly seacoast towns, used such simple direct methods as "warning out" strangers (Deutsch, 1946), monthly alms, boarding out with local families, or poor houses and other forms of indoor relief. Although ours was a pluralistic society it was, nevertheless, dominated by an English-speaking, Protestant, middle-class, white, individualistic culture. In the colonial era the odd-people—the variant ones, the indigent ones, the deviant ones, the immoral ones—were usually members of this dominant culture, who were taken care of by their own "people." The custom-carriers made little categorical differentiation among these unfortunate human conditions. The social welfare programs were also categorically undifferentiated. Local settlement laws were enough to keep out undesirable strangers. If such a human condition as mental illness was singled out as a special condition, it was usually regarded as a medical problem, with such explanations as an accumulation of bile. The belief in demonic possession had also accompanied the colonists to the New World. So, although it is not clear how many "possessed" people may have been involved, it is probable that many were victims of the witch trial hysteria, which climaxed at Salem, Massachusetts, in 1692.

Designing the Melting Pots

The tidal wave of eastern and western European refugees which began to inundate this nation just prior to the Civil War provoked a radical change in the American view of human services and human problems. Obviously these refugee peoples had to be absorbed and integrated. They overwhelmed the new society and its social mechanisms. They also provoked progressively complex concepts of, and attitudes toward, human differences.

The melting pot not only became a national ideal, it also became a crisis instrument to deal with the fear for the stability of society. Growth of cities was rampant. Strange people with strange customs, alien religions, strange clothes, and strange institutions swarmed to the cities, entrenched themself in the poorer sections, and clung together against the influences of their host culture. Their children filled the streets.

In the Massachusetts Senate Documents of 1847, it was recorded that the Irish are displacing

... the honest and respectable laborers of the State; and ... from their manner of living ... work for much less per day ... being satisfied with food to support their minimal existence alone ... while the latter (the native American workers) not only labor for the body but for the mind, the soul, and the State. (Handlin, 1959, p. 185)

In 1893, *The New York Times* reported on the Jewish community in the Lower East Side of New York City:

This neighborhood, peopled almost entirely by the people who claim to have been driven from Poland and Russia, is the eyesore of New York and perhaps the filthiest place in the Western Continent. It is impossible for a Christian to live there because he will be driven out, either by blows or the dirt and stench. . . . They cannot be lifted up to a higher plane because they do not want to be. (Bernard, 1973, p. 19)

The sentiment of many in the indigenous culture was voiced in the Boston's *American* in the midst of the heavy Irish migration into that city:

Instead of assimilating at once with the customs of their country of adoption, our foreign populations are too much in the habit of retaining their national usages, of associating too exclusively with each other and living in groups together. These practices serve no good purposes, and tend merely to alienate those among whom they have chosen to reside. (Handlin, 1959, p. 185)

The most plausible way of integrating these alien populations into the mainstream culture was to educate them, or rather, their children, into the qualities, behaviors, and values that would represent the previously chosen pattern of the new nation. The only recourse was to make education a compulsory government vehicle to accomplish the melding of such diverse elements.

The city child, especially the child of the newcomers, had generated both compassion and fear. He was unkempt, uncared for, and untutored. He was in need of help. But he was also a threat. . . . Partly from fear and partly from compassion, thirty-one states enacted some form of compulsory education law by 1900. (Perkinson, 1968, p. 70)

So long as certain classes or certain individuals refuse to recognize their natural relations to society, that is, are unsocialized, so long will they retard the advances of society toward its ultimate goal. The great problem of the age is how to get rid of our unsocialized classes. Obviously, the only way to get rid of them is to socialize them. And this may be done by education and this should be, we contend, its main object. (McMurray, 1899, pp. 75-76)

The Protestant Infusion

One of the critical dimensions on which the in-migrant cultures differed from the predominant English-speaking cultures was religion. This nuclear dimension was significant in the general ethos of colonial America because even among the dominant Protestant sects, religious persuasion was one of the reasons for coming to the new country. Therefore, religious freedom was an important ethic in the general ethos of the nation. However, as pointed out by Pekarsky (1974):

Exacerbated by religious differences, the difference between the socially and economically dominant protestant population and the immigrants was profound. The immigrants, escaping from famines, revolutions, and pogroms, clung tenaciously to communal and religious forms that guaranteed the continuity of their experience. The dominant Protestant population viewed with alarm the intrusion of alien culture-bearers that resisted assimilation.

Prior to the mid-nineteenth century the several states differed in religious emphasis among the various Protestant sects. The line between church and state had not been clearly drawn. However, after the Fourteenth Amendment to the Constitution was ratified in 1868, and due process and equal protection became the law of the land, the Supreme Court construed these concepts to include national disestablishment.

Whether this was prompted by the fear that non-Protestant sects might gain control of government power, or whether this was a humanitarian device to assure against the persecution that many Americans had experienced in their extruding countries, is a tangential issue to the way in which this new legal mandate effected the development of education and other human services in this nation.

Although there was uniform sentiment in favor of separation of church and state, the sentiment was not uniform in the separation of state and instruments of socialization. The development of the unity between state and human services became much more strongly supported by the ensconced Protestant groups than the more recent non-Protestant settlers. (Pekarsky, 1974) Furthermore, the general ambience of these new government services was Protestant in nature; and this fact is important to the understanding of government controlled care in this nation.

22

Even the basic bureaucratic form of corporate organization that was employed in developing these new government functions seems to reflect the prevailing character of Protestantism in that period of history. Pekarsky (1974, p. 455) says:

For, if Max Weber is correct, the distinctive Western rationality that consists of devising the most efficient means to given ends, and which involves making systematic, precise calculations on the keeping of records, has its roots in the Protestant's quest to assure himself of his Election through worldly success. (Weber, 1958)

Also the very definition of such conditions as "madness" and the types of confinement facilities and treatment programs prescribed at this point seem to have their roots in Protestant England. As Foucault (1973, pp. 57-60) points out in his book *Madness and Civilization*, segregation and/or confinement of the mad in England was not related to their irrationality, but rather to their "sloth." The Protestant community was bound to eject all forms of social uselessness. It was the violation of the frontiers of bourgeois society he says, and not irrationality, that led to the confinement of the insane. In the English Protestant view, crossing of the frontiers of social order resulted in the weakening of discipline and the relaxation of morals. God cursed the state that did not punish libertinage, that tolerated crimes and vice, that allowed its citizens to live in ignorance of religion. Platt (1969, p. 55) reports a similar flavor in the efforts of prominent Protestant leaders in the child-saver movement in the United States. In the reformatories they sponsored for children they felt that "the value of sobriety, thrift, industry, prudence, 'realistic ambition,' and adjustment must be taught." Abell (1962) says: "Protestants persisted in believing that human sufferings were the 'penalties of idleness, disease or similar causes, in great measure the fault of the sufferers.'"

Trait and State

This country, groaning under the weight of its invited sufferers from other cultures, was at a crossroad in the latter part of the nineteenth century. Its agrarian society was becoming urbanized and there was a growing distaste for city life. The immigrants flowing into these cities were generally impoverished and untrained in industrial skills. The Civil War and rapid industrialization further weakened the social order. There were also railroad scandals, bank scandals and the Credit Mobilier affair which involved the vice-president of the United States. Domestic order became an overwhelming priority for the nation's expenditure of energy and resources.

Traditional America was becoming increasingly reluctant to trust in an informal family and community. It turned to the state to gain direct and formal control over the socialization process. It turned to the courts to regulate the lives of children, and the juvenile court system was born (Platt, 1967). It discovered confinement and a wide array of institutions were born. Rothman (1971), in the history of the asylum in the United States, writes: "The almshouse, the penitentiary, the reformatory, and the insane asylum all represent an effort to insure the cohension of the community in new and changing circumstances" (p. xviii). By this period in history twenty-three of the thirty-three states had already established asylums for the insane, a phenomenon which really only began with the turn of the century. Now in the midpoint of that century, as pointed out by Rothman (1971), the aftermath of a Jacksonian society riddled with vice appeared even more sharply in the national images of the young victims of poverty, orphans, and vagrant children.

The lack of confidence in the informal enculturation processes of the family and its pluralistic communities was accompanied by dismay over youth. State institutions for delinquents, residential schools for the mentally retarded, and other types of closed congregate care facilities grew up rapidly alongside the religiously controlled orphanages. The need for supplementary socialization institutions resulted in the inaguration of compulsory education in this nation, a movement with its strongest, almost hysterical support, in the large cities.

Between 1852, when Massachusetts was the first state to initiate compulsory public education, and 1918, when Mississippi followed suit, all the states in the Union enacted compulsory school attendance legislation. The school was transformed, "from a relatively minor institution, catering largely to the middle class, to one which was not only available to all segments of the society, but which was legally impowered to compel children to attend" (Hoffman, 1973, pp. 19-20).

This state instrument became more and more important as the nineteenth century wore on.

The Harpur report, which evaluated the Chicago schools near the end of that century, said:

There are also a large number of children who are constantly dropping out of our schools because of insubordination and want of cooperation between the parents and the teachers and they are becoming vagrants upon the streets and a menace to good society. The welfare of the city demands that these children be put under restraint. (Harpur Report, 1899, p. 163)

Paul Hanus, a professor of education at Harvard, in a report to the New York Commission on School Inquiry wrote (1913),

Whatever it costs, the city cannot safely perpetuate the inadequate measures of discovering and caring for its mental defective children and run the further risk of allowing the present progressive increase of mental defectives to continue unchecked. (pp. 20-21)

The introjection of the state into the internalized processes of individual formation and socialization took multiple social routes and avenues in this country. In writing about the child saver movement in the late 1800s and early 1900s Platt (1969) said:

The juvenile court movement went far beyond a concern for special treatment of adolescent offenders. It brought within the ambit of government control a set of youthful activities that had been previously ignored or dealt with on an informal basis. It was not by accident that behavior selected for penalizing—sexual license, drinking, roaming the streets, begging, frequenting dance halls and movies, fighting and being seen in public late at night—was most directly relevant to the children of lower-class migrant and immigrant families. (p. 29)

Ethno-Religious Resistance

This rapid extension of the state into socialization and caretaking areas formerly reserved for the family was strongly supported by representatives of the dominant culture. Platt (1969) said: "Child saving may be understood as a crusade which served symbolic and status functions for native, middle-class Americans, particularly feminist groups" (p. 26).

However, the newcomers to this land viewed these developments with suspicion and even alarm. Pekarsky (1974) says, "Thus the Catholic response to the efforts of the first child-savers was to seek ways of multiplying their own provisions for children" (p. 461).

The Catholics saw themselves in a defensive position. In the new country in the pre-nineteenth-century period there had been mass desertion of the Catholics from the church (O'Grady, 1930). The heavy individualism inherent in the Protestant ideal of "the priesthood of believers" was antithetical to the Catholic ideal of community in the Church. According to Pekarsky (1974):

The efforts of John Carroll, the First American Bishop, to establish schools for Catholic children at the end of the eighteenth century represents the first of a long series of Catholic efforts to ensure that the disturbing early history of the Church in America would not repeat itself. (p. 459)

The Catholic reaction to the Protestant dominant child saver movement was to multiply their own provisions for caring for children.

According to Pekarsky (1974, pp. 471–474) Jewish immigrants were somewhat divided in their resistance to the intrusion of the State. Although the principle of communal responsibility for the care of its own members was well established, both theologically and in practice, there was a division in their view of the growing public policy of state care. The Sephardic Jews had settled in this country in the seventeenth and eighteenth centuries. The German Jews, who came in large numbers in the early nineteenth century, sought to assert their authority and independence of this group by establishing their own welfare and service provisions embodying their own beliefs and values. They had suffered through the history of isolation in Europe and, with the relaxation of medieval constraints, had sought to win wider arenas of freedom by making themselves indistinguishable from west European non-Jews. Therefore, in the new country, espousing the course of assimilation, they adapted the ways of the dominant culture. Having secularized themselves in Germany, where social life no longer revolved around the Synagog and the Jewish community, they transplanted this "modern" Jewish pattern to the new country. They separated welfare or care and religion. It was, therefore, not difficult for the German Jews to support the Protestant view of separation between care and ethnic community. By the time the eastern European Jews came to this country in large numbers after 1880 the pattern had been set.

Pekarsky (1974) says:

It was also a consequence of the German outlook that their (own) welfare institutions, which served later immigrants, embodied an assimilationist ideal. In contrast to the nineteenth-century Catholic welfare institutions which sought to protect traditional cultural and religious outlooks, those promoted by the German-Jewish community were largely instruments of Americanization. (p. 423)

The Century of the Mental Ethic

During the twentieth century the ideal of the chosen American type took an unusual twist. The white-Anglo-Protestant American typology appears to have firmly established itself as the representative pattern. The melting pot process took strong roots in the growing hierarchical governmental structure of the new republic. The nationwide system of public education became the accepted central instrument of Americanization. With this century, however, two new interrelated developments occurred to profoundly influence the patterning of the chosen ideal. As in all cultures, this development was the product of critical historical shifts. One of these twin developments was the elevation of science to a pinnical position in the world, and, hence, in the cultural patterning institutions; this brought the sudden emergence of a new breed of social pattern interpreters and gatekeepers—the social scientists. The other development was the torsion by which the scientific revolution transformed the Puritan ethic into a mental ethic for the nation.

Cultures have always entrusted this choice of trait-patterns into the hands of institutionalized interpreters. In this relatively new nation, where there was such a clear separation between church and state, so that the church could not be the interpreter, and where pluralistic cultures tried to blend their diverse patterns through the melting pot ideal, it would seem inevitable that a new secular breed of social interpreters and gatekeepers would grow up within the society.

This new breed brought into the enculturation arena a point of view that seems very much like a secular version of the older Protestant-American views for grouping people. This took the form of a social translation of the biological theories of Charles Darwin. Herbert Spencer had analyzed Darwinian theory of natural selection and survival in terms of the interference of man-made environments. Spencerian philosophy argued that mankind's survival and evolution was being disturbed by such unnatural prostheses as "poor laws," public health, and education. Biological principles, if left alone, would naturally select the most fit members of the species for breeding the future race. The weaker members, through their innate inferiority, detracted from man's progress, and their unnatural preservation was, therefore, a threat to the future of mankind. Particularly in Protestant nations, this new view of mankind's progress seemed to fit hand-in-glove with a view of bourgeois order in which to be chosen and materially flourish in this world was a sign of having been equally chosen in the other. However, in the new egalitarian nation, with its population skewed in the direction of persecuted, deviant populations of old nations, old systems of social class were anathema to its people. If such a system were to reemerge it could not appear in any of its previous editions.

The way in which it seems to have reappeared in this new nation, hidden from public consciousness by the powerful justification of the new social science, was in terms of gradations of "fitness." Certain segments were less fit than others, as demonstrated by their proportionate contributions to certain newly invented social inferiority entities. These newly constructed entities were located more frequently, by the new breed of scientific gatekeepers, in specific undesirable populations and the poor, the unassimilated, and the culturally alien. A high correlation existed and continues to exist between those labeled by the new technology and those who reside in poor, unassimilated, culturally segregated groups, the hidden class system of the young nation.

Spokesmen for the new science of human origins and human progress quickly sounded the eugenic alarm in this nation. H. H. Goddard, the renowned psychologist, who introduced intelligence testing to the United States and who established the first laboratory for the study of mental retardation, wrote in a book on delinquency (1921):

There are two million people in the United States who, because of their weak minds or their diseased minds, are making our country a dangerous place to live in. The two million is increasing both by heredity and by training. We are breeding defectives. We are making criminals. (p. iv)

His voice was joined by others. Paul Hanus (1913), a professor of education at Harvard, in a report to the New York City Commission on School Inquiry, worried that mentally defective children were a serious problem:

... the danger of allowing such children to grow up at large is a grave one. Such persons not only become a burden to society themselves, but propagate their kind in large numbers ... whatever it costs the city cannot safely ... run the further risk of mental defectives to continue unchecked. (pp. 20–21)

The drive toward perfection and the threat of imperfection was not a new impulse in Western cultures. For the first time, however, the concern with perfectability and the identification and treatment of imperfect characteristics moved from the spiritual realm into the natural realm. It can be debated whether this was an actual break with an older tradition, or whether the tradition now reappeared in another guise. The language was certainly different, since analytic rather than generalistic explanatory concepts were employed by this new group of social interpreters. The prevailing public belief composite, which lumped together an undifferentiated mass of unfit and socially contaminating citizens such as "immigrants," "libertines," "beggars," "criminals," and "lunatics," was now put under the naturalistic microscope and subjected to clinical and laboratory scrutiny by these scientist-practitioners. They tried to differentiate among these human states and conditions and having differentiated, to work out solutions to the threat they presented to the social body. Education, settlement, charity, protection of morals, and treatment and cure, which had already begun to be separated by the state into specialized corporate structures such as compulsory schools and asylums of various sorts, now became the environmental laboratories of this newly emergent group of professional specialists who aligned themselves with the methods, philosophies, and theories of the new science.

During the first quarter of the twentieth century the emergent scientist-practitioner breed consolidated their own identity by organizing into associations and developing training programs. This is the period in which American social work became a profession. In 1893 Anna Dawes presented a paper to the International Congress on Charities entitled *The Need of Training Schools for the New Profession*. Edward Devine and the New York Charity Organization society established its summer school of philanthropy in 1896. After 1900 the National Conference of Charities and Corrections gradually began referring to its members as "social workers" and by 1905 the term social work was in common use (Devine, 1914, pp. 15-16). In 1919 the New York School of Social Work grew out of the New York School of Philanthropy, which had been founded eight years before. This new breed of social workers worked in charity organizations, in corrections, in settlement houses, and, after 1905, in mental units of general hospitals and psychiatric hospitals (Grinker, 1961, p. 116). This profession of social work was very much involved in socializing ethnic groups into the representative type for the nation. By 1911 there were four hundred settlement houses in the vicinity of shifting urban ethnic populations. One of the major goals of the National Foundation of Settlements was the establishment of programs to actively aid the Americanization of the immigrant multitude in these areas. The settlement houses were dedicated to research and reform of the ethnic settlements.

In the public compulsory schools, psychology was becoming a body of norm clarifiers and definers. Binet and Simon had constructed the first intelligence test in France at the beginning of the century to differentiate nonaverage from average pupils. In 1908 Goddard presented his translation and adaptations of the instrument for American children. In 1907 a Child Study Department, for the rise of individualized tests, was set up in Rochester, New York. In 1911, in Cincinnati, a psychology laboratory was established in the public schools. In 1912 the University of Pittsburg School of Education established a program for "mental deviates" in the surrounding school communities.

Also, during this period, the medical model began to emerge as a strong influence in the area of human variance. During the first decade of the twentieth century many organizations devoted to preventive medicine came into being (Fraser, 1973). Psychiatry and neurology emerged as a new branch of medical science and oriented itself to social problems. The National Committee for Mental Hygiene sprang into existence in 1909. Clifford Beers wrote *A Mind that Found Itself* (1921) and described his recovery within a mental hospital, thus capturing the negative human fantasies of the public in the imagery of mental states. Many professionals reacted favorably, including William James and Adolph

Meyer, who actually recommended the term "mental hygiene" for the new movement. In 1909, Sigmund Freud and C. G. Jung traveled to the United States to deliver a series of lectures on mental alienation and its cure. In 1912 a donation of $50,000 was made to the National Committee on Mental Hygiene to study existing facilities and create new ones. Dr. William Healy, a psychiatrist, founded the first Juvenile Psychopathic Institute, in Chicago, in 1909. A national conference on the Prevention of Juvenile Delinquency, sponsored by the Commonwealth Fund and the National Committee on Mental Hygiene was held in 1921. By then the young "criminal" element had been analyzed by the new behavioral sciences as a source of social infection which could, and should, be subjected to early identification and scientific cure. In this medical model of scientific cure, the Puritan ethic appears to have been translated into a new psychiatric ideal—the mental ethic. Poverty, criminality, libertinage, and all forms of irrationality and alien, urban, inner-city life styles were subsumed under this new ambient ethic. All of these were determined to be mental diseases which could be diagnosed and cured. Spurred by this medical mental model, the principle action recommended by the national delinquency prevention conference was to establish an experimental pattern of child guidance clinics for juvenile delinquents. This experiment was implemented and the results reported in the Healy and Bronner Report (1936), which resulted in the nationwide development which spread child guidance clinics throughout urban America.

The Great Catalysts—World Wars

Although there were wide differences in theory and research approaches among the various breeds of scientist-practitioners during the first part of the century, they generally agreed upon a major final operational model for prevention of the spread of imperfection, that is, public segregation under government supervision. Between 1918 and 1932 separate facilities for deviant children within the governmental controlled and financed public school system grew very rapidly. By 1930 sixteen states had passed legislation relating to the mentally handicapped and their segregation in or directly under the public schools (Schleier, 1931). By 1932 thirteen states had established a state division or bureau for administering special education services. By 1933, 75 percent of the nation's high schools had some form of special assistance for exceptional children, primarily for children who failed regular classes (Heck, 1940). However, such classes were perceived frequently as a means of identifying the mentally retarded, the mentally sick, and the delinquents for subsequent institutionalization. Just prior to World War I, Fernald (1915) stated,

The modern public school class for defective children ensures diagnosis and treatment at an early age, helps to inform parents as to the dangers of mental deficit, and admirably serves as a clearinghouse for permanent segregation. (in Keugel & Wolfensburger, 1969, p. 127)

In 1915 the National Conference of Charities and Corrections devoted most of its proceedings to the discussion of "Prevention of Mental Defect." The practical solutions offered were basically segregation and prevention of procreation (Keugel & Wolfensburger, 1969). It was the consensus of the committee that the survival of the society demanded that the mentally retarded be segregated from society through involuntary committment to institutions. During this period there was also a proliferation of reformatories for delinquents.

The World Wars and Bureaucracy

The government-supervised model of segregation, enhanced by scientific measures for detection and isolation, supported the consolidation of chosen cultural patterns. The various forms of segregation through asylums lent themselves to the organization of state welfare and correction bureaus for funding and administering this effort. The utterances of the scientific fraternity mobilized the general society to press for such protective services and to provide the tax support necessary to create and maintain them. The federal level of the government hierarchy began to take on responsibility of detecting and separating those who deviated from mental standards. The U.S. Public Health Service became the first federal agency involved in detecting and isolating mental undesirables. It instituted a program of inspection of aliens at Ellis Island to detect such characteristics. This public health service was expanded with the entry of the United States into World War I, when the Surgeon General's Office created a division of neurology and psychiatry to (1) examine new recruits for mental disorders, (2) develop programs and facilities for observation and treatment of soldiers, and (3) design and implement after-care facilities for veterans. Mind watching now became a federal concern and completed the hierarchical structure of the bureaucracy for protecting the mental status of society. The first World War thus played a part in collecting large masses of population into a special social institution where it could be subjected to the new detection measures and separated into special facilities or programs to help ameliorate adaptive imperfections. World War I gave great impetus to the development of all sorts of mental and social measurement procedures. This measurement philosophy resulted in a totally new type of social stratification, unique to the United States. Ideal models for accomplishing this stratification were incorporated into the major cultural melting and social-sorting institution of the democratic society—the school.

In the 1920s the new standardized intelligence and achievement tests were urged as the basis for restructuring school systems. Lewis Terman, creator of the extensively used Stanford-Binet scale and a leader in the educational testing and measurement movement proposed the first scientifically engineered model for social stratification by culturally chosen traits. It was a multiple track plan based upon the new scientific instruments for early mental and cognitive screening of children, to prepare them precisely for their future life role. The proposed blue print seems to be a direct transposing of the economic usefulness element of the Protestant ethic into the new mental ethic. Terman (1923) laid out his own vision for a scientifically, determined socioeconomic class system based on mental gradations as follows:

The present writer would urge the widespread adaption of a multiple-track plan, adapted according to the size of city and according to other circumstances . . . at present vocational guidance is too largely an end process, an afterthought. . . . At every step in the child's progress the school should take account of his vocational possibilities. Preliminary investigations indicate that an IQ below 70 rarely permits anything better than unskilled labor, that ranges from 70 to 80 is preeminently that of semiskilled or ordinary clerical labor, from 100 to 110 or 115, that of semiprofessional pursuits; and that above all these are the grades of intelligence that permits one to enter the professions or the larger fields of business. Intelligence tests can tell us whether a child's native brightness corresponds to the median of (1) the professional classes, (2) those in the semiprofessional pursuits, (3) ordinary skilled workers, (4) semi-skilled workers, or (5) skilled laborers. This information will be of great value in planning the education of a particular child and also in the differentiated curriculum here recommended. (pp. 74, 75-76)

World War II and its aftermath greatly accelerated the growth and expansion of both the scientific body and its involvement in public policy, and the proliferation of and hierarchical structuring of the bureaucratic care system in this country. For instance, Margaret Fraser (1974) writes,

at the time the U.S. entered World War II, there was very little federal preparation for the preservation of good mental hygiene in either the armed forces or the civilian population. In fact World War II interrupted the development of a federal Mental Health program, but it did alert the populace to the tremendous toll mental illness cost in terms of national welfare. Neuro-psychiatric disorders caused more medical discharges than did any other disability. Seventeen percent of American men of draft age were rejected by selective service or received medical discharges due to medical or educational deficiency (Brand & Sapir, 1964). The testimony of Major General Lewis Hershey, Director of the Selective Service System before congress about this situation precipitated the nation's interest in a comprehensive mental health program. (Deutsch, 1946)

Edward Hoffman (1974) describes the rapid growth of special education following World War II.

It has been in the period from approximately the end of World War II to the present that public schools in the United States have dramatically increased their degree of involvement with children viewed as mentally retarded, emotionally disturbed, or socially maladjusted, and most recently as learning disabilities. (p. 64)

World War II consolidated the mental ethic of our society and finalized the federal hierarchical structure of the bureaucratic administration of that ethic in the United States.

The federal Public Works Administration had earmarked $12 million for the construction of state hospitals in 1934. The Social Security Act of 1935 had authorized funds for public health in all the states, and as pointed out by Margaret Fraser (1974)

These innovative programs were symptomatic of a radical new philosophy about the nature of federal involvement in areas which had traditionally been left to the states. (p. 264)

After this period in history the nation slowly began to turn away from social segregation as the cure of its social ills; and, at the same time, quietly, almost unobtrusively, began to lose its faith in the melting pot. Somehow these two factors are intertwined. When there was a firm belief in a single ideal representative character pattern, it seemed simple to pick out those who deviated from this pattern. It seemed logical to conclude that those few deviants spoiled the purity of society and would multiply to further contaminate the social body. Segregation or sterilization would prevent further impurities. Now, slowly and imperceptibly, doubts began to grow. Two interacting factors seemed to be involved. First, the previously sharp social model was beginning to blur; and second, even though the mental ethic grew stronger, the separation between "them" and "us" became less clear. The genetic strain was no longer the decisive dividing line between the rational and irrational. Irrationality refused to be segregated.

In the years immediately after World War II, the public embraced special education with a growing sense of desperation. The number of mentally retarded children, served by the schools, for instance, increased from 87,000 in 1948, to 113,000 in 1952, to over 213,000 in 1958. By 1956 all states had provisions for state assistance to local special education programs focusing on such children.

Children who violated the social ethic of mental acceptability because of irrational or asocial behavior were attended to by counseling and guidance services on a one-to-one basis in the newly emergent nationwide mental health services, except where they were viewed as "culturally deprived."

World War II made the society deeply, self-consciously, anxious about its own general mental decline. Seventeen percent of American men of draft age had been reported to be rejected by the Selective Service or received medical discharges due to mental-educational deficiencies. By 1946 Veteran Administration facilities were flooded with psychiatric patients who comprised 60 percent of the hospitals' residents.

The nation was alarmed. Something had to be done. With the depression-born dependence on federal bureaucratic solutions, the country turned to the federal level to take action against its perceived worsening mental condition.

In 1944, Dr. Robert Felix was appointed the Director of a Division of Mental Hygiene in the U.S. Public Health Service. His first action was to develop an outline of a comprehensive community-based mental health program, which, in 1946, was translated into national legislation. The National Mental Health Act was passed by Congress and signed by the president in July, 1946. It outlined a national attack upon "mental disease." A National Institute of Mental Health was created. A grants-in-aid program made funds available for local mental health programs. Each state was required to name one of its agencies as the State Mental Health Authority.

The obsession with disordered psyches of self and others began to spread rapidly throughout society. As irrational events increased across the world and within the nation, irrational forces seemed to have a greater control over individual lives. The end of World War II did not end the martial holocausts that overtook the land. Poverty did not end even though the economy boomed. The nation seemed to discover more and more mental conditions which infected it—minimal brain damage, neuroses, emotional disorders, and behavioral disorders, social maladjustment, sociopathy, cultural disability, autism, alcoholism, drug addiction, etc. It discovered social discrimination, deprivation, segregation. Dissolution and decay seemed to characterize the environment of the cities. These cities discovered ghettoes in their midst.

Then suddenly the country entered the frightful Sixties. This decade had the existential quality of a schizophrenic nightmare. The Community Mental Health Act of 1963 was passed by Congress. It instituted a massive federal committment to the growth of community mental health programs in the United States. Hordes of new mental science practitioners were trained in University Programs. Mental health research burgeoned. In 1958 and 1959 public laws had been created to foster the development of higher education training programs in special education. In 1963, under PL 88-164, Section 301 and 302, support was extended for the training of professionals in several areas of exceptionality, including emotional disturbance.

Nineteen hundred sixty-three was also the fateful year in which John F. Kennedy, the 35th president of the United States, was assassinated. Next a chain of riotous explosions wracked the newly discovered ghettoes. In rapid succession came the assassination of Reverend Martin Luther King and presidential candidate Robert Kennedy. The nation seemed to itself to be infected with madness. Students revolted. Some were killed by the national guard. The abortive Great War on Poverty ground to a halt. The society felt dismayed rather than great. And then came Watergate; and the shared illusions of perfection began to come apart. The great uniform Ego Ideal, the model American type, was shattered into splinters. Irrationality could no longer be projected onto the imperfect few who violated the heroic myth. It resided in us all. The nation was face to face with the false God of Normalcy.

The Melting Pot Melts

In place of the melting pot ideal a new concept of cultural pluralism began to assert itself. It expressed itself in very strange ways; through the national move toward antidiscrimination and desegregation which was so greatly accelerated by the judicial process.

Psychosocial philosophy and the human measurement movement had provided a scientific structure for the American progeny of social Darwinism and the English Protestant bourgeois ethic at the turn of the century. Now, at midcentury the Judiciary took over from the psychologists and sociologists. They translated newer scientific doctrine into social policy which reversed the process. This turn began with the profound Supreme Court decision in 1954 to desegregate schooling. The lifting of repression of nonrepresentative types spread to become a civil rights movement that soon encompassed the mentally ill and mentally retarded. Schools were the principal institutional target of antidiscrimination. However, alienating elements of other social structures such as mental institutions were also under attack.

"Civil Rights" legislation and litigation burgeoned in the land. The tracking concept, invented in the Twenties by the psycho-educational measurement experts such as Lewis Terman, was struck down in the famous *Hobson* v. *Hansen* decisions in Washington, D.C. in the Sixties. Litigation was spawned in the area of "labeling," "psycho-educational testing," and "segregated placement"(*Guadalupe* v. *Tempe Elementary School District, Diana* v. *State Board of Education, Covarrubias* v. *San Diego Unified School Dis-*

trict, Larry v. *Riles, Stewart* v. *Phillips*, etc). The right to education and right to treatment of labeled children became an issue (*Pennsylvania Association for Retarded Children* v. *State of Pennsylvania, Mills* v. *Board of Education of the District of Columbia, Lebank* v. *Spears*). A national act was passed by federal legislation to insure the right to public schooling of all handicapped children (PL 94-142, Education of the Handicapped Act of 1976).

Discrimination-Segregation Consciousness

Discrimination and segregation were an integral part of the mental ethic of the early twentieth century. It had been accomplished by a profound public denial of its own psycho-social discrimination and segregation practices. Now in the last quarter of that century, the denial itself was being brought into focus. Awareness processes and movements asserted themselves strongly. This current fostered group-consciousness and self-consciousness: "I am Woman," "Black is Beautiful," "Gay Liberation," "Indian Rights," "Chicano Rights." The hyphenated Americans came back in style—"Mexican-Americans," "Italian Americans," and so on.

Now, as we move into the last quarter of the twentieth century it is difficult to predict clearly what direction we will take in relationship to our concepts of deviation and differences. At the moment, however, it does seem clear that hidden class designation through labels of unfitness has faltered and that we have moved from "melding" to "pluralism." It seems very difficult at this time in history for the nation to maintain a unified trait preference. Under such circumstances it would also deem difficult to continue with the present public belief in perfecting the "imperfect" or "unfit" societal members. The illusory image-ideal of the representative cultural type which was defensively concretized in the great immigration tidal wave of the late nineteenth and early twentieth centuries, seems to have been shattered by the explosion into conscious awareness of self-protective bias and discrimination. This older ego-ideal no longer seems tenable. The whole question of normalcy and abnormalcy is at issue as it never has been since the advent of gatekeeping sciences. This question shakes the foundation of the bureaucratic edifices erected upon it.

We seem to be poised upon the brink of a new torsion in our human history, a torsion which may or may not be determined by the human sciences and their social admonitions on public policy. The suspense is almost unbearable.

References

ABELL, A. *The urban impact of American Protestantism*. London: Archon, 1962.

BEERS, C. *A mind that found itself*. New York: Longmans, Green, 1921.

BENEDICT, R. *Patterns of culture*. Boston, Houghton Mifflin, 1961.

BERNARD, J. *The children you gave us: A history of 150 years of service to children*. New York: Jewish Child Care Association of New York, 1973.

BRAND, Jr. & SAPIR, P. An historical perspective on the National Institute of Mental Health. Unpublished monograph prepared as Section I of the NIMH Report to the Wooldridge Committee of the President's Scientific Advisory Committee, February 1964.

DEVINE, E. *The principles of relief*. New York: Macmillan, 1914.

DEUTSCH, ALBERT. *The mentally ill in America: A history of their care and treatment from colonial times*. New York: Columbia University Press, 1946.

FOUCAULT, M. *Madness and civilization*. New York: Vintage Books, 1973.

FRASER, M. Treatment of deviance in the mental health system. In W. Rhodes & S. Head. (Eds.), *A study in child variance*, Vol. 3, *Service Delivery Systems*. Ann Arbor: University of Michigan Press, 1973.

FRAZIER, SIR JAMES. *The golden bough: A study in magic and religion*. Vol. 1 abridged, tenth printing. New York: Macmillan, 1969.

GODDARD, H. H. *Juvenile delinquency*. New York: Dodd, Mead, 1921.

GRINKER, R. *Psychiatric social work*. New York: Basic Books, 1961.

HANDLIN, O. *Boston's immigrants*. Cambridge, Mass.: Belknap Press, 1959.

HANUS, P. *School efficiency: A constructive study applied to New York City.* Yonkers, N.Y.: World Book, 1913.

HARPUR, W. *The report of the Educational Commission of the City of Chicago.* Chicago, Ill.: Lakeside Press, 1899.

HEALY, W., & BRONNER, A. *New light on delinquency.* New Haven, Conn.: Yale University Press, 1936.

HECK, A. O. *Education of exceptional children.* New York: McGraw Hill, 1940.

HOFFMAN, E. Treatment of deviance by the educational system. In W. Rhodes & S. Head, (Eds.) *A study in child variance,* Vol. 3, *Service Delivery Systems.* Ann Arbor: University of Michigan Press, 1974.

KEUGEL, R., & WOLFENSBURGER, W. *Changing patterns in residential services for the mentally retarded.* Washington, D.C.: President's Committee on Mental Retardation, 1969.

McMURRAY, M. *Yearbook of the National Herbart Society,* 1899.

O'GRADY, J. *Catholic charities in the United States.* Washington, D.C.: National Conference of Catholic Charities, 1930.

PEKARSKY, D. Treatment of deviance by religious institutions, in W. Rhodes & S. Head, (Eds.) *A study of child variance,* Vol. 3, *Service Delivery Systems,* Ann Arbor: University of Michigan Press, 1974.

PERKINSON, H. J. *The imperfect panacea: American faith in education.* New York: Random House, 1968.

PLATT, A. *The child savers: The invention of delinquency.* Chicago, Ill.: University of Chicago Press, 1969.

ROTHMAN, D. *The discovery of the asylum.* Boston: Little, Brown, 1971.

SCHLEIER, L. *Problems in the training of certain special-class teachers.* New York: Teacher's College, Columbia University, 1931.

TERMAN, L. *Intelligence test and school reorganization.* New York: World Book, 1923.

PART TWO

Logical
Positivistic Views

The two chapters that follow present the views most frequently used today in guiding school programs for children who are seen as deviant or disturbed. Both learning theories and psychoneurological theories are logical-positivistic in that they confine themselves to the data of behavior and biogenetics. The data that such theories use in looking at deviation is restricted to the sphere of observation and observable phenomena. The child is seen as an ordered organism governed by causal laws. Any assumptions not based on empirical philosophy which may be inherent in the processes and procedures growing out of the behavioral or the psychoneurological views are studiously avoided by their practitioners.

Neither set of views considers or admits into its sphere of activity the contribution of the observer into what is observed in children. Their methodologies do not consider the "eyes of the beholder" in determining the problem itself. In these two sets of views, the bi-location of deviance does not seem to be at issue.

Neither set of views will admit metaphysical speculations into its treatment of the conditions that it defines as deviance. Value issues are put outside the realm of both theory and intervention as being tangential or "metatheoretical."

These views stress experimentation, evidence, data, general principles, specified outcomes, and specific interventions. Such factors are treated as though they are independent of the viewer.

CHAPTER THREE

Behavioral Views and Approaches

Maladaptive Behavior

Maladaptive behavior, whether disturbance, delinquency, retardation, learning disability, etc., as viewed from the point of view of the modern behavioral theorist, takes its meaning from the environmental context in which it appears. Except in a pure Pavlovian interpretation, it is rarely viewed as a condition of deviation from a psychobiological standard. Instead, it is a behavior that departs from the expectations and customs of the culture surrounding the individual marked as a deviator. Ullman and Krasner (1965), representing this point of view, express the problem this way:

The person whose behavior is maladaptive does not fully live up to the expectations for one in his role, does not respond to all the stimuli actually present, and does not obtain the typical or

43

maximum forms of reinforcement available to one of his status. (p. 20)

Such a point of view has a profound meaning for the practitioner working with children who are designated disabled or disordered. It directs him to the place in which he must look for the determination of which children are disturbed and which are not. Instead of locating the condition within some categorical state or process within the child, he looks to the discrete environments within which the child is functioning. He does not expect to find a universal syndrome, or a characteristic of the organism which will determine who is maladapted and who is not. If he expects to find any generalized set of syndromes at all, he will have to classify characteristics of environments and of the relationship of human organisms to environments.

Also, in contrast to the typical medical-functional point of view, maladaptation is not treated as a biological insufficiency that accounts for the lack of adaptation of the individual to his surroundings. Rather, it is usually handled as though a particular environmental-organismic pattern of exchange is the maladaption. This is most explicitly stated within the Skinnerian framework (1965), but it is implicit in almost all of learning theory, that theory which undergirds the behavioral model. Current extensions of this thinking would go even further, and say that the state of maladaptation existing between the organism and his immediately surrounding environment is being created by the current contingencies occurring in the impinging environment. One can look to the environmental side of a current exchange in order to understand what is maintaining a condition of maladaptation between the organism and his surroundings.

From this point of view, any classification system which is developed by the practitioner, must look into these connections between environments and organisms. It is here that one can locate the categories of maladaptation. In general practice the modern behavioral theorists do not rely upon classification systems. The followers of the learning framework view this effort of classification as a somewhat superfluous effort. They feel that if the practitioner is concerned with changing a particular individual who is looked upon as emotionally disturbed, the classification of the individual offers nothing useful for determining how to change him. Rather, particular principles of learning are the guide that will locate the source of maladaptation and determine the direction in which a program of change must proceed.

In the determination of what it is that has to be changed in the individual's interchange with the environment, the practitioner has to look into the cultural standards and expectations surrounding him that are being violated. From the behavioral learning frame of reference, the furor created over disturbances is understandable only within the context in which the individual is functioning. The furor is a manifestation of the behavioral codes, beliefs, legends, etc. held by the people surrounding the child.

Since the practitioner's concern and empathy focus more directly on the individual child and his particular needs, the practitioner operates differently within the predominant behavioral model than within other major explanatory models of emotional disturbance. He would not, for instance, concern himself with inner processes or conditions of the child who is being labeled maladaptive. Rather, his empathic concern would be with the fact that the child's current activities are not gaining maximum benefit from the environment. He is not sharing fully in the stimulation and reinforcements available in the environment. In a sense, the child is being grossly deprived of the environmental benefits in relationship to other children within the same settings. His deprivation stems from the fact that he has learned certain kinds of behaviors and these are being maintained by the conditions which exist at the present time in his own personal interactive exchange with that environment. The deprivation is being maintained by a maladaptive coupling system, or connecting arc, between the individual and the environment.

For those who are concerned about such children, one can benefit from the objectivity of the psychological science of learning, and still orient one's passions and human empathy toward the preventable or alterable condition of deprivation which the child is currently suffering relative to this environment.

In order to grasp the process whereby the condition of maladaptation between the child and his environment has been constituted and continues to be maintained, one must understand the way in which coupling exchanges or connections are established and maintained between the two open systems of individuals and environments. The creation and maintenance of such functional connections which exist as ongoing interchange patterns between individuals and environments lie in the conditioning concept first developed by Pavlov.

The connection between the stimulus and the responding organism had been known since early times, and was called a reflex long before Pavlov's investigations. Gantt (1944a) reported that the concept had been fully developed by Sechenov, the father of Russian physiology in his book *Reflexes of the Brain* published in 1863. However, it was Pavlov who established and demonstrated the idea of the *conditional* or individually *acquired* reflexes— "variable, fluctuating, appearing, disappearing, symbolizing, substituting reactions, whence a delicate equilibrium is maintained in a system surrounded by a changing environment where the system is itself perpetually changing." (Gantt, 1944a, p. 6) It was Pavlov who established that this was the central building block for the plastic and delicate adjustments which keep the organism in equilibrium with its environment.

Pavlovian Conditioning

Ivan Petrovich Pavlov (1849-1936) encountered the phenomenon of conditioning while studying the salivary glands and their relationship to digestion. In a speech delivered to the International Medical Congress in Madrid in April, 1903, he gave the first major account of the conditioning process.

Pavlov was studying the activity of the salivary glands of dogs in reaction to the application of various specific, material, substances to the glands. He was interested, more precisely, in the salivation of the animal to these various substances which included dry bread, sand, meat, etc. In the course of experimenting with these familiar, salivary-specific substances, he noticed a very strange and unaccountable phenomenon. In addition to the specific reactions of the animal to these palpable substances, there were extraneous stimuli of a nonspecific, nonmaterial nature, which began to produce some of the same salivary reactions in the animal as the material substances that he expected to activate the salivary glands. Somehow, other organs and organ systems in the animal began to receive and respond to other aspects of the environment that were impinging upon the animal at the same time as the experimental stimulus materials. Furthermore, these other organs and organ systems (i.e. the ears, eyes, etc.) began to refer the messages to the responding subsystem of the salivary glands so that they acted as though these simultaneous components of the environment had some equivalency with the stimulus properties of the bread, meat, sand, air, etc. that were being applied to the salivary glands at the same time. By additional experimentation, Pavlov and his associates discovered that these extraneous aspects of the environment such as the smell of food, the dish, the people, the room and even sounds at a distance would produce the same reactions as the original substances. This was true, even though previously, these parts of the environment failed to have any effect at all upon the salivary glands. Something was happening to cause a generalized reaction on the part of the animal to generalized aspects of the environment.

Later, Pavlov found that in addition to this connection between external environmental aspects, which caused the extraneous conditions occuring at the time of stimulation to become stimulus equivalents, another kind of equivalency also could be induced. Responses that the animal made during the same time that he was salivating, also could be reproduced when the salivary stimulating properties of the environment were introduced. Thus, not only did environmental properties gain functional equivalencies in becoming stimulus producers under a set pattern of circumstances, but also, nonessential responses of the organism could become connected to the "natural" or essential response of salivation.

Pavlov was paving the way for later studies of "learning." He was concerned with how the animal learned, for instance, to salivate upon hearing the step of his feeders. And although he did not use the term "learning" he was fully conscious of the importance of such connections being developed out of the basic unconditioned, "natural" connections between the properties of certain substances and distant, connected properties of the object or of its setting. He was aware that aside from any innate or unlearned appropriate adaptive responses to the environment, it was out of such couplings of environmental messages and organismic responses that the animal becomes adept at seeking its food, avoids environmental dangers, etc.

The classical conditioning paradigm thus developed by Pavlov and his colleagues in these researches went as follows:

1. An unconditioned substance (such as meat or bread) produced a flow of saliva as an *unconditioned reflex (response)* of the organism to this matching part of the environment.
2. An extraneous part of the environment, by being paired with the environmental releasor or unconditioned stimulus (food, sand, meat, etc.) during the time of the releasable, inherent, or unconditioned response (salivation) becomes connected with and becomes a functional equivalent of or substitute for, the unconditioned stimulus. Thus, it becomes a *conditioned stimulus*.

The pairing of the conditioned stimulus and the unconditioned response was called a *conditioned reflex*.

This simple basic paradigm has developed into a rather complicated schema, where the various pairings of environmental stimulus aspects and organismic response aspects can produce an astoundingly varied set of environmental-response pairings. Various combinations of conditioned and unconditioned stimuli and conditioned and unconditioned responses can be carried out to profoundly alter or modify the functional coupling or connecting systems between environmental and behavioral properties. This has been elaborated and developed into a much more sophisticated and manipulable schema by the manipulating of "reinforcers" or conditions which have the capacity to stamp-in the functional connections created by these directed environmental-organismic interactions.

A *reinforcer*, or *reinforcement*, is any property of the organism or the environment that has the capacity either to intensify or maximize these functional couplings, or to attenuate or interfere with these couplings. Some researchers working within the conditioning framework are convinced that a reinforcement is any condition which is tension releasing for the organism (such as sexual discharge, feeding when the individual is hungry, or drinking when thirsty). Others believe that a reinforcement is any condition (which needs not be tension-reducing) that satisfies the individual (like mastery of a problem, achievement of various kinds, or exploring and investigating new aspects of the environment). Still others are much more pragmatic in their approach and call any identifiable condition or circumstance that strengthens or reduces the established bond between environmental aspects and organismic responses a reinforcement.

Reinforcements are called either *positive* or *negative*, depending on their actions upon the functional couplings between stimuli and responses, and upon their aversive or positive qualities for the individual receiving them. The more frequently encountered view of reinforcement has led to experimentation with specific agents that are satisfying to basic tissue needs, such as food when the individual is hungry, water when he is thirsty, a sexually reciprocating partner when there is sexual deprivation, etc. These are frequently called *primary reinforcements*. Other reinforcements that can become directly connected with these, such as social reinforcements, are referred to as *secondary reinforcements*. In learning research conducted within the last few years it has been demonstrated that almost any satisfying state of affairs, or even an individual's own behavior can act as a reinforcement when one is trying to condition or bring into existence other, more socially prized behavior. In the Premack "principle" (Premack, 1959) an individual's own frequently emitted behavior can be used as a reinforcement for behaviors which are less frequent in the individual's repertory.

Thus, we see that out of the early work of Pavlov, investigating the conditioned reflex and the process whereby it is brought about, a basic set of events or factors is all one has to use in understanding how individuals learn behaviors that are not in their original repertoire, whether this be adaptive or maladaptive to the specific microenvironment in which they are acting and being evaluated for their acts. In the interchange between the individual and the environment, certain stimuli impinge upon or are directed to the individual, certain responses are called out by these stimuli, and certain reinforcers act to achieve a functional coupling system between stimuli and responses. Such coupling systems have a tendency to perpetuate themselves. If, for some reason inherent in the social and cultural context, these functional coupling systems are looked upon as maladaptive, a special effort or outside intervention has to be instigated in order to interrupt, change, modify or eliminate them. This, then, is the essential logic of the classical conditioning, Pavlovian conditioning, or "respondent" conditioning view of the problem of emotional disturbance as maladaptive behavior.

Behavioral Disorders: Early Research

The relationship between the conditioning procedure and the problem of behavioral disorders and emotional disturbance did not spring full-blown from the early observations of conditioning. The use of the conditioning schema in modern practices of behavioral therapy and behavior modification did not make the leap from these simple, general experiments to the clinic or classroom. Instead, the parallel drawn between conditioning and behavioral disorders resulted from a long series of research and experimentation carried out in the area of experimental neurosis in laboratories across the world. Like the conditional reflex, the concept of "experimental neurosis" and the demonstration of the methods by which it could be established were initiated in the laboratory of Pavlov. Although Pavlov did not specifically report upon this phenomenon under the title of experimental neurosis until 1923 (Pavlov, 1941), it was observed as early as 1912 by one of Pavlov's colleagues conducting experiments having to do with pathological changes following conflicting stimuli. (Yerofeyeva, reported in Pavlov, Vol. 1, 1941.)

These special neurotic conditions were seen by Pavlov as pathological disturbances resulting from functional interference. He defined a neurosis, for experimental purposes, as:

... a chronic deviation of the higher nervous activity, lasting weeks, months, and even years. For us the nervous activity is manifested chiefly in the system of conditioned positive and negative reflexes to any stimulus and partially, but to a lesser degree, in the general behavior of our animals (dogs). (1941, p. 73)

The technique worked out in Pavlov's laboratory, and one that is the major process employed in various studies of experimental neurosis, is that of establishing a conditioned reflex between a stimulus and a response and then to switch to a conflicting stimulus, or to set up a laboratory situation of conflict in which the animal is required to differentiate between two stimuli so similar that they cannot really be distinguished.

In the first experiments from Pavlov's laboratory in 1912 having to do with pathological changes following conflicting stimuli, Yerofeyeva (in Pavlov, Vol. 1, 1941) reported the following procedure: A conditioned food reflex was developed in connection with a stimulus that would ordinarily evoke a defensive or avoidance response. An electric shock was applied to the skin of a dog at the same time that he was being fed. A weak current was used in the beginning and gradually it was increased. The dog developed a good conditional or acquired response to this strange stimulus response pairing. In other words, he would begin salivating in anticipation of the reception of food when the current was applied to his skin. The usual defensive or avoidant responses such as changes in breathing or heart rate, gave way entirely to the anticipatory salivation response. This in itself was pathological. What had happened was that the natural defensive reactions of the organism to environmental insult or danger were inhibited, and in its place a positive or excitatory response was called out.

The experimenter, having established a stable excitatory or food response, began to shift the electric irritation at every excitation to another new point on the skin. When the number of these points became considerable, one of the dogs suddenly changed. Everywhere, beginning with the first location of the skin stimulus, and even with the weakest current, every trace of the food reaction disappeared and all that could be elicited was only the strongest defensive reaction.

Later, the experimenters in Pavlov's laboratory developed the technique of impossible differentiations between two very similar stimuli. The conditioning task set for the dog was differentiation of a circle from an ellipse of the same size and visual intensity. The circle was always accompanied by feeding, the ellipse, never. The circle called out or released a food reaction, but the ellipse released an inhibition of the food response. In the procedure the experimenter began with marked differences between the circle and ellipse until the appropriate responses were well established. Then, gradually, the ellipse was brought closer and closer in form to the circle. At first there was increasing acuity in the animal's capacity to differentiate between the circle and the ellipse as they began to come closer together. However, a point was reached, when the two forms became increasingly similar, where the differentiation disappeared altogether. The dog became increasingly excited, struggled, fought his bonds, and displayed many other symptoms of agitation. In some dogs catalepsy or pathological sleep was elicited by the undifferentiable stimuli.

Further experimentation with "experimental neuroses" in the Pavlovian laboratories established certain facts about this phenomenon or condition:

1. Behavioral disturbances could be brought about in experimental animals by a variety of causes or conditions. Pavlov identified three circumstances that could elicit it.
   (a) extremely strong stimuli used in place of those that are weak or moderately strong and which ordinarily determine the animal's activity.
   (b) the animal is required to exert a very strong or very protracted inhibition.
   (c) a conflict between these two processes is produced by the experimenter in which conditioned positive and negative stimuli are produced one right after the other.
2. At least two types of susceptible animals succumbed to the same stimulus conditions:
   (a) the excitatory type, which loses almost completely its ability for any inhibition and generally becomes unusually excited.

(b) the inhibitory type who, though hungry, refuses to eat under the influence of the conditioned stimuli and generally becomes exceedingly ill at ease and passive with the least change of its surrounding environment.

3. "Natural" emotional shocks can produce disturbances in behavior so that previous adaptations to the environment can be radically altered. As a result of a great flood in Petrograd in 1924 Pavlov's kennels were inundated. During the terrific storm, amid the breaking of waves against the walls of the buildings, the noise of falling and breaking trees, etc. the animals had to be quickly transferred by making them swim from the kennels to a safe place in the laboratory. As a result some of the dogs later showed extremely disturbed reactions in the experimental conditions.

Gantt (1944b), in a review of some of the findings of studies in experimental neurosis (which we prefered to call behavioral disorders), up to the period of 1944, reports on the variety of causes and methods noted in these various researches. He groups these under external factors and internal factors:

Under internal factors he lists the emotional or constitutional state of the animal. Under external factors he includes *natural* severe emotional shocks, such as situations involving extreme fear, explosions, unusual scenes, fierce fights, physiological states like parturition, disturbance in the male from the presence (or withdrawal) of a rutting female.

Under external factors he also lists *artificial* methods of producing experimental neuroses:

1. By creating a conflict between emotions, or in the concept of Pavlov, the tensions between subcortical centers, or two unconditional reflexes, as between food and pain.
2. By the conflict between opposing conditional stimuli—either a conflict in space and time, e.g., differentiations too difficult for the animal, or simultaneous application of positive and negative conditional stimuli.
3. Changes in the daily order and time relations of the routine.
4. Excessive increase of intensity in the conditional reflexes.
5. Change in relation between conditional and unconditional reflexes: failure to follow the conditional reflex by the usual unconditional stimulus. Though this is a method of producing extinction it may, instead of leading to extinction, become a chronic state of disturbance.

In a twelve year study of the nervous disturbances of dogs in his laboratory Gantt (1944b) replicated some of the phenomena observed in the Russian laboratories. His contribution was, in many ways, even more significant since it provided a longitudinal and life-context report on a small group of dogs which were permanent subjects in his researches.

In discussing the general symptoms of "behavior disorder" shown by his research animals and those of contemporary researchers, Gantt reports the following categories. First, *general behavior* was affected—refusal of the animal to perform the problem correctly or marked deviation from the performance previously established. Reluctance to enter the experimental environment was reported both in animals and children when the difficult differentiation method was used. Second, *gross emotional disturbance* appeared—whining, barking, attempting to escape. Defense reactions might replace the food reflex. Third, *motor phenomena* that were not components of definite emotion were noted. These varied from great hyperactivity to sleep, catalepsy, convulsions, tics, etc. Fourth, *autonomic responses* were affected—change in heart rate, frequency of urination, defecation, change in respiration, sexual symptoms. Fifth, there were changes in the special relations between positive and negative conditional reflexes. One or both were suppressed, or one predominated at the expense of the other.

In terms of the classes of deviations from the "appropriate" reactions of excitation or inhibition, Gantt observed that the following had occurred: (1) direct active defense reactions aimed at escaping the experimental situation; (2) passive defense, leading to immobility and various motor disturbances (catalepsy, etc.); (3) entirely unrelated and extraneous symptoms, having neither characteristics of the appropriate response nor an active or passive defense reaction (permanent abnormal changes in the separate physiological systems such as circulatory, sexual, respiratory, alimentary changes); (4) changes observable only in the special measurements of autonomic functions.

Gantt, in reporting these classes of symptoms, makes the important observation, not usually made by other experimenters who are focusing their attention only upon the specific, tiny microcosm of stimuli and responses that he has singled out for his study:

in any measurement that we make—whether general behavior, motor, secretatory, respiratory, cardiac, metabolic—it is imperative to recognize that *no single measure represents the whole picture*. We are, so to speak, fishing in the stream of life, and bring up only that for which we have the appropriate bait. (1944b, p. 16)

As shown in one of his experimental dogs, Nick, many profound effects are occurring as a result of the tiny, highly controlled research procedure, which are not observed in the limited effects which the usual laboratory researcher is attending to.

In studying Gantt's report, as contrasted with the work of Pavlov, Jules Masserman (1943), Norman Maier (1935), etc., one is more likely to grasp the Gestalt of the interplay between environmental and organismic events. One is more likely to perceive the intricacy and complexity of the flow of exchanges between the individual and the external milieu.

Nick was a mongrel male born about 1929 or 1930. In early 1931 he became one of the experimental animals in Gantt's Pavlovian Laboratory at the Phipps Psychiatric Clinic in Baltimore, Maryland. For about a year before any work was done on him he was brought into the experimental room for casual observations. He was kept in the paddocks of the laboratory with the other experimental dogs. He was studied until his death in 1943. He was originally selected because of his very normal behavior and demeanor as an appropriate animal in whom to create an artificial "neurosis." Before the experimental work began he appeared to be a very good natured and friendly animal.

The major procedure used for most of the experimentally-intended research in the Pavlovian Laboratory of Gantt was the same as the salivary method developed in the Russian laboratory.

Nick's task was to differentiate between auditory sounds. After the positive and inhibitory conditioning (differentiation between tones) was established, the differentiation was made increasingly difficult. The experiments began in January, 1932, and by July of that year behavioral disorders began to appear. In October of the same year the differentiations were made even more difficult, and from that point on Nick refused the dry food in the experimental room, even when very hungry, until the end of his life.

In April of 1933, when impossible differentiation was introduced, Nick's restlessness greatly increased, as evidenced by howling, barking, marked trembling, scratching off salivary disc, refusing to eat, etc. He had to be taken by force into the experimental room. He ran in the opposite direction when told to jump on the stand. His heart rate increased considerably. At the end of January, 1934, he was given three weeks rest to see if he would improve.

No improvement occurred, and beginning in August, 1934, to July, 1936, he was allowed to rest in the laboratory paddock. These two years of rest caused only slight temporary improvement when he was returned to the same experimental environment. A number of other experiments were tried with Nick. He developed a very peculiar, loud, raucous, asthma-like breathing, which showed up most intensely in the experimental room. Also he developed a very significant symptom of a behavioral nature. The tone sound had, during the two-year interval, been shifted from another part of the room than that which had been used in the original conditioning of Nick. The first few days Nick reacted appropriately to this new source of sound. However, suddenly Nick began to react to the past rather than to the reality of the present. When the tone was sounded, Nick began to whine as before, but now instead of looking toward the source of the tone, he stared fixedly in the opposite direction, in that corner of the room whence the tone had previously come and backed away from the old location of the tone and actually toward its present position.

At this time his sexual responses were still very "normal." They were appropriate in response to a female dog when she was introduced into the experimental situation. He engaged in coitus and showed no atypical sexual behavior. This is mentioned at this point because a little later unusual sexual responses developed, which became a more or less permanent part of Nick's behavior under tension.

In the middle of December, 1936, during a demonstration of Nick before several people, the reciprocal relationship between sexual reflexes and anxiety first appeared. The inhibitory tone produced the usual anxious responses in Nick, but the appearance of an experimental female dog in estrus overcame the inhibitory tone to this sexual stimulation, while at the same time overcame the excitatory response to food. At this time Nick showed intense excitement and interest in the female dog and in her urine. The intensity of the sexual stimulation and its capacity to overcome the inhibitory responses was the forerunner of the interplay between anxiety and sexual responsiveness in Nick, which marked the rest of his life.

Having noted this inhibitory effect of sexual stimulation on the anxiety reactions to the tone and to other aspects of the experimental environment, a small female dog was put in the paddock with Nick. She was left there from December 22, 1936, until January 5, 1937. During this whole period, when Nick was brought down to the experimental room he was much quieter, there was less hyperactivity, he went into the experimental room more readily, ate the meat without hesitation and urinated only twice in the room during a three month period. On December 31, it was noted for the first time in several years that Nick did not pant or breathe raucously in the experimental room.

Nick's improvement in the experimental situation lasted until the end of March, 1937. Due to the fact that neither rest nor food had much effect upon the behavior, it seemed justifiable to conclude that the companionship of the female in his paddock was responsible for this striking improvement. This, combined with the observation that sexual stimulation of the dog in estrus during the December demonstration was capable of overcoming his inhibitory responses where food had not been able to do this, indicated the reciprocal relations existing between sexual excitation and the anxiety-like state in this animal. By May of that year, most of his old symptoms reappeared, including the loud panting and abnormal breathing.

On May 20 a new phenomenon became visible. In addition to producing all of the anxiety indicators previously noted to the sound, there was a sexual erection to the tone. This stereotyped involvement of the sexual system from there on in, took its place alongside the respiratory and urinary system in prominence, intensity, and perverse stability. Any anxiety state occurring within Nick developed the power to elicit sexual erections and even ejaculation.

A series of experiments were then instigated between June and August, 1937, to bring out clearly the relations between the anxiety-like state and sexual excitation. In addition to the tone, other stimuli that aroused defensive reactions in Nick such as those mentioned above, plus crouching, whining, etc. also produced the sexual symptoms of erection and occasional spontaneous ejaculation. The appearance of Gantt and other members of the laboratory staff also produced an erection plus the other symptoms. Gantt concluded, with considerable evidence, that any experience event, or circumstance that would elicit anxiety in Nick also excited a sexual response.

In order to determine the effect of a complete change of environment Nick was removed from the laboratory and brought to Dr. Gantt's farm. He remained there from August 1, 1937, until

October 3, 1937. On first arriving in the country he showed a marked degree of antipathy toward people associated with the laboratory, including Dr. Gantt. However, he was much more friendly with strangers, showing the kind of behavior he had exhibited to all people prior to his use as an experimental animal. Gradually, he became more friendly with Gantt during his stay.

On three occasions, during this stay on the farm, he demonstrated an intense return of all of his old anxiety symptoms. These three occasions were threatening or disagreeable experiences. Once he was thrown in the water, once his foot got caught in the chain of a bicycle and he was dragged some distance, and once he became entangled in the chain on which he was tied. After each event, during a walk with Dr. Gantt immediately after his experience, he was restless, scratched vigorously, growled and had penile erections.

In October, 1937, he was returned to the laboratory and experiments began again. During the next month his behavior was much more normal and showed very little in the way of former symptoms, and when they did appear they were much milder. However, by January 3, 1938, all of the old symptoms of inhibition, whining, retreating, erections, etc. were evident with great intensity even though petting by strangers or by Dr. Gantt was sufficient to inhibit these reactions.

A year after his return to the laboratory in January 1939 he showed marked avoidance of Dr. Gantt, plus erections whenever Dr. Gantt or the handlers who assisted him came near Nick. The reciprocal relationship between anxiety and the sexual symptoms was well established by this time.

On August 25, 1939, Nick was transported to the farm again. During 1940 he was kept on a leash most of the time on the farm. When Dr. Gantt visited in February, 1940, and again in March, 1940, Nick crouched when he saw the experimenter approaching, lay on his back and had an ejaculation. His heart rate increased considerably. His behavior toward Dr. Gantt and a farm attendant was markedly in contrast. He crouched and rolled on his back with the approach of the experimenter, but he jumped up upon the attendant in a friendly manner and there was no erection.

Gradually, as in the previous stays, Nick's behavior toward Dr. Gantt began to change. By the end of May he was showing a mixture of the different behavioral patterns he had exhibited toward the farm attendant and the experimenter. He would alternately jump up upon his master and crouch away from him. The heart rate and the erections began to diminish in intensity. By September, he would come into the house, accept food, exhibit markedly friendly behavior, and even when whipped by Dr. Gantt for jumping on the table, he did not have an erection. His devotion was more marked than two other dogs on the farm. He followed Dr. Gantt everywhere, jumping into his car or running after it. When Dr. Gantt was working at his desk Nick would lie quietly at his feet.

After this period, there were several shifts of Nick back and forth between the laboratory and the farm until he died in 1943.

Other major researchers have experimented with the production of disordered behaviors in various animals. Masserman (1943) produced experimental neurosis in cats, Bajandurow (1932) produced it in pigeons, Maier (1935) in rats, Anderson and Liddell (1935) in sheep, Jacobsen (1936) in chimpanzees.

These early laboratory studies of behavior provided the base upon which current practices of behavioral therapy and behavior modification are built. In them we are faced with the amazing plasticity of behavior as the mediator between the individual and the environment. At the same time that behavior is shaped by the environment, it is also shaping the environment (for example, Nick's behavior shifted Gantt's research toward the study of the reciprocity between anxiety and sex). At the same time that it is a stereotyped representation or expression of the organism, it is also quite capable of great flexibility and change (e.g., Nick's changing behavioral pattern toward his master, Dr. Gantt). At the same time that there may be pronounced changes within subsets of behaviors, the outline and overall pattern remains integral and recognizable for an individual (e.g., Nick's general, characteristic orientation toward human beings in social conditions). At the same time that it obeys ancient directives from within the genetic structure of the organism, it is quite capable of undergoing dramatic transformation (e.g., Nick's sexual system changes).

The Bias of Organismic Modification

In his Nobel speech, delivered in Stockholm in 1904, Pavlov said that animal organism, as a system, exists in surrounding nature thanks only to the continuous equilibration of this system with the environment, i.e., thanks to definite reactions of the living system to stimulations reaching it from without, which in higher animals is effected mainly by means of the nervous system in the shape of reflexes. This equilibration, and consequently, the integrity of both the individual organism and of its species, is ensured first of all by the simplest unconditioned reflexes (such as coughing when foreign substances enter the larynx), as well as by the most complex ones, which are usually known as instincts—alimentary, defensive, sexual, and others. The reflexes are caused both by internal agents arising within the organism and by external agents, and this ensures the perfection of the equilibration. The equilibrium attained by these reflexes is complete only when there is an absolute constancy of the external environment. But since the latter, being highly varied, is always fluctuating, the unconditioned, or constant connections are not sufficient; they must be supplemented by conditioned reflexes.

It remained for Skinner to fully emphasize the significant part played by the environment in the reciprocal exchange between organism and the environment. Further, as will be discussed shortly, he pointed out the spontaneity of behavior. That is, behavior can be a spontaneously initiated action of the organism operating upon the environment. Such operant behavior is produced by, not elicited from, the individual and is affected by the way in which it is met by the environment. He conceives of an active role being played by the environment in response to the individual's spontaneously produced behavior. Skinner (1953) has thus been led into and has led modern behavioral therapy and behavior modification theorists into a consideration of the environment: particularly the culture of the environment. It has also led to a different interpretation of emotional disturbance.

Whereas Pavlov and his followers have referred all neuroses to dysfunctions between excitor and inhibitor processes within the nervous system, the followers of Skinner have pictured behavioral disorders as a culturally relative or community-relative phenomenon. What is considered disordered depends upon the particular microenvironment in which the individual is functioning.

Although Skinner has not, in his theories, moved beyond these new emphases in conditioning to articulate the complex interchangeable functions of individual and environment, he has demonstrated them in his theoretically consistent novel, *Walden II* (1948). In *Walden II* he shows, by design and orderly process, the mutuality between man and environment. He shows how the tranquility or turbulence of life ensues from the interplay or mutual action of one upon the other. He shows that the design or structure that organizes this interchange must embrace both individual and environment as though they were a unitary, amalgamated system.

Operant Conditioning

In his book on the behavior of organisms, B. F. Skinner (1938) discusses a conception of conditioning that places the behavioral modification process in a new perspective.

In the Pavlovian or classical conditioning experiments, the emphasis was upon stimulus substitution. The unconditioned stimulus (the meat) produced the unconditioned response (salivation). After the conditioning procedure, a conditioned stimulus (a bell, a light, etc.) paired with the unconditioned stimulus, produced the same unconditioned response as the meat.

However, according to Skinner (1938), there is a different kind of conditioning, which is much more concerned with behavior, which has some of the effect upon the surrounding world. Such behavior, he says, raises most of the practical problems in human affairs and is also of particular theoretical interest because of its special characteristics. This type of behavior, spontaneously occurring behaviors for which there is no obvious stimulus, and which are under the control of the organism, operate upon the environment and produce a consequence to the organism. Such behaviors are called operants, and they are emitted rather than elicited. They are distinguished from "respondents" or stimulus elicited behaviors that are produced by a stimulus.

In order to bring operant behavior under environmental control, all that one needs to do is to provide appropriate reinforcing stimuli to follow their appearance. Instead of looking for the stimulus-response connections, one waits for the operant behavior or takes opportunistic advantage of their appearance in the natural situation and then manipulates reinforcers or stimulus aspects of the environment in order either to increase the probability of the occurrence of behavior in this form, or to shape it in certain directions of greater utility to the organism.

By manipulating the environment one can gain a certain amount of control over behavior. Positive reinforcements (such as food, drink, praise) can increase the rate of frequency of the emission of that behavior if it is applied immediately after each response. A negative reinforcement (undesirable consequences or stimuli) can also increase the probability of that behavior by removing it immediately after each response. In Skinner's terms, *punishment* is defined either as the removal of a positive reinforcer, or the application of a negative reinforcing stimulus. As suggested in the above paragraph, by the proper manipulation of the contingencies of reinforcement, one can shape or modify behavior quite drastically in a particular direction. As an example, a pigeon can be taught to play ping-pong by careful observation of its behavior and by careful reinforcement of that behavior.

By waiting until the pigeon moves in any direction toward the ball and reinforcing even that slight movement, one can increase the frequency with which the pigeon will produce that movement. Then, by *successive approximations*, one begins to reinforce only after the pigeon has produced turning plus drawing back the foot. After this sequence is stabilized, reinforcement is provided only after turning, drawing back the foot, and kicking the foot forward. Gradually, through these bits and pieces of behavior, one gradually builds up the kick-ball response.

In Pavlovian or "respondent" conditioning, according to Skinner, we simply increase the magnitude of the response elicited by the conditioned stimulus and shorten the time that elapses between stimulus and response.

In operant conditioning we "strengthen" an operant in the sense of making a response more probable or, in actual fact, more frequent.

According to Skinner (1953):

While we are awake, we act upon the environment constantly, and many of the consequences of our actions are reinforcing. Through operant conditioning the environment builds the basic repertoire with which we keep our balance, walk, play games, handle instruments and tools, talk, write, sail a boat, drive a car, or fly a plane. A change in the environment—a new car, a new friend, a new field of interest, a new location—may find us unprepared, but our behavior usually adjusts quickly as we acquire new responses and discard old. (p. 66)

From the operant conditioning point of view, as expressed by Skinner, disturbance is conceptualized quite differently from the Pavlovian point of view. However, in actual fact, the presentation offered by Skinner is very close to the experimental phenomenon of neuroses created and studied within the Pavlovian laboratories. Pavlov's description posited a chronic deviation of the higher nervous activity, lasting weeks, months, and even years. Behavior was a reflection of such nervous activity. Skinner on the other hand, sticks pretty closely to the behavior. He sees it as behavior which is inconvenient or dangerous to the individual himself or to others (1953, p. 367). He sees disturbances as an emotional byproduct of control of various social agencies of control such as the religious, family, governmental, and legal agencies. This byproduct has come about as the result of punishment.

What is "wrong" with the individual who displays these by-products of punishment is easily stated. A particular personal history has produced an organism whose behavior is disadvantageous or dangerous. In what sense it is disadvantageous or dangerous must be specified in each case by noting the consequences both to the individual himself and to others. (1953, p. 372)

From Skinner's point of view, the methods of treating these behaviors is replete with explanatory functions. He says that behavior itself has not been accepted as a subject matter in its own right, but rather as an indicator of something wrong somewhere else. He says that the terms "neurotic" and "neurosis" still carry the implication of a derangement of the nervous system, and are unfortunate examples of an explanatory fiction. It has encouraged the belief in a single cause for multiple disorders and implies a uniformity which is not found in the data. It has encouraged the belief that treatment consists of removing inner causes of mental illness as the surgeon removes an inflamed appendix or as indigestible food is purged from the body. He says that: "It is not an inner cause of behavior but the behavior itself which—in the medical analogy of catharsis—must be 'got out of the system'" (1953, p. 373).

He says that the traditional treatment consists of exorcising the Devil and that the lesser demons of modern theory are anxieties, conflicts, repressed wishes, and repressed memories. The belief that certain kinds of "pent-up behavior cause trouble until the organism is able to get rid of them" is at least as old as the Greeks.

In the alternative point of view which states the trouble as a by-product of punishment in which a particular personal history has produced an organism whose behavior is disadvantageous or dangerous, one must look to the consequences of this behavior both to the individual and others in order to determine in what sense the behavior is disadvantageous or dangerous. From this point of view, the problem of therapy is to supplement a personal history in such a way that behavior no longer has these characteristics.

Skinner says that the community functions as a reinforcing environment in which certain kinds of behavior are reinforced and others are punished. The reason why certain behaviors are reinforced and others rebuked by a particular community is sometimes difficult to analyze. However, it is possible that a given form of deviant behavior was aversive for good reasons under an earlier condition of the group. Foodstuffs, for instance, are generally selected by contingencies which follow from their physical and chemical properties. Foods that are unpalatable, inedible, or poisonous come to be left alone. A child who starts to eat such a food receives powerful aversive stimulation from the group. "Good" and "bad" foods are eventually specified in ethical, religious or governmental codes. When, through a change in climate or living conditions, or through a change in preparation and preservation practices, a "bad" food becomes safe, the classification may nevertheless survive.

Skinner claims that no matter how we ultimately explain the action of the group in extending the ethical classification of "right" and "wrong" to manners and customs, we are on solid ground in observing the contingencies by virtue of which the behavior characteristic of a particular group is maintained. As each individual comes to conform to a standard pattern of conduct, he also comes to support that pattern by applying a similar classification to the behavior of others. Moreover, his own conforming behavior contributes to the standard with which the behavior of others is compared. Once a custom, manner, or style has arisen, the social system that observes it appears to be reasonably self-sustaining.

The last few observations of this section have been an extension of Skinner's thinking. In Skinner's conception we can see the significance of the particular context of behavior. The environment becomes a much more significant referent than it was under the Pavlovian conception of conditioning. In order to determine what behavior is maladapted one has to refer to the specific surrounding environment of the organism. Unlike the Pavlovian ideas of conditioning, that which is maladaptive is not referrable to the neurological functioning of the organism, but rather, is much more reliant upon the culture in which the specific behavior is occurring.

The problem lies in particular behaviors which either do not pay off, in terms of cultural rewards, or which bring on punishing consequences in that particular microculture. The task is to change those behaviors or to provide other behaviors that will be "advantageous" to the individual and/or the group. Emitted behavior of the organism acts upon the environment and is fed back consequences. The consequences, if positive, have a way of engaging behavior and increasing its probability of emission in the future. These repeated pairings create a behavior-environment exchange circuit that maintains a certain behavior in a certain environment that then becomes characteristic of the individual emitting it.

The Two Patterns of Conditioning

Essentially, then, there are two basic patterns for making and unmaking behavior, and for explaining the problem of emotional disturbance. Both are subsumed under the general concept of conditioned learning. From both points of view the disadvantageous behavior was acquired through learning, and new or modified behaviors can be brought about by unlearning and relearning.

Skinner has referred to Pavlovian conditioning as "respondent" conditioning. A previously neutral stimulus acquired the power to produce a response that was originally elicited by another stimulus. This change occurs when the neutral stimulus is followed or "reinforced" by the effective stimulus. Such reflexes are mainly concerned with the internal physiology of the organism.

"Operant" conditioning, on the other hand, is interested in behaviors that have some effect upon the surrounding world. These behaviors that operate upon the surrounding world, Skinner believes, raise most of the practical problems of human affairs. The consequences of such behavior feeds back into the organism. When they do so, they may change the probability that the behavior that produced them will occur again. Skinner, therefore, as opposed to Pavlov, is interested in consequences-producing behavior.

Instrumental Learning

Before moving on, we must mention another type of learning, instrumental learning, which is frequently included under the general heading of conditioning. This type of learning is seen as goal directed, and is instrumental in either producing a reward or avoiding a punishment. The responses that are learned are related to a goal that is either actively sought, or actively avoided by the individual involved.

For instance, an individual in a certain specific situation is hungry and seeking to obtain food. There are a number of possible responses that can lead to the obtaining of food in such a situation. However, he happens to choose one response over the others, and it leads to food. Thereafter, whenever he finds himself in the same or a similar situation, he is much more likely to use that particular response which led to the food than all the other possible ones which could also obtain food for him. In this type of learning example, the act that precedes the reward is instrumental in the delivery of reward.

The same general principle is also involved in another type of instrumental or goal-directed learning to avoid a particular goal or outcome. In the avoidance form of the same type of learning, the individual is in a situation which leads to a particular outcome that is noxious. By responding to a signal that precedes the noxious stimulus, he can prevent the appearance of the noxious stimulus. For instance, in some of the laboratory experiments on avoidance training, the experimental subject learns to avoid a shock by jumping, by pressing a lever, or by turning a wheel, which prevents the shock from occurring. In the original experiment of this sort by Bekhterev (1933) withdrawal responses of hand or foot, in which the responding member rested on an electrode, would prevent the shock from occurring. Unlike the classical conditioning procedure, the individual has control over the appearance of the reinforcement.

A variation of this, and one that has been widely used as a paradigm for neurotic response learning, is escape training or escape learning. In this type of learning, the individual, by accident or trial and error, discovers that when in a situation where a noxious stimulus is delivered (say, a shock) this stimulus can be turned off by a particular response so that it does not increase in intensity and duration.

In another variation of this, reward is withheld when a particular response occurs. That is, if the reward is food or candy, and the individual's response is reaching; with each reaching response the food is withheld, the individual may soon make a definite withholding response antagonistic to reaching.

Another type of instrumental learning is involved in direct punishment. In avoidance learning, the punishment follows only if the to-be-learned response fails to occur. Also, in avoidance learning, the noxious stimulus, if it is administered at all, occurs before the response. In punishment learning, on the other hand, the noxious stimulus appears after the response has occurred. This is like a slap on the wrist after the hand is extended or reached out.

Instrumental, or goal-directed, learning reintroduces certain inner dynamics of the organism, which Skinner has put aside in his particular theoretical construction of behavior. It introduces the phenomenon of *purpose*. The behavior of concern in disturbance thus becomes purposive behavior, behavior with a sought-after endpoint. However, instrumental learning, like operant conditioning, can be studied and influenced without resorting to the neurology of the organism. It makes no assumptions about the neurological substrate. Furthermore, it is not dependent upon either the "reflex" concept, or the "conditioning" concept in explaining and controlling the interactions between the organism and the environment. It claims that behavior is purposive and that the organism, in striving to achieve these individual, organismic purposes, learns that certain behavioral patterns, acting upon the environment, achieve these purposes for him. Thus, in his future encounters with the environment, he will be more likely to resort to these particular behavioral patterns.

Ullman and Krasner (1965) say that the significance given to a certain behavior is dependent on the social context. Maladaptive behavior is that behavior which does not fit the expectations set up in the context, does not respond to all the stimuli actually present, and does not obtain typical or maximum forms of reinforcement available to the status of the behavior.

Behavioral Therapy and Modification

In some of his later work Pavlov emphasized the roles of the excitatory and inhibitory system in the problems of psychiatry. In modern American psychotherapy, Andrew Salter (1961) comes closest to the Pavlovian concepts. Salter contends that higher nervous activity, as manifested in the conditioned reflex, consists of a continual change of three fundamental processes—excitation, inhibition, and disinhibition.

Within Salter's paradigm, it is these reflexes, rather than the higher level abstractive processes of the human being, which make for trouble. The cognitive and abstractive processes are subservient to these more primitive mechanisms in man. Man is basically an emotional animal, like his animal ancestors. He does not act because of intellectual reasons, but attaches intellectual reasons to his actions. Reasoning follows emotional habit. Whether we like it or not, the brain case has been permeated by the viscera. "In the beginning was the gut, and the gut was law, and it is still so" (Salter, 1961, p. 35).

We run into trouble when the conditioned inhibitions gain ascendancy over our basic excitatory nature. The disturbed individual is an individual who "suffers from constipation of the emotions" (Salter, 1961, p. 47).

Therefore, Salter works to free people from these conditioned inhibitions of their emotions through a process of disinhibition. He asks that inhibited people stop using their intelligence as the driver of their lives, and to start living their emotions, their basic excitatory nature. He stresses six techniques of conduct as a means of freeing people to act upon their excitatory nature:

1. Stress feeling talk in your daily life. That is, strive for spontaneous expressions of feelings and emotions under all circumstances.
2. Use facial talk. That is, emotions should be allowed to show themselves in the face.
3. Contradict and attack when differing with someone. Instead of pretending to agree and instead of using socially acceptable subterfuge to avoid disagreeing with someone, express your differences strongly and spontaneously. Do not hesitate to contradict and attack.
4. Use the word "I" as much as possible. Instead of politely excluding oneself from engagements with other people, do not hesitate to use the pronoun "I." I like this. I read this book.
5. When in agreement with someone, express it with praise. Praise of self should also be volunteered wherever one feels justified.
6. Be and act spontaneously. Live now. Use improvisations as much as possible.

These six personal procedures follow directly from Salter's convictions. In his concept of disturbance, personal maladjustment is a result of malconditioning, and treatment consists of reconditioning. Since the individual's problems are a result of his social experience, changing his techniques of social relations will change his personality. Not only is experience the best teacher, it is the only teacher. One cannot substitute symbolic or abstract understanding of one's behavior for direct experience and direct action.

Wolpe (Wolpe, 1958, Wolpe & Lazarus, 1966) has a more complex and theoretically elaborate translation of respondent conditioning as applied to emotional disturbance. Like Pavlov, he sees the phenomenon of emotional disturbance as neurotic behavior. Neurotic behavior is any persistent habit of unadaptive behavior acquired by learning in a physiological normal organism. He also incorporates many of the conclusions drawn from large sectors of the literature on experimental neurosis. He pictures the central constituent of neurotic behavior as anxiety. Anxiety is invariably present in the causal situation of maladaptation. In dealing with neurotic behavior one always has to deal with a central core of anxiety. In general, however, the salient feature of neurosis is the persistence of unadaptive behavior, its failure to extinguish as one might expect it to on the basis of the lack of positive reinforcement or the presence of negative reinforcement from the environment. Since most maladaptive behavior violates cultural taboos or cultural prescriptions, one should expect it to be extinguished by the feedback it receives from the environment or through satiation. The fact that it does not is due to "drive-reduction." That is, the behaviors being exhibited are those which have occurred simultaneously with the reduction of a basic drive in the person. The most salient drive in neurosis being anxiety, most of the confusing behaviors observed in disturbance are associated with the reduction of anxiety. If a situation produces anxiety, this anxiety is reduced by retreating from the situation. Any response or behavior on the part of the person occurring at that time will be reinforced by the reduction of anxiety. Hence, many behaviors that look maladaptive to the observer who sees the individual acting in ways completely inappropriate to the objective situation are behaviors associated with anxiety-reduction. Strange, ritualistic behaviors, self-defeating behaviors, etc. fall into this category of behaviors that are maintained on this basis.

One uses this knowledge in therapy. If a response that reciprocally inhibits anxiety can be made to occur in the presence of anxiety-evoking stimuli it will weaken the bond between these stimuli and the anxiety. Wolpe calls this process *"reciprocal inhibition."* He attempts to reciprocally inhibit anxiety or fear by eliciting a response antagonistic to anxiety in a previously anxiety-provoking situation. In carrying out this principle, for instance, a child can be taught to inhibit his anxiety in a fear-provoking situation in the classroom by practicing responses antagonistic to anxiety. Included in reciprocally inhibiting responses used by Wolpe are assertive responses, relaxation responses, pleasant responses, etc.

A major technique of behavioral therapy developed by Wolpe is desensitization. The desensitization paradigm is based upon the classical study of Mary Cover Jones with Peter, in which she used hunger and food reinforcement to countercondition Peter's fear of the rabbit. As the reader will remember, she gradually reduced the fear associated with the white, furry rabbit by balancing anxiety and hunger satisfaction. She placed the rabbit in the extreme periphery of the room and moved him closer only gradually at a rate which could be tolerated by Peter while he was being fed. Desensitization uses the same principle of "reciprocal inhibition." Desensitization also conforms to one of the methods suggested by Guthrie (1938) for learning through associative inhibition. According to Guthrie,

All learning involves associative inhibition. Acquiring a tendency to respond in any manner whatsoever to a situation must involve losing other conflicting tendencies already established. Breaking one habit always means establishing another. In many cases it is a matter of indifference what the new habit shall be, just so that it is not a new annoyance. (p. 54)

One of the three ways which he suggested to prevent a particular stimulus complex from eliciting a given response is the "method of inhibition." In this method the stimulus is introduced at such weak strengths that it will not cause the response, and then the intensity of the stimulus is gradually increased, always taking care that it is below the threshold of response.

In Wolpe's method of Systematic Desensitization (Wolpe & Lazarus, 1966) he first teaches his patient the art of progressive relaxation. Once this is learned, he constructs a hierarchy of anxiety provoking situations. This, he feels, is the most difficult and taxing procedure in the desensitization technique because it requires accurate recognition of the stimulus sources of unadaptive anxiety response. An anxiety hierarchy is a graded list of stimuli incorporating different degrees of a defined feature that evokes anxiety. The defined feature common to the listed stimuli is known as the theme of the hierarchy. Phobic themes are easy to recognize—fear of high places, of dogs, of death, etc. are examples.

Others are quite difficult to recognize, depending sometimes on a common internal response that disparate stimulus situations may evoke, such as a rejection hierarchy or a guilt hierarchy, etc.

When these sources of "neurotic disturbance" are listed, the therapist classifies them into themes. Once the major themes are identified and the hierarchy constructed, desensitization begins. Relaxation is used first and the patient is then presented symbolically with situations that arouse anxiety. This presentation can either be under hypnosis or with the patient merely imagining himself in the stimulus situation. Scenes low on the hierarchy, that is, those that produce lesser anxiety, are presented first. The stimulus hierarchy is then presented in an ascending order until the patient feels anxiety. The session is terminated at this point. Through a succession of sessions (as in the Mary Cover Jones experiment with Peter) the patient is deconditioned to anxiety.

Wolpe and Lazarus (1966) report upon a number of other techniques used in behavioral therapy. These include: (1) methods involving concept control; (2) intensive neurotic response evocation, or "flooding"; (3) aversive conditioning and a major technique developed by Wolpe for problems in achieving sexual satisfaction, the use of sexual responses in a counter conditioning and positive reconditioning framework.

Wolpe and Lazarus say that an explicit assumption of the behavior therapist is that human behavior is subject to causal determination no less than that of billiard balls or ocean currents. Consequently, the general attitude of the therapist to his patients is in accord with this deterministic outlook. He regards the patient as a joint product of his physical endowment and of the molding influence of the succession of environments through which he—an organism—has passed. Each environment, each exposure to stimulation, has modified the character of the organism to a greater or lesser extent.

This attitude is transmitted to the patient and he is assured that the processes by which he developed the maladaptive behaviors which brought him to the specialist is a logical and known process of learning. The patient is given an understanding of the learning process and is told precisely how he is to modify his behavior through this process. Within this frame of reference the patient is given the following kind of statements:

1. You are not mentally ill and there is no chance of your going insane.

2. All your reactions are explicable.
3. There is no virtue in confronting your fears.

The responsibility for the patient's recovery is placed unequivocally in the therapist's hands. If he does not improve under the regime set up for him, the fault lies with the therapist.

Adjusting the Functional "Fit"
Between Organism and Environment

Both of these sets of ideas presented here with respect to therapy can be seen as direct descendents of the Pavlovian view of the nature of the problem with which they are dealing. They, like all of the other behavioral technologists addressing themselves to emotional disturbance, are concerned with individual adaptation to the environment. They are involved in perfecting ways of adjusting the functional "fit" between organism and environment. Two separate systems, organism and environment, in mutual dependence, are engaged in the major task of life—reciprocal adaptation. Gantt (1944b) stated the Pavlovian concept of the problem as follows:

The neurosis was considered by Pavlov a disturbance of the balance between a system and its environment, whose equilibrium was preserved through the mechanism of the conditional reflex; by virtue of its ability to change, this relation in a changing environment or a changing organism is preserved. (p. 8)

The delicate interdependence between an organism in flux and an environment in flux is preserved through the conditional reflex. Whether the functional fit between organism and environment is in balance or out of balance the constant exchange between them is channeled through these dynamic mechanisms of exchange.

Behavior, both innate and acquired, can be viewed by all of the various methods of behavioral intervention, as a major fulcrum upon which the exchanges between a fluctuating organism and a variable environment are balanced. From this point of view behavior is both a functional exchange channel and a product of the kind of interflow which is coming from the fluctuating environment and fluctuating organism. In talking about the variable environment we usually refer to its actions upon the organism that release or trigger action potentials as "stimuli." In a time sequence stimuli come prior to the reciprocal action of the organism when organism and environment are engaged in exchange. When the action of the environment follows after the action firing of the organism in the exchange, we usually talk about the released environmental response as a consequence, reinforcement, reward, etc. When the environment is the releasor or excitor of a return action from the organism, we talk about a response on the part of the organism. When the initiation or provocation of the exchange comes from the organism we speak of "operants." As in a tennis match or football game we use these different terms to distinguish who is serving and who is receiving.

In a particular situational configuration of exchanges between organism and environment, the behavioral therapists have mapped out a number of ways of intervening in, effecting, and revising the exchange. Although behavior, within all of these methods, is seen as the sole property of, or expression of the human organism, it might also be looked upon as having property contributions from both the organism and the environment. In this way behavior becomes a shared system reflecting both environment and organism. When an individual outside this exchange system (the therapist) chooses to intervene he may be seen as modifying, extinguishing, substituting, or repressing particular patterns of exchange between the fluctuating organism and the variable environment.

The therapist, or intervention specialist, when operating within the behavioral model framework, must make his adjustments at some point within the exchange channel. In addition to the two published systems presented so far for intervention into this exchange, numerous methods and ways of effecting the exchange have been developed (Phillips & Wiener, 1966; Eysenck, 1960; Rotter, 1954; Cameron & Magaret, 1951).

Current and Future Trends

As we look at the vast outpouring of literature on behavioral therapy and behavior modification, it is difficult to realize that its first applications outside the experimental psychology laboratory are very recent, actually beginning in the late 1950s and early 1960s. Initially the move was toward the laboratory-like settings of mental hospitals, correctional institutions, and special classrooms. As examples: Theodore Ayllon and Nathan Azrin used behavioral procedures in Anna State Hospital in Illinois, not publishing *The Token Economy* until 1968. Harold L. Cohen and James Filipczak wrote about the project at the National Training School for Boys in 1971, in *A New Learning Environment*.

In the area of special education, behavior modification has been accepted with unbridled enthusiasm. Winters and Cox edited a book in 1972 entitled *Behavior Modification Techniques for the Special Educator*. This book discussed the use of behavioral techniques with the retarded, the brain-damaged, neurotic, and psychotic individuals, etc.

Two other books published specifically discussing behavior modification techniques with the mentally retarded are Thompson and Grabowski's *Behavior Modification of the Mentally Retarded* (1972) and Nesworth and Smith's *Modifying Retarded Behavior* (1973). James J. Gallagher, in *Classroom Behavior Modification Techniques Applied to Educationally Deprived, Primary Children* (1967), did a special study on classroom behavior and found the techniques successful in behavior management of educationally deprived children.

In the last five to ten years behavior controllers have continued their move away from the laboratory-like settings and special classrooms into the "real world"—public schools, half-way houses, private homes, and community mental health centers. In Kansas they have helped vitalize a large urban ghetto housing project named Juniper Gardens. The project, in the poorest section of Kansas City served as a testing ground for the ideas of Baer, Hall, Wolf and Risley. The association was mutually fruitful providing a better environment and services for the residents and several packaged teaching models such as Wolf's teaching family model to help communities set up homes for delinquent children and Hall's responsive-teaching model to help teachers learn techniques (Fixen, Phillips & Wolf, 1973; Risley & Hart, 1968; Hall, 1971; and Baer, 1971).

The behaviorist's move into the larger world has given rise to numerous publications and programs aimed at the layman or nonpsychologist. Principally, the books and pamphlets have been written for two groups—teachers and parents. For example: *New Tools for Changing Behavior* (Deibert & Harmon, 1970); *Modifying Children's Behavior* (Valett, 1969); *A Primer of Behavior Modification* (Weinrich, 1970); *Managing Behavior* (Hall, 1971).

Many books are directed specifically at classroom management:

Motivating Children (Vernon, 1972)
Constructive Classroom Behavior (Sarason & Sarason, 1974)
Behavioral Management in the Classroom (Morreau & Daley, 1972)
Any Teacher Can . . . (Shipman & Foley, 1973)
Managing Problem Behavior in the Classroom (Kress & Gropper, 1970)

There have been a few books written for educators explaining the use of behavior modification techniques for instructional purposes, i.e., *Instructional Applications of Behavior Principles* (Gentile, Frazier, & Morris, 1973) and *Behavioral Objectives* (Plowman, 1971).

Basically these publications contain an explanation of behavior principles followed by more specific "how-to" and/or case studies. Some are directed toward parents:

Helping Your Child to Learn: The Reinforcement Approach (Wittes & Radin, 1969)
Parents Are Teachers (Becker, 1971)
Parent Groups with a Focus on Precise Behavior Management (IMRID, 1970)

Other titles of note published in the past few years with the same purpose are:

Operant Conditioning Techniques for the Classroom Teacher (Ackerman, 1972)
Behavior Modification in the Classroom (Fargo, Behrns, & Nolen, 1970)
How to Use Contingency Contracting in the Classroom (Homme, et al., 1969)
Operant Conditioning in the Classroom (Pitts, 1971)
Behavior Modification: A Practical Guide for Teachers (Poteet, 1973)
How to Make Johnny Want to Obey (Beltz, 1971)
How Your Children Can Learn to Live a Rewarding Life (Bannatyne & Bannatyne, 1973)

Leland C. Swenson (1973) applied contingency management principles to the college classroom. He developed a system of teaching based on the principles of the token economy. It was successful and it was suggested that this approach might allow both effective teaching and a flexible, creative educational environment.

Gerald P. Patterson has developed his interest in the past few years in behavioral intervention procedures in the classroom and at home. His methods are based on a social learning approach which takes advantage of the fact that people learn most of their behavior from other people. *Living With Children* (Patterson & Gullian, 1968) was a primer for changing behavior for teachers and parents. The second volume, *Families* (Patterson, 1971), concerns itself with the details and the technology of how one changes one's own behavior and the behaviors of those living in the immediate social environment.

Another current trend in the field is toward the development of greater self-control (Kanfer & Phillips, 1970). David Watson and Roland Tharp have written a practical book entitled *Self-Directed Behavior: Self Modification for Personal Adjustment* (1972). The purpose of the book is to teach readers to self-direct or self-modify their behavior.

With the move of the behaviorist into the natural environment also comes an expanded view of therapy. The view of man is more flexible and encompasses the world around him and includes his various relationships—e.g., Sheldon Rose in *Treating Children in Groups: A Behavioral Approach* (1972).

Recently, behavior modification is beginning to be questioned through legal channels.

David B. Wexler (1973), Professor of Law at the University of Arizona discussed the natural flow of legal concepts from the prisoner's rights movement into the area of the rights of the institutionalized mentally ill, more specifically the use of token economies with chronic psychotic mental patients. He notes the "remarkable turnabout in the willingness of courts to scrutinize living conditions in total institutions."

From the sparse legal precedents there is a definite trend and the emerging law bears rather directly on the rights of patients subjected to a token economy. Although work assignments in mental institutions often specify goals in therapeutic terms, critics view the jobs as simple labor-saving devices which exploit the patients and even sometimes make hospital retention of particular patients almost indispensable to the functioning of the institution.

The Second Circuit in *Jobson* v. *Henne* (1966) made it clear that the law will not tolerate forced patient labor that is lacking therapeutic purpose.

In a 1972 decision, *Wyatt* v. *Stickney*, the court barred all involuntary patient labor involving hospital operation and maintenance, whether therapeutic or not, but permitted voluntary institutional work of either a therapeutic or a nontherapeutic nature, so long as the labor was compensated according to the federal minimum wage laws. The Judge further ordered that payment to patients for work shall not be applied to offset hospitalization costs. The only type of work exempt from minimum wage coverage is therapeutic work unrelated to hospital functioning. Patients may also be required to perform personal housekeeping tasks such as making their beds according to *Wyatt*. The *Wyatt* court specified that "privileges or release from the hospital shall not be conditioned upon the performance of labor involving hospital maintainance."

As the article discusses, if the law's general direction in the patient rights area proceeds uninterrupted, token economies may well become legally unavailable even if they are therapeutically superior to other approaches.

If one examines current trends and developments, the future directions of the behaviorists seem to be:

1. A move toward whole systems, i.e., whole schools as opposed to the present individual and specific classroom approach.
2. In education—a move into high schools and college classes.
3. In business—almost virgin territory.
4. Greater interest in individual management of one's own behavior, finding new ways for persons to practice self-control.
5. The direction of new research is toward longitudinal and follow-up studies; side effects; and research on "normal behavior."
6. There is a trend toward new multiple measurement on a wide range of interrelated behaviors rather than isolated change.

References

ACKERMAN, J. *Operant conditioning techniques for the classroom teacher*. Glenview, Ill.: Scott, Foresman, 1972.

ANDERSON, O. & LIDELL, H. Observations on experimental neurosis in sheep. *Archives of Neurology & Psychiatry*, 1935,*34*, 330–354.

AYLLON, T. & AZRIN, N. *The token economy: A motivational system for therapy and rehabilitation.* Englewood Cliffs, N.J.: Prentice-Hall, 1968.

BAER, D. Behavior modification: You shouldn't. In E. Ramp & B. Hopkins (Eds.), *A new direction for education: Behavior analysis* (Vol 1). Lawrence: University of Kansas Support and Development Center for Follow Through, Department of Human Development, 1971.

BANNATYNE, A. & BANNATYNE, M. *How your children can learn a rewarding life: Behavior modification for parents & teachers.* Springfield, Ill.: Charles C Thomas, 1973.

BAJANDUROW, B. Zur physiologie des schanalysators bei vogeln. *Zsch Vergl, Physiol*, 1932, *18*, 298-306.

BECKER, W. C. *Parents are teachers.* Champaign, Ill.: Research Press, 1971.

BEKHTEREV, V. *General principles of human reflexology.* London, Jarrolds, 1933.

BELTZ, S. *How to make Johnny want to obey.* Englewood Cliffs, N.J.: Prentice-Hall, 1971.

BURROW, T. *Biology of human conflict.* New York: Macmillan, 1937.

CAMERON, N. & MAGARET, A. *Behavior pathology.* Boston: Houghton Mifflin, 1951.

COHEN, H. & FILIPCZAK, J. *A new learning environment.* San Francisco, Calif.: Jossey Bass, 1971.

DIEBERT, A. & HARMON, A. *New tools for changing behavior.* Champaign, Ill.: Research Press, 1970.

EYSENCK, H. *Behavior therapy and the neuroses: Readings in modern methods of treatment derived from learning theory.* New York: A Pergamon Press Book, Macmillan, 1960.

FARGO, G., BEHRNS, C., & NOLEN, P. *Behavior modification in the classroom.* Belmont, Calif.: Wadsworth, 1970.

FIXEN, D., PHILLIPS, E., & WOLF, M. Achievement place: Experiments in self-governments with pre-delinquents. *Journal of Applied Behavioral Analysis*, 1973, *6*, 31-47.

GANTT, W. *Experimental basis for human behavior.* New York: Paul B. Huber, Inc., Medical Books Department of Harper Bros., 1944(a).

GANTT, W. Experimental basis for neurotic behavior. *Psychosomatic Medical Monograph*, 1944(b), *3*, 3-4.

GALLAGHER, J. *Classroom behavior modification techniques applied to educationally deprived, primary children.* Durham, N.C.: Duke University, 1967.

GENTILE, J., FRASER, T., & MORRIS, M. Instructional applications of behavioral principles. Monterey, Calif., Brooks-Cole, 1973.

GUTHRIE, E. *The psychology of human conflict.* New York: Harper, 1938.

HALL, R. V. *Managing behavior.* Lawrence, Kansas: H.N.H. Enterprises, 1971.

HALL, R. V. Responsive teaching: Focus on measurement and research in the classroom and home. *Focus on Exceptional Children*, 1971, *3*, 1-7.

HOMME, L., ET AL. *How to use contingency contracting in the classroom.* Champaign, Ill.: Research Press, 1969.

I.M.R.I.D. Parent groups with a focus on precise behavior management. Peabody College, 1970.

JACOBSON, C. Studies of cerebral function in primates. *Comparative Psychological Monographs*, 1936, *63*, 13.

JONES, M. A laboratory study of fear: The case of Peter. *Pedagogical Seminary*, 1924(b), *31*, 315-328.

KANFER, F., & PHILLIPS, J. *Learning foundations of behavior therapy.* New York: John Wiley, 1970.

KRESS, G., & GROPER, A. *Managing problem behavior in the classroom.* New York: Appleton-Century-Crofts, 1972.

MAIER, N. *Principles of animal psychology.* New York: McGraw-Hill, 1935.

MASSERMAN, J. *Behavior and neurosis: An experimental psychoanalytic approach to psychological principles.* Chicago, Ill.: University of Chicago Press, 1943.

MOHRER, A., & PEARSON, L. *Creative development in psychotherapy*, Vol. 1. Cleveland, Ohio: The Press of Case Western Reserve University, 1971.

MORREAU, L., & DALEY, M. *Behavioral management in the classroom.* New York: Appleton-Century-Crofts, 1972.

NESWORTH, J., & SMITH, R. *Modifying retarded behavior.* Boston: Houghton Mifflin, 1973.

PATTERSON, G. *Families: Application of social learning to family life.* Champaign, Ill.: Research Press, 1971.

PATTERSON, G., & GULLIAN, M. *Living with children: New methods for parents and teachers.* Champaign, Ill.: Research Press, 1968.

PAVLOV, I. *Lectures on conditioned reflexes, Vols. I & II.* New York: International Universities Press, 1941.

PHILLIPS, E., & WIENER, D. *Short term psychotherapy and structured behavior change.* New York: McGraw-Hill, 1966.

PITTS, C. (Ed.) *Operant conditioning in the classroom.* New York: Thomas Y. Crowell, 1971.

PLOWMAN, P. *Behavioral objectives.* Chicago, Ill.: Science Research Association, 1971.

POTEET, J. *Behavior modification: A practical guide for teachers.* Minneapolis, Minn.: Burgess, 1973.

PREMACK, D. Toward empirical behavior laws: to positive reinforcement. *Psychological Review,* 1959, *66,* 213-233.

RISLEY, T., & HART, B. Developing correspondence between the non-verbal and verbal behavior of preschool children. *Journal of Applied Behavioral Analysis,* 1968, *Vol. 1,* 267-281.

ROSE, S. *Treating children in groups: A behavioral approach.* San Francisco, Calif.: Jossey-Bass, 1972.

ROTTER, J. *Social learning and clinical psychology.* Englewood Cliffs, N.J.: Prentice-Hall, 1954.

SALTER, A. *Conditioned reflex therapy: The direct approach to the reconstruction of personality,* 2nd ed. New York: Capricorn Books; Farrar, Straus, & Giroux, 1961.

SARASON, I., & SARASON, B. *Constructive classroom behavior.* New York: Behavioral Publications, 1974.

SHIPMAN, H., & FOLEY, E. *Any teacher can. . . .* Chicago, Ill.: Loyola University Press, 1973.

SKINNER, B. F. *The behavior of organisms: An experimental analysis.* Englewood Cliffs, N.J.: Prentice-Hall, 1966.

SKINNER, B. F. *Science and human behavior.* New York: Free Press, 1965.

SKINNER, B. F. *Walden II.* New York: Macmillan, 1948.

SKINNER, B. F. *Beyond freedom and dignity.* New York: Knopf, 1971.

SWENSON, L. *Application of contingency management principles to the college classroom.* Paper presented at the Western Psychological Association, Spring, 1973.

THOMPSON, T., & GRABOWSKI, J. *Behavior modification of the mentally retarded.* New York: Oxford University Press, 1972.

ULLMANN, L., & KRASNER, L. (Eds.) *Case studies in behavior modification.* New York: Holt, Rinehart & Winston, 1965.

ULLMANN, L., & KRASNER, L. *Psychological approaches to abnormal behavior,* 2nd ed. Englewood Cliffs, N.J.: Prentice-Hall, 1975.

VALETT, R. *Modifying children's behavior.* Palo Alto, Calif.: Fearon, 1969.

VERNON, W. M. *Motivating children.* New York: Holt, Rinehart & Winston, 1972.

WALDER, L. ET AL. *Learning of aggression in children.* Boston: Little, Brown, 1971.

WATSON, D. & THARP, R. *Self-directed behavior: Self-modification for personal adjustment.* Monterey, Calif.: Brooks, Cole, 1972.

WATSON, J. & WATSON, R. *Psychological care of infant and child.* New York: W. W. Morton, 1928.

WEINRICH, W. *A primer of behavior modification.* Belmont, Calif.: Brooks, Cole, 1970.

WEXLER, D. Token and taboo: Behavior modification, token economics and the law. *California Law Review,* January 1973, *Vol. 61,* No. 1.

WINTERS, S. & COX, E. *Behavior modification techniques for the special educator.* New York: M.S.S. Information Corp., 1972.

WITTES, G. & RADIN, N. *Helping your child to learn: The Reinforcement Approach.* San Rafael, Calif.: Dimensions Publishing Co., 1969.

WOLPE, J. *Psychotherapy by reciprocal inhibition.* Stanford, Calif.: Stanford University Press, 1958.

WOLPE, J. & LAZARUS, A. *Behavior therapy techniques: A guide to the treatment of neurosis.* New York: Pergamon Press, 1966.

CHAPTER FOUR

Psychoneurological Views and Approaches

Introduction

One of the major theoretical formulations explaining the origin and nature of behavior problems in children emerged from specialized study concerned with the behavioral consequences of brain dysfunctions. This particular view of "abnormal" child behavior has been called by various names, including psychoneurological, neurosensory, sensory-neurological, and neuropsychological.

The psychoneurological view incorporates several points of view that are related, either by implication or by explicit formulation, to the functions of the central nervous system and to the behavioral correlates of those functions. Some of these views are typically more descriptive than explanatory in nature, more addressed to the questions of what and how than of why.

81

In part, these different orientations are accounted for by the diversity in goals and training of the professional group or groups involved. For example, physicians or medical researchers, and special educators, clearly have different responsibilities, which require the pursuit of very different types of information.

The interface of these orientations and the general child view advanced by the psychoneurological position is that of a receiver, processor, and responder to stimuli. The child is a complex organism occupying at any given point in time a stimulus field that includes a set of response demands. In addition, there are social expectations and task requirements, some more explicit than others.

The child then is an actor-reactor or an organism with a very specialized capability for maintaining himself in that environment. He is decoding complex stimulation while he is simultaneously exerting his own particular influence on that environment. Thus, he is both a stimulus and a responder to that field.

The psychoneurological view of children has been elaborated in terms of the adaptive capability vis-à-vis the central nervous system. The relative integrity of the receptor, integrator (including storage and retrieval), effector, and feedback apparatus of the organism is significantly correlated to the organism's adaptability to various environments. Maladaptation, then, is explained in psychoneurological terms, that is, psychological consequences of central nervous system dysfunction.

No other prominent theoretical concept of deviation in child growth and development requires more interdisciplinary effort than does the psychoneurological view. While many of the primary constructs are neurological, neurology is only one of many disciplines involved in the diagnosis, treatment, and research to generate new knowledge about these children (Rappaport, 1969, p. xvi). The various professional points of view brought into the case conference or into the research laboratory differ in terms of knowledge base, means for developing new knowledge, specialized language, and in terms of the questions of what, how, and why. All, however, have a common dilemma with reference to the question of who. The problems of defining and labeling the dysfunctional child have been significant ones for concerned professionals and continue to resist acceptable resolutions.

The following discussion will present a number of dilemmas which have arisen in attempts to accurately define and label these children. When viewed from a psychoneurological perspective there are many proposals for both labeling and defining children whose behavior is maladaptive. No one label or definition is either accurate or inaccurate in a broad or generic sense, but rather has a relative fit to each particular orientation or philosophical perspective. This is not to suggest that disagreement exists only between disciplines or professional groups; much of the controversy surrounding these issues has centered within disciplines as well. This attests to the relative status of theory and knowledge within as well as between the related science areas.

There have been several attempts at resolution by individuals and by professional groups, each suggesting a label that might have more general interprofessional support. The National Society for Crippled Children and Adults, Inc., and the National Institute of Neurological Diseases and Blindness, part of the National Institutes of Health, cosponsored a task force appointed in 1964 to study the issues of terminology and identification. This task force, composed primarily of physicians, adopted the term *minimal brain dysfunction* (Clements, 1966). The report of the task force included the following statement:

A review of selected literature revealed a total of 38 terms used to describe or distinguish the conditions grouped as minimal brain dysfunction in the absence of findings severe enough to warrant inclusion in an established category, e.g., cerebral palsies, mental subnormalities, sensory defects.

Similarly, Cruickshank (1966, pp. 10-18) convened a group of distinguished professionals that addressed themselves to the question of labels. Out of this discussion came yet another term, *developmental imbalances*, suggested by Gallagher (1966, p. 28). Recognizing the inadequacy of a single term for all purposes, Cruickshank suggested that the term *brain-injured* be used until a more acceptable label could be adopted. As evidence of both the growing concern for these children and the changing perceptions reflected in the labels used, it may be noted that the 1962 edition of Cruickshank's *Psychology of Exceptional Children and Youth* contained no discussion of this disability group. A later revision (1971) addressed the issue of the psychological characteristics of brain injured children, and the most current revision (1977) refers to these children as "learning disabled."

Numerous other labels have been suggested but the problem is sufficiently complex that a single label will probably never suffice. Much of the concern for the appropriate label has more recently shifted from a focus upon technical accuracy to the social consequences of labeling. A thorough analysis of this issue is included in *The Futures of Children* (Hobbs, 1975). Wiederholt (1974) has also pointed out that current research and litigation in the field of mental retardation make labels and definitions extremely unattractive. He notes further that labels and definitions should be, but currently are not, educationally relevant in programming instruction.

Definition has been as problematic as labeling. If behavioral difficulty is to be understood in terms of the integrity of the central nervous system, then the definition of children so impaired should reflect this frame of reference. However, much controversy has centered on this issue. Theoreticians have questioned the ability to validly determine the precise nature of brain-behavior relationships. Certainly, the empirical support for the existing postulates, which will be reviewed in this chapter, does not bring consensus.

The brain-injured child was defined by Strauss and Lehtinen (1947) as

... a child who before, during or after birth has received an injury to or suffered an infection of the brain. As a result of such organic impairment, defects of the neuromotor system may be present or absent; however, such a child may show disturbances in perception, thinking and emotional behavior, either separately or in combination. These disturbances can be demonstrated by specific tests. These disturbances prevent or impede a normal learning process. (p. 4)

Based upon research conducted with mentally retarded children and the clinical differentiation between exogenous and endogenous groups, Strauss and Lehtinen indicated that a child could be diagnosed as brain-injured on the basis of behavioral characteristics even when biological signs were negative.

Much of the discussion has centered on the question of whether children diagnosed as brain-injured, based on behavioral criteria, do, in fact, have an injured or defective brain. Dunn (1967, p. 121) argued that the unfortunate equation of the "Strauss Syndrome" child (Stevens and Birch, 1957) with a neurologically impaired child has generated controversy that does not take into account the precise Strauss conceptions as communicated in his work with Lehtinen.

A distinction between the *fact* of brain damage and the *concept*, "brain-damaged child" (Birch, 1964, pp. 3-5; Reger, 1969), the latter being a label for the child with a behavioral syndrome associated with brain damage without physical verification of organic etiology, is one way of sorting definitions. That is, some professionals focus their definitions on the behavioral incompetence of the child while others are more concerned with the accuracy of the etiological implications.

Birch (1964) stated,

It is essential that we recognize that the disturbed behavior seen in the clinic is not "due to" brain damage as such . . . we see individuals with damage to the nervous system which may have resulted in some primary disorganization, who have developed patterns of behavior in the course of atypical relations with the developmental environment, including its interpersonal, objective, and social features. The behavioral disturbances of children who come to our notice are developmental products and not merely manifestations of a damaged portion of the brain. (pp. 8-9)

This focus on the interaction over time between the adaptive incapacity of the child and the environments to which adaptation is required characterizes several basic definitions in the literature (Rappaport, 1966; Gallagher, 1966).

One of the most prominent definitions associated with the problem of brain injury in the education and psychology literature focuses on the disability in learning. The specific relationship between learning disability and injury to the brain has occasioned much debate. To some writers it has become less important to speculate on the relationship between the two; rather, they have argued that etiology is important only to the extent that it aids in the development of corrective procedures.

In 1962, Kirk and Bateman stated:

A *learning disability* refers to a retardation, disorder, or delayed development in one or more of the processes of speech, language, reading, writing, arithmetic, or other school subjects resulting from a psychological handicap caused by a possible cerebral dysfunction and/or emotional or behavioral disturbances. It is not the result of mental retardation, sensory deprivation, or cultural or instructional factors. (p. 73)

Bateman (1964) later defined the problem more specifically in terms of language dysfunction without specifying probable cause.

Several professionals have been more concerned with the neurological substrate of the problem, which locates the definitional bias in the integrity of the CNS. From a scientific point of view, this approach cites neurology as the source of important knowledge. From a social point of view, the label communicates deficit inside the child, which has implications for responses received from parents and teachers.

Cruickshank (1966) has suggested that any definition of brain-injured children should recognize etiology, include the concept of developmental imbalances, focus attention on the importance of the child's development of self, and indicate the necessity of interdisciplinary programming (pp. 17-18). He defines brain-injured children as:

(a) those with a definite diagnosis of a specific or diffuse neurological injury and who are also characterized by a series of significant psychological problems; (b) those with no positive diagnosis of neurological injury (although such may be suspected by the neurologist), but whose psychological and behavioral characteristics are identical with those children for whom a diagnosis can be definite; or (c) some children in specific clinical groups such as cerebral palsy, epilepsy, aphasia, mental retardation, cultural deprivation, emotional disturbance, and others whose members show the common psychological characteristics of brain injury and where it is either definitely known or logically suspected that some neurological deficit is present.... These children may be of any intellectual level whatsoever.... The problem is almost always complicated by an emotional overlay in the child.... The issue is a complicated one with many dimensions—physical, intellectual, and emotional. (Cruickshank, 1967a, p. 29)

There are two general topics that need to be examined with reference to the current status of neurosensory theory: the history of the area, and normal child growth and development from a neurosensory point of view.

History

The history of the development of the neurosensory area is a complex blend of professional thinking, personalities, empirical data, and clinical practices. As with the development of other major theories, *zeitgeist* considerations have been important.

The social as well as professional contexts of work have either facilitated or inhibited the development of knowledge. The existence of resources, the sanction to examine certain phenomena in certain ways, the availability of technical procedures and instrumentation, and public values of inquiry are examples of such influences.

One of the primary landmarks in the development of neurosensory theory and methodology, as described by Hewett (1968), is the work of Itard early in the nineteenth century. Victor, "the wild boy of Aveyron," was approximately eleven years old when he was found living in a forest near the Province of Aveyron in France. Itard worked for five years with Victor, at that time considered an incurable idiot, utilizing exercises designed to help him discriminate differences in taste, touch, vision, sound, and temperature. While much of the training was successful, particularly as judged by the knowledge of behavioral change methodology at that time, Itard was not successful in "humanizing" Victor. Victor did not learn to talk and to appropriately accommodate himself to society. The failure to teach adaptive social behavior was a minor one, however, when viewed in terms of Itard's successes. He exerted considerable influence on the thinking of those who would follow, including Seguin, one of his students. In fact, some of the sensory training methodology Itard developed is still used with exceptional children.

Seguin (Talbot, 1964) continued to develop sensory-motor training and influenced Montessori's (1965) important "scientific approach to pedagogy." Montessori further refined and created procedures and materials for training visual, auditory, tactile, and olfactory sensitivity.

The work of Goldstein and Sheerer (1941) with traumatically brain-injured soldiers provided a significant thrust in the concern with brain functions and behavioral correlates. Based on their clinical experience and observation, they suggested one behavioral taxonomy for brain-injured adults, which included catastrophic reaction, rigidity, distractibility, and concrete thinking. In terms of their contributions to the theory of brain functions, Goldstein and Sheerer, along with Head (1926), helped shift thinking to a broader concept of generalized brain damage—in contradiction to the theory of specific localization of psychological functions in the brain.

The theory of localized function had developed as a result of the discovery by Broca (1861), a French anatomist at the

Academy in Paris, that a lesion on the third frontal gyrus destroyed the expressive phase of speech. This theory was furthered by the plethora of research activity on brain functions and their behavioral correlates that followed. The brain was viewed as sectioned into discrete physical units, each having specific capabilities.

Critchley (1953) noted the fallacy of confusing sign-producing lesions with localization of function, and suggested specialization of function as a more accurate term.

Other very basic work in the area of brain injury attempted to understand more about the value of neurological explanations of deviance. Utilizing the psychoneurological model, this work sought to develop a science to understand and modify abnormal behavior.

Much of the impetus to the study of brain-injured children came from the work of Heinz Werner and Alfred Strauss at the Wayne County Training School, Northville, Michigan. Their research with retarded children resulted in a delineation of patterns of learning and behavior that had considerable effect on research in the field of mental retardation. Their endogenous-exogenous typology has been widely used. The exogenous or brain-injured child, estimated by Strauss and Lehtinen in 1947 to constitute 15 to 20 percent of the mentally retarded population, can be differentiated from the endogenous group when the broad characteristics of perception, thinking, and behavior are compared.

In the perceptual area, exogenous children were found to be less systematic and to reproduce designs characterized by more discontinuity and incoherence in the patterns (Werner & Strauss, 1939). This difficulty was accounted for by specific deficits such as a disturbed visuomotor perception (Strauss & Lehtinen, 1947), problems in figure-ground relationships (Werner & Strauss, 1941), and perseveration (Werner, 1946).

In the area of thinking, the exogenous children performed differently on certain conceptual tasks. In object groupings, for example, the exogenous child made typical or uncommon associations on the basis of unessential detail (Strauss & Werner, 1942).

The behavior of the exogenous children also distinguished them from other retarded children. Based on observer ratings these children were differentiated in terms of being erratic, uncoordinated, uncontrolled, uninhibited and socially unacceptable (Strauss & Kephart, 1940). In general, they were found to be more hyperactive, disinhibited, and perseverative, characteristics that have both behavioral and perceptual implications. Strauss and Lehtinen (1947, pp. 34-35) also noted "catastrophic reactions": exaggerated emotional reactions to tasks or situations that the child experienced as insoluble or inordinately unpleasant.

Lewis, Strauss, and Lehtinen pointed out that the perceptually disturbed child may receive distorted images resulting in endless perceptual errors or misconceptions of reality (1960, p. 17). This applies to social as well as sensory perceptions. They also indicated that, "the brain-injured child's physiologically based behavior anomalies may result in emotional disturbance inasmuch as they increase his environmental difficulties and influence the attitude of others toward him" (p. 62).

In 1955, Strauss and Kephart wrote the second volume of *Psychopathology and Education of the Brain-Injured Child*, which included significant expansion of the clinical syndrome of exogeneity to include brain-injured children who are not mentally defective. An excellent critique of the work of Strauss and Werner and their colleagues is provided by Sarason (1959).

In studying the psychopathology of the brain-injured child who was not mentally retarded, Cruickshank initially explored the applicability of the behavioral taxonomy derived from the Werner and Strauss work with exogenous children. His research and the research of his students on idiopathic epileptic children (Shaw, 1955; Shaw & Cruickshank, 1956) and cerebral palsied children (Cruickshank, Bice & Wallen, 1957; Cruickshank, Bice, Wallen & Lynch, 1965; Dolphin & Cruickshank, 1951a; Dolphin & Cruickshank, 1951b; Dolphin & Cruickshank, 1952; Qualtere, 1957) led him to further develop the concepts of psychopathology of brain-injured children without measurable intellectual deficits and to translate these concepts into educational methodology (Cruickshank, Bentzen, Ratzeburg, & Tannhauser, 1961; Cruickshank, 1967a).

Rappaport (1961; 1964; 1965; 1966; 1969) and his colleagues have made significant contributions to the development of understanding the child with brain dysfunction from an ego psychological point of view. He has provided a conceptual model for understanding the basis of disabilities in these children, that includes the proprioceptual, preceptual, perceptual, and cognitive levels of functioning. Rappaport (1961) pointed out that:

behavior disturbance (1) . . . is not due solely to damaged brain tissue per se and therefore is not necessarily irreversible; (2) but it is due to a considerable degree to the disturbance which that damage causes in the epigenesis of the ego; (3) the deviant ego maturation fosters a disturbed parent-child relationship that in turn inhibits proper ego development; and (4) the disturbance both in ego development and in the parent-child relationship can be alleviated by psychotherapy and adjunctive therapies. (p. 425)

This view of the brain-injured child in terms of his ego struggle for adaptive capacity, even when the child's neurologic adaptational equipment does not function in the service of that struggle, added new dynamic life to neurophysiological constructs.

Eisenberg's (1957, 1964) contributions to understanding the psychiatric implications of brain damage in children have been of major importance. He views brain injury as

a psychological disorder affecting the child on three levels, namely: (1) on the level of quantitative and qualitative alterations in brain function produced by damage to its structures, (2) on the level of behavior influenced by the reorganization of the previous personality of the patient in the face of his functional deficit, and (3) on the level of the social environment which has a profound influence on the patient's performance and, under certain conditions, might be considered the decisive influence. (Adamson, 1966, p. 276)

The studies out of Bellevue Hospital in New York City have made substantial contributions to the development of theory and clinical procedures. Schilder (1950, 1964), Bender (1949, 1956, 1961; Bender & Silver, 1948) and others have developed the position that specific lesions have both negative psychological and motor consequences.

Body image is a crucial issue in both the psychological and motor characteristics of the child. Psychological problems arise in the "organically sick" child, according to Bender (1949), because (1) motor disorders cause prolonged dependency on the mother; (2) perceptual or intellectual problems lead to frustrations, misinterpretations of reality, and bizarre behavior patterns in efforts to make contact with the world; (3) disturbed patterning of impulses leads to distortion in action patterns with compulsive features; and (4) anxiety due to physiologic disorganization and frustration is central to the problem. The recommended method of treatment is prolonged mothering, avoidance of isolation, and specific aids for motor, perceptual, and interpersonal disabilities. A strong drive for normality in development and independence is present in these children as in normal children.

Another major stream of influence has been the work of those researchers concerned with the location of brain lesions in adults through the use of psycholinguistic diagnostic tests. Halstead (1947), Luria (1961), and Reitan (1959, 1962) have made substantial contributions in this area.

The broad area of psycholinguistic abilities in children has been conceptualized, and assessment procedures developed by another group of scholars interested more in the specific abilities than in their neurological substrate. The focus here has been on the utility of the data for suggesting remedial or habilitative procedures. The outstanding example here is the work of Kirk and McCarthy and their associates who developed and refined the *Illinois Test of Psycholinguistic Abilities* for children (Kirk, McCarthy, & Kirk, 1968; McCarthy & Kirk, 1961).

Frostig (1966; Frostig & Horne, 1964; Frostig, Lefever, & Whittlesey, 1961) and others have made major contributions in understanding the visual perceptual implications of brain injury in children. Her developmental test of visual perception includes the following areas: (1) eye-motor coordination, (2) constancy of form, (3) figure-ground relationships, (4) position in space, and (5) spatial relationships.

Getman (1962, 1964; Getman & Hendrickson, 1966; Getman & Kane, 1964; Lewis, 1961) and others from the field of optometry have aided the clinician and the researcher in understanding vision and the visuomotor complex with reference to the visual-perceptual and visuomotor problems of these children.

Reading, a complex process, has occupied a prominent place in the development of psychoneurological theory. Money (1962, 1966), Critchely (1964), Thompson (1966), and others have made major contributions to thinking about dyslexia, an inability to read due to cerebral dysfunction. The work of Orton (1937) on cerebral dominance as a basic issue in learning difficulties is worth noting. Adequate lateralization was considered essential to the organism's proper adjustment to visual stimuli such as in reading. Reversals, for example, indicated mixed or incomplete dominance.

Fernald's (1943) multisensory approach to learning constitutes another important chapter in the history of this area. Her use of the kinesthetic sense, in having the child trace a word with his finger while looking at and saying the word aloud, has become a familiar procedure to many pedagogists.

The technical, professional, political, personal, and social streams of influence have been and continue to be numerous in the development of thinking in this area. It should be clear from the discussion that the history is not a simple linear series of events and that what is "known" and believed is not limited to the outputs of laboratories.

Growth and Development:
A Psychoneurological Frame of Reference

The psychoneurological perspective postulates the origin and development of behavior in terms of variables *primarily* internal to the organism. When behavior is inappropriate or unexpected, it is not "unlawful," but rather a consequence of damage or injury to the central nervous system. This constitutes the basis upon which disorder and disability is understood and provides a frame of reference for explaining aberrations in the expected sequence of psychobiological events in childhood.

There are a variety of ways in which to approach normal growth and development from a psychoneurological point of view. These variations in perspective account, in part, for the varying conclusions regarding appropriate labels and definitions of abnormal behavior and learning patterns in children. Some of the areas of research that have contributed to the development of psychoneurological theory include: motor development (Kephart, 1960); a behaviorally oriented frame of reference and model of the human organism as developing competencies in the processing of information (Gallagher, 1966); technical issues of neural development in biophysical terms (Luria, 1966; Eisenberg, 1960, 1964); intellectual development (Piaget, 1952a, 1952b; Piaget & Inhelder, 1969); and neuropsychological dimensions (Reitan, 1959, 1966; Reitan & Heineman, 1968; Pribram, 1964).

The following description relies most heavily on the work of Rappaport and his colleagues (1964, 1965, 1966, 1969), who employ ego psychological constructs in accounting for the dynamic consequences of organicity. His conceptual model proposes a view of the organism as a dynamic psychobiological entity and includes specific analysis of the systems through which learning takes place. While this model is described by Rappaport specifically with educators in mind, the conceptual and empirical support for his work is extensively developed in technical, mathematical, and neurophysiological areas (Rosenblith & Allensmith, 1962; Penfield & Roberts, 1959).

Rappaport (1969) states that:

In the normal child, the primary guarantees of his adaptation are built in at conception. Just as genetic coding tells certain cells to become differentiated into specific tissues and organs, it tells those organs what their functions should be. It also indicates the means by which those functions will become practiced, refined, and organized to prepare the organism for what will be demanded of it through successive stages of development. Actually the exploratory practice, refinement, and organization of the various basic functions begins during intrauterine development, to ready the fetus to cope with its emergence into its new, extrauterine environment. Similarly, after birth the child goes through a series of developmental stages in preparation for the increasing demands for self-sufficiency that life will make upon him. During both the intrauterine and extrauterine development of the organism, what is being practiced, refined, and organized are the basic tools by which the child's ego is fashioned. (p. 37)

The child with an intact central nervous system has the capacity to develop an adequate ego. Primary skills of the ego include motility, perception, concept formation, and language. The development of these basic skills provides the condition for developing higher ego skills, which include awareness of others, impulse control, frustration tolerance, or the ability to mediate between biological drives and environmental demands (Rappaport, 1969, p. 38).

The infant has to learn how to act volitionally, how to master his own gross motor responses. Getman (1965, p. 74) has pointed out that "children must first *learn to act*, and when they have achieved magnitudes of skill in these actions, they will *act to learn*." The infant must explore and practice his own movement until he succeeds in obtaining some control and satisfaction.

Cortical inhibition, made possible by further neural maturation, provides the child with increasing ability to act upon his motor discharges and to volitionally practice those actions. The mastery of one's own body in a specific cultural context is the basis for the child's development of self-esteem. As Rappaport (1969) states:

The first few years of life—during which the child learns such skills as walking, talking, feeding himself, and being toilet trained—provide him with literally hundreds of opportunities a day for being pleased with himself, for the budding of positive identity that later will bloom into the conviction "I am one who can." (p. 38)

The demands of the culture are mediated by significant others in the environment. Initially, the mother expects the infant to nurse, to cuddle, and to respond with contentment or joy when obvious biological needs are satisfied. These responses, in turn, help to satisfy her need and wish to be a good mother. An "all's well" signal exchange is crucial for both mother and infant and will continue to provide the basis for new growth as expectations change and new developmental levels are obtained.

Because the brain is the primary organ of adaptation, many children with brain dysfunction do not experience this continuity of development (Rappaport, 1969). The improper development of the primary ego skills militates against higher order ego skill development. The sense of mastery is supplanted by mystery and frustration. The absence of success gives rise to the conviction of "I am one who cannot," and, inevitably, to negative concepts of self.

These children's sense of safety in the world and their development of trust in the dependability of that world are prevented. They have no sense of reliance on their own physical structure and its functions, and their patterns of acting preclude eliciting the approving support of the environment. When a skill is gained, for example, it may be practiced in exaggerated pace and intensity, which exceeds the tolerance threshold of the environment and thus robs the child of external gratification.

Psychopathology

This section, concerning psychopathological characteristics of learning disabled children, includes the following major topics: inadequate impulse control, disturbances in perception and movement, in conceptualization and abstract thinking, of body image and self-concept, and in socioemotional adjustment.

Inadequate Impulse Control

Inadequate impulse control is used here to indicate the organism's relative inability to respond appropriately to stimuli.

The locus of control is in the stimuli and not in the cognitive ability of the responding organism.

The relative freedom of response existing within the child is variable and may be viewed as a function of the integrity of the mechanisms of the central nervous system. Efficiency of response, management of stimuli, or impulse control could then be viewed as a grouping of several characteristic phenomena, such as distractibility and hyperactivity, often considered separately in other behavioral taxonomies.

Attention is a complex psychological adjustment that has two dimensions. Eisenberg (1964, p. 65) has defined attention in terms of enhancing responsiveness to a limited field, on the one hand, and inhibiting responses to the numerous environmental stimuli, on the other. The structure of the central nervous system allows simultaneous attending and unattending, selectively focusing attention on certain stimuli and not responding to others.

In a typically active classroom situation, however, distractible children do respond to "noise" or nonrelevant stimuli in the environment. A variety of nonrelevant auditory and visual stimuli may prevent the child from being able to attend to a specific assigned task.

Cruickshank et al. (1961), Haring and Phillips (1972) and Hewett (1968) have noted the importance of attention in the learning process. Educational planning for emotionally disturbed and learning disabled children must be based on assessment information that includes an examination of the child's ability to attend. The educational environment and curriculum must accommodate attention deficits with program structure that compensates for the deficit.

Another aspect of poor impulse control, *hyperkinesis*, is perhaps the most common characteristic of brain-injured children. Hyperkinetic children are constantly in motion and, as Hirt (1964, p. 45) points out, the motion is in double time. The issue is not simply one of surplus behavior but, rather, of the quality of the behavior which is likely to disregard the typical time and place conventions.

Schulman et al. (1965) studied the level of total day activity of brain-injured children and found no significant correlation with any of the diagnostic or behavioral clusters of brain damage. Their research indicated that most brain-injured children have total activity levels that are essentially similar to those of normal children. The brain-injured child, however, responds to behavioral rule-oriented social situations with either hypoactivity, perhaps an overcompensation for an inability to control his behavior, or hyperactivity. Hyperactivity was found in this study to correlate with brain injury only in highly structured situations.

Kahn and Cohn (1934) described this phenomenon as "organic driveness," a result of what they called "surplus inner impulsions." Eisenberg (1964, p. 64) suggested lack of inhibition as a more parsimonious hypothesis than excess drive.

Eisenberg (1964, p. 67) has also pointed out that the hyperkinetic syndromes are likely to diminish by childhood and almost disappear entirely by adolescence, which presumably reflects an increased capacity for inhibition normally associated with maturation (1964, p. 74). He further noted the need for research to differentiate between overactivity derived from patterns of neural dysfunction in the child, and behavior that is socially inappropriate in certain settings but not the result of organic defect in the child. If the types of environments that tend to result in nonhyperkinetic functioning could be studied, information may be developed on how to modify environments to reduce hyperkinetic behavioral disturbances (pp. 74-75).

Figure-ground pathology. A phenomenon that has similar functional components and has been described extensively in the literature as a characteristic of brain-injured children is figure-ground pathology. This may be expressed as any one or a combination of the following: 1) a confusion of the figure and background, 2) an inability to differentiate the two, and 3) a reversal of figure and background. This disturbance has been demonstrated with cerebral palsied children in the visual and tactual modalities (Dolphin & Cruickshank, 1951a; Dolphin & Cruickshank, 1952; Cruickshank, Bice & Wallen, 1957; Cruickshank, Bice, Wallen, & Lynch, 1965).

Birch and Lefford (1964), studying visual differentiation, intersensory integration, and voluntary motor control, obtained results indicating that the ability to separate figure from background is of a developmental nature.

Several studies have indicated the difficulty brain-injured children have in tasks that require them to identify figures from a complex background (Cobrinik, 1959; Teuber & Weinstein, 1956). In a study of two groups of mentally retarded children, one diagnosed as brain-damaged and the other as familial, Vegas and Frye (1963) found that the organic group made fewer total responses but named significantly more objects hidden in the background than the familial group.

Dissociation. Another variation of the stimulus management issue is what Cruickshank (1967a, Cruickshank et al. 1961) has called dissociation, the inability to conceptualize a gestalt.

A word, a sentence, and a picture are examples of stimuli that have meaning as a unity, meaning that does not exist in the component parts. The organism must, therefore, adjust to the pattern if it is to obtain the relevant information or intended meaning. If the organism "gets caught" on the parts and cannot see the existing configuration, the adjustment will not be appropriate.

Perseveration. Perseveration, included under inadequate impulse control by Rappaport (1964), and Cruickshank and Paul (1971), is another frequently observed aspect of the psychopathology of brain-injured children. Hirt (1964, p. 46) has defined it as an "idea, either spoken or written, which is continuously repeated . . . until a child can free himself from it and move on to another idea." He pointed out that, when it occurs, perseveration interferes with "all basic thought processes." In a discussion of the control of motor responses in relation to the development of cognitive structures, Gardner (1966, p. 148) has stated, "like the controls of attention . . . the capacity to inhibit irrelevant motoric responses is an important aspect of cognitive control in learning and remembering tasks."

Disturbances in Perception and Movement

Visual-motor disturbances. Considerable data exist that demonstrate that learning disabled children often exhibit inadequate visual-motor performance (Bensberg, 1952; Frostig, Lefever, & Whittlesey, 1961). Visual perception is a complex phenomenon that represents the visual dimension of the organism's adaptation. Unlike sight, which is the limited function of recognizing light, its contrasts and patterns, vision involves the interpretation of that light in relation to the total organism's present and past experiences.

Getman and Hendrickson (1966, pp. 53-83) have pointed out that the purpose of the visual system is one of guidance and monitoring. Many writings describe the primary importance of vision in providing information about the space occupied by an organism and the relationships between the organism and other objects in that space, and among those other objects (Hebb, 1937; Held, 1959; Riesen, 1947; Smith & Smith, 1962).

Frostig, Lefever, and Whittlesey (1961) included eye-hand coordination in their investigation of visual perception in children. Although the perception of form was the central area of concern in their design of a developmental test of visual perception, eye-hand coordination was included as a result of the following considerations:

1) Perception is never divorced from motor activity; 2) minute eye movements are a precondition of form perception (Hebb, 1949); 3) perception proper develops out of the sensory-motor behavior of the infant and in small children depends to a great degree on exploratory movements; 4) while perception "originates" in motor behavior, it is also followed by motor events. The pupil dilates and contracts with light perception; grasping with the hand follows grasping with the eye. (Gessell, 1941)

The human organism is so designed that movement is necessary for obtaining information. It is only as the genetically blueprinted integration and balance of perceptual and motor systems is realized that the organism's adaptive potential is realized. For sensory data to continue to be received, movement must be involved. In the absence of movement, the organism accommodates itself to the environment and new data are not received.

The inability to translate visual experience into an appropriate motor event, to mediate a satisfying (to the child and his environment) response to usual stimuli, constitutes one of the major issues in the psychopathology of brain-injured children. The diagnostic problem is complex, and judgments based solely on the product performance of the child grossly oversimplify the requirements of the task of psychodiagnosis. The child may or may not possess accurate visual information; if not, the process is impaired before coordination is initiated. If the motor system is not intact, then the quality of its attachment to the visual system is difficult to assess. To complicate the issue even further, the input, integrating, and performance systems are not functionally autonomous, and an assessment based on this assumption could be misleading (Rappaport, 1969). The close relationship between the characteristics of visual-motor disturbance and distractibility, depending on the test being used or the circumstances under which the observation is made, also poses additional questions for the diagnostician.

Auditory Disturbances. The auditory mode is another crucial dimension of perception that must be intact in order to support adequate adjustment of the developing organism. The organism must learn the culture's codes for sounds, since a basic part of socialization is the accurate decoding of the "messages" transmitted in those sounds and the efficient social adaptation to those messages. This is, however, only one side of the process. Adaptation requires that the organism acquire encoding competence, an ability to generate a response, including a sonic response, that matches the code received. This capability is part of the normal genetic design of the organism.

The response ability of the organism in relation to the auditory dimension of perception is predicated on its precise integration with the motor system. This constitutes another important part of the organism's genetically blueprinted potential for unity.

Auditory disturbances are difficult to separate from disturbances in the area of language, and both are often discussed with reference to the broader area of communication disorders (Zigmond & Cicci, 1968).

Strong (1964) and Boshes and Mykelbust (1964) found that auditory processing problems were very significant in differentiating normal from poor learners. Sebatino (1969a, 1969b) has pointed out that neurologically handicapped children may not be identified if the auditory modality is not included in the evaluation.

The issues, discussed in relation to visual-motor disturbances, concerning ability to attend to relevant stimuli and repress response to irrelevant stimuli, to concentrate, to incorporate the temporal flow of stimuli, to "get the message" or gestalt without getting caught on a single stimulus or aspect of the message, have also been used in the analysis of the auditory mode.

There are other basic questions involved in auditory perception in the presence of an intact end organ. Deutsch (1964), for example, has pointed out that children from homes that are noisy, but offer little experience with meaningful verbal interaction, may experience difficulty in discrimination. Eisenberg (1960) has stated: "It is not a question of heredity *or* experience, physiology *or* culture, but how much of the observed variance in specific behaviors is ascribable to each and how much to their interaction" (p. 39).

Language Disturbances. Luria (1966) indicated the importance of an intact central nervous system in pointing out that speech is the result of "highly complex integration of nervous processes. All complex forms of human mental activity involve direct or indirect participation of speech." Luria further states that it is the higher mental processes in the hierarchy of complexity that are the most easily deranged by local or general brain lesions (Goldstein, 1939). It follows that language processes should be among those behaviors that are most significantly affected (Cruickshank & Paul, 1971).

There is some evidence that disturbances in the motor area of speech production appear early in language development and can be recognized in the types and rhythms of sounds produced by infants (Fisichelli, 1966; Karelitz, Karelitz, & Rosenfeld, 1960).

Cruickshank and Paul (1971) have pointed out that these and similar early disturbances in the motor area of speech production "might later be concomitant with language disturbances of a conceptual nature."

Bateman (1967) views the language area so central to the functioning of these children that her definition of the general problem is stated in terms of language functions. She subsumes dyslexia, verbal communication disorders, and visual-motor integration problems under the concept of learning disabilities as a language problem.

Hardy (1967), writing on language disorders, describes two groups of language-deviant children:

One group commonly reflects basic interferences with mechanisms of attention, which often show as inadvertent shifts between distractibility and perseveration; a child is prone to be stimulus-bound or fleeting, and seems best to learn within very limited boundaries of stimulus and attention. Children in the other group are gregarious enough but have fundamental difficulties in sensory integration, in memory-storage, and in recall. (p. 40)

No distinction is made here between the broadly defined group of brain-injured children with variable psychopathology and a more specific group of brain-injured children with a primary language disturbance, i.e., the aphasias. The specific problems of aphasia will not be discussed here. The reader is referred to the works of Wepman (1951) and McGinnis (1963) for detailed treatment of this topic. The distinction has to do with the theoretical foci with reference to language function in brain-injured and/or learning disabled children.

Intersensory Disburbances. Belmont, Birch and Karp (1965) have observed that the ability to integrate information obtained from a single sense modality "is phylogenetically more primitive and appears earlier in ontogenesis than does the capacity to integrate information arriving through two or more sense systems" (p. 410). This general position has been supported by the work of Maier and Schneirla (1935), Sherrington (1955) and others.

Ayres (1968) has pointed out that man has five times as many nerve fibers bringing information into his central nervous system (CNS) as he has for directing his body to respond. The central nervous system filters, organizes and integrates the sensory information for use in developing and executing the brain's functions. One of these functions, Ayres notes, is learning.

Goldstein (1939) described a "hierarchy of disintegration," which suggests that more complex behavior is first impaired by cortical injury. Birch and Lefford (1964) have pointed out that the emergence of intersensory organization is, at a minimum, delayed in brain-injured children. This deficit in the information processing system makes it difficult for the child to obtain a satisfying psychological balance with the environment. They also note the possibility that such a primary defect may enhance the opportunity to develop bizarre integrations and result in the reinforcement of aberrant paths of development (p. 59).

Major contingencies here, as with other aspects of psychopathology, are the specific demands imposed by the child's environment. If the intersensory combinations that have not been adequately integrated are not required by the environment for adaptation, then in that particular situation the child may not be disabled. The importance of engineering the environment to facilitate the child's successful adaptation and to make possible organized responses to stimuli have been described by Cruickshank and others (Cruickshank et al., 1961, 1966, 1967a; Cruickshank & Paul, 1971).

Disturbances in Conceptual and Abstract Thinking

Brain-injured children have frequently been characterized by their inability to deal with ideas, to form concepts, and to understand relationships and similarities (Rappaport, 1964; Burks, 1960; Strauss & Werner, 1942; Dolphin & Cruickshank, 1951b).

The child must symbolically manage environmental information provided by his sensory modalities as a basis for action (or nonaction). This requires appropriately integrating and sorting data from the different modes. The brain-injured child's deficiency in abstract thinking and concept formation forces him to rely on concrete operations (Paine, 1966) and formalistic behavior.

Reed and Reed (1967) studied concept formation and nonverbal abstract thinking in children with cerebral dysfunction. They found that when the level of intellectual functioning was controlled, there was no evidence of selective impairment in the brain-damaged group. They concluded that the general lowering of intellectual ability, rather than specific impairment in the realm of concept formation or nonverbal abstract thinking was a concomitant among older children with chronic cerebral dysfunction. They pointed out the need to investigate variables such as type of lesion, its age of onset, lateralization, location, rate of progression or severity, in order to determine the consequences of selective impairment if it does occur (p. 160).

Gallagher (1957), reviewing the literature comparing brain-injured and non-brain-injured children, observed that the research trends indicated that brain-injured children may have difficulty in concept formation only when they are distracted from the central task by outside stimuli and unstructured situations. He also noted that, in the perceptual area, these children are more likely to have a deficit in attending to relevant tasks than a deficit in perceiving or organizing.

Body Image

Body image is an area of difficulty for brain-injured children. From the point of view of normal child growth and development, all children must learn about their biological equipment, how the various parts function separately and in concert. As they learn how the body parts function, they can learn how to control them and thus act volitionally. They must develop an awareness of where they are and what they can do as a dependable point of reference before they can learn about the physical space occupied by their body. To get somewhere, to know how far one must go, and eventually to have multiple sensory data about distant objects that are processed by a single sensory modality, such as vision or audition, depend upon the development of functional body knowledge.

This knowledge is developed by practicing movement in a space with a constant gravity. The movement of a limb, for example, is accomplished with elaborate kinesthetic, and often visual, feedback. The feeling of movement becomes the basis of preliminary data for how the action might be repeated. The repetitions provide additional information not only about that particular movement but about how nonmovement or supportive movement is simultaneously accomplished. Tentative hypotheses about movement are tested, refined, and retested until a reasonable certainty exists in what he is, where he is, and how he acts. This is a dynamic interplay of developing biological systems that support movement (neurosensory, skeletal, and muscular) and the gravity-dominated physical space in which that movement occurs. The child's contest with gravity is a battle that can be won if his genetically coded maturation follows a reasonable normal and expected course.

Bender and Silver (1948), among the first to attend to the problem of body image of brain-injured children, pointed out the dependence of body image development on biologic growth and the integration of physical and psychological experiences. Characteristics such as hyperactivity and figure-ground disturbance (Cruickshank, 1967) and significant deviations in sensory-motor development (Schilder, 1964, p. 53; Strauss & Kephart, 1955, p. 48) militate against the development of an adequate body image. Schilder has also pointed out the importance of optic development to support the acquisition of an adequate body image. Getman (1964) has written extensively on the importance of visual development to the total organism, including the initial guidance and tracking functions.

The concept of body image was dealt with initially by neurologists in efforts to explain correlates of brain lesions. Critchely, Gerstman, Bartlett, and others including Head (1926), a British neurologist who developed specific theoretical formulations of the phenomenon, did considerable experimental work on the organization and development of body attitudes. Since then, many definitions have been suggested.

One definition of body image refers to "the picture of our own body which we form in our mind, that is to say, the way in which the body appears to ourselves" (Schilder, 1950). Myers and Hammill (1976) have described body image as a fluid and dynamic internal conceptualization that, like self-concept, is an important aspect of the learning ability of children. Freud's formulation of the ego in body terms, which underlines the importance of feelings about body knowledge, success, and integrity, represents one aspect of the problem in defining body image and its close relationship to self-concept (Freud, 1960). Wylie (1961) has also pointed out the probable relationship between value ascribed to body characteristics and general self-concept.

Hallahan and Kauffman (1976) have noted the vagueness of the body image construct. As a psychological construct, body image has not had the definitional clarity to support extensive research interest. While of relatively little utility so far in the development of new knowledge, body image has provided a conceptual aide in the analysis of behavior and a useful basis from which the practitioner might consider disability.

While this discussion has focused primarily upon the integrity of internal events, the obvious needs to be stated about the external environment. Except for gravity and working principles of space objects such as size, kind of relationships, movement, direction, etc., that environment is not a constant. Part of the process of adapting involves the environment to which adaptation is made. The quality of the particular influence of those with whom the child interacts is infinitely variable. Opportunities for practice and experimentation, expectations, rules, and limits of the environment all vary.

Self-Concept

One of the major characteristics of brain-injured children is their negative or inappropriate concept of themselves. Here the essential psychoorganic unity of the child is particularly visible. That is, *what* he can do and understand with the neurosensory equipment he has is fundamentally related to who he experiences himself to be in the world.

Wylie has observed that constructs of self "have been stretched to cover so many cognitive and motivational processes that their utility for analytic and predictive purposes has been greatly diminished" (1961, p. 318). In the context of a discussion of brain-injured children, a term also lacking precise conceptual boundaries, the problem of definition is compounded.

Despite conceptual problems, self-concept has long occupied an important place in literature on personality theories (e.g., Rogers, 1951). It has been considered a significant aspect of the learning process (Fennimore, 1968) and has been a prominent issue in early education (Goodlad, 1964; Sears & Sherman, 1964).

Generally, the view of self has been adopted as a relevant concern in understanding the developing child and his/her behavior; the positive self-view being more supportive of his adjustment to others, to task demands, and to learning.

Davidson and Lang stated, "the child's self concept arises and develops in an interpersonal setting" (1960, p. 107). Feelings about self emerge in relation to the child-environment interactional process.

Each failure experienced in that process reinforces the negative self-view and militates against the probability of success in future tasks. Ross (1976) has pointed out that failure in early childhood experiences can have a negative impact on the child's perception of himself, self-confidence, and his response to school. The child who failed to develop trust in himself and his world does not have the psychological basis for establishing autonomy and experiencing his separateness. Continual failure may extinguish serious attempts at succeeding in socially acceptable areas, and devious behavior designed to protect the child from further failure may develop. Wallace and McLaughlin (1975) and others have indicated the apparent relationship between self-concept and low achievement with these children. The fear of being unable to accomplish anything correctly causes them to resist work on tasks. Success becomes translated into the acts of distracting others from an activity in which failure is feared, threatening and overpowering others before unattainable demands are made, gaining attention even if it is negative, withdrawing successfully prior to competing unsuccessfully, etc. Rappaport (1964) has outlined five reaction patterns associated with defective self-concept and narcissistic hypersensitivity. These include low frustration tolerance, flight from challenge, overcompensation, control and manipulation of others, and power struggle or negativism.

This child's energy goes into protecting a very fragile ego, leaving little for ego development. Time is taken defending against further failure, allowing little opportunity for the accumulation of new information and possible success experiences. The defenses are strong because the stakes for the child are very high.

Socioemotional Disturbances

The social history of the brain-injured child is often one of failure. This child learns to defend against further insult to a fragile ego and those very defenses militate against his growth and social development. His fear of further failure robs him of experimental behavior which could serve as a basis for developing competence. The child who has adopted the view that his psychobiological equipment is untrustworthy, is often "ego bankrupt" (Rappaport, 1966), and receives little psychological support from home, school and/or neighborhood environments.

Birch and Lefford (1964) presented three case studies in an attempt to determine why one child with brain damage makes a positive social adjustment and gains mastery over his environment, while another cannot adapt and develops severe psychopathology. It was found that parental attitudes and their methods of management were not markedly different during the early infancy of children in the study. The most useful behavioral predictor of subsequent development was temperamental organization. That is, children primarily positive in mood, rhythmic in functioning, moderate in activity level, mild in intensity, with no significant lowering of response threshold, and readily adaptive, had good behavioral outcomes. Children who were primarily negative in mood, arhythmic, high in activity level, intense reactors with low thresholds, and nonadaptive, followed an increasingly disturbed behavioral course. They concluded that the behavioral development of the children was the result of the interaction between their response tendencies and the environment.

In his comparison of brain-injured and familial children, Gallagher (1957) found the most impressive area of difference to be personality ratings. Differences were found between the groups on almost all of the personality variables in favor of the familial children. The brain-injured children were rated as being "hyperactive, lacking attention, being fearful, less popular and generally more uninhibited children than their familial pairs" (p. 65).

Gallagher suggested two possible explanations of this data. One, the brain-injured child may not be able to correctly perceive social situations or to distinguish between socially appropriate and inappropriate behavior based on an adequate perception of the social cues. Two, impulsivity and unpredictable behavior, as a result of general lack of inhibition, made the brain-injured children unacceptable to peers and adults. The distrust and rejection caused by the disinhibition then produced secondary effects of fearful behavior and inordinate demands for attention.

Whatever the more salient explanation of the behavioral discordancy, the association of negative behavioral characteristics and inordinate demands on others in the child's environment is well established in the literature on learning disabled children

(Bender, 1956; McCartney, 1956; Gallagher, 1957; Rappaport, 1964; Farnham-Diggory, 1966; Jacobs & Pierce, 1968). Fouracre (1958) described the dilemma of the brain-injured child who is driven by need for affiliation and recognition to continue in unsuccessful attempts to enter a group. Research has pointed out that the child's inability to adequately perceive and comprehend physical and abstract structure accounts for part of the child's inability to enter group situations (Fouracre, 1958; Lewis, Strauss, & Lehtinen, 1960).

The degree to which perceptual deficit or disinhibition accounted for the negative social behavior is yet undetermined. Knoblock (1966) raised the question of whether the etiology of maladaptive behavior was in the brain injury or in the personality development in the presence of limited adaptive capacity. It is reasonably clear, however, that the environmental responses elicited by the disturbing behavior reinforce the negative behavior cycle, and that this disturbed exchange produces data for the child's regarding himself and his world. Wallace and Kauffman (1973) have pointed out the importance to academic learning of the child entering school with a repertoire of adequate emotional and social behaviors. If the child is unable to learn those affective and social responses necessary for succeeding in school, he or she is more likely to develop maladaptive behavior. Learning disabled children manifest more aggressive behavior problems than immature or neurotic problems (Hallahan & Kauffman, 1976).

Their behavior problems are more likely to alienate them from sources of social and psychological support including their peer group, teachers, and parents. For example, Kronick (1974) has described the loneliness of the child whose experience is not shared with other family members.

TREATMENT

The professional, educational, and psychological treatment and management of brain-injured children is, for the most part, predicated on a functional analysis of their existing strengths and weaknesses. Several basic and emerging themes can be identified in the treatment of these children.

One major theme found in the literature on treatment is the lack of self-satisfying experiences and the need for success. The child expects failure and is programmed for defense. Any intervention into the accustomed failure "system" of the child must insure the child's psychological success. The teacher or therapist has only the child's need for success as an ally, while the behavior that has been so futile for this child will persist as a foe.

Another major theme in the treatment literature is that of structure. These children have been managed by environments in which they have failed to participate successfully. In their desperate attempts to optimize their participation, they frequently make explicit bids for control of the environments; the prospect that they might win such control is terribly frightening. Structure, as it is used in the literature on the treatment of brain-injured children, means a careful, explicit design for experiences intended to minimize the futile conflict and maximize the child's chances of successful adaptation and learning—thus endowing the environment with an essential reliability.

The need to consider the twenty-four hour adjustment/maladjustment of the brain-injured child is still another theme. That is, any system of intervention must accommodate the total life of the child. A focus on the therapy hour, for example, is not sufficient. The school and home environments, their demands and potentials for important failure or gain, must be examined carefully (Cruickshank, 1977).

A more recent theme that is emerging has to do with diet. Valentine (1971) has observed, for example, that hyperactive children need nutrients, not drugs. Hallahan and Cruickshank (1973) have reviewed much of this literature as it relates to learning disabilities. Important questions have been raised and research interest in the area is beginning to generate useful information (Martin, 1974; Cott, 1971). Several possible relationships are being investigated including that between hypoglycemia and brain damage (*Journal of Learning Disabilities*, 1974). The *Pediatric News* and *World News Report* reported growing recognition that many inherited disorders affecting the central nervous system have been found to respond to vitamin therapy (*Journal of Learning Disabilities*, 1974). While long-term uncritical use of pharmacologic dosages of vitamins is still ill advised based on the limited knowledge available, this certainly represents one of the promising research areas that would have important consequences for treatment.

Kirk and Bateman (1962), Black (1973), and Kenny et al. (1972) have pointed out that remediation is generally based on behavioral symptomatology rather than neurological findings.

That is, the functional disability, not the neurological substrate, is the focus of intervention.

There are two general approaches to treatment. One is directed at the strengths of the child and involves tasks designed to minimize performance demands that involve deficient or dysfunctional areas. Developing areas of strength, and providing the child with opportunities to experience success and to feel good about himself and his acts can help the child to acquire more adaptive compensatory behavior. He will be released from his psychological battle to hide his disabilities and the energy previously required for self-protection will be freed to develop behaviors that will compensate for his deficits.

The other approach involves what Cruickshank has called "teaching to the disability" (1967, p. 101). In this view, the intervention is equally directed at helping the child succeed. In fact, minimizing failure is essential. The difference is that the dysfunction is recognized by the child and the teacher or therapist, and a program, based upon ability level, is planned to remediate that specific disability. Kirk and Bateman (1962) have suggested developing the areas of major deficit since "a part of the deficit in the child is the result of psychological withdrawal from activities requiring use of the deficient ability" (p. 77).

While there is some variation in professional opinion on this issue, there is little disagreement on the complexity of the diagnostic and treatment problem, and the need for a multidisciplined orientation (Cruickshank, 1966). Haring and Schiefelbusch (1967) cited the need for a total medical, psychological, and special education approach to help children with the syndromes of cerebral dysfunction.

Parents are crucial in a total treatment plan. Their feelings are closely attached to the failure and successes of their child. Their own sense of adequacy and ego resources have been challenged directly by this child's experience of constant failure. No one knows better than the parent the anger and resentment, the disappointment, the intensity of hope and frustration that resonates to the demanding activity of these children. No one needs to tell many of these parents that they should have been more understanding and helpful when their child ruined an evening with friends, demanded responsiveness with excessive activity when everyone else had experienced a long, tiring day and was ready to relax, could not get his sleeping habits adjusted to others in the house, simply did not seem to understand anything, was up and active in the morning waking parents still tired from the previous day and dreading the present, and so on.

Educative counseling oriented toward helping parents better understand the behavior of their child and how to better engineer the home activities can be extremely useful (Adamson, 1966). Information that can help the parents understand a specific course of action and alleviate guilt energy for positive action can make an enormous difference in the home life for the child and others.

At times, intense interaction can endure sufficiently long that the parents need psychological support beyond educative counseling. Ego battles, and countering defensive, self-protective tactics can set up a spiraling and futile dynamic in which both the child and the parents ultimately lose. It is in these primary transactions that the child first learns about the world, its trustworthiness, and who he is in it. And, it is here that the parents learn what they are like as parents. The psychological importance of the predominance and reciprocity of positive messages or responses over negative ones is critical.

The literature on education and treatment of brain-injured children includes several ways of viewing the matter of adjusting the environment to the child. Cruickshank (1967) has described the multiple environmental dimensions and eloquently described the impact of the child's disability on the parents. The importance of structure, including reduced environmental stimuli, reduced space, a structured school program and life plan, and an increase in the stimulus value of the teaching materials that are constructed to accommodate specific characteristics of psychopathology has been pointed out (Cruickshank et al., 1961). The concept of structure was later elaborated to include other aspects of the child-environment linkage such as the quality of the relationship between the teacher and child (Cruickshank, 1967).

The teaching-learning environments in public schools are typically arranged so that vital information about who one is, the raw experience data for a concept of self, is derived principally from how well one acts with reference to "normative" performance criteria. The hurt of failure and the constant loss of esteem are a part of the environmental fabric for children who do not have an intact central nervous system to support their successful adaptation. Positive messages are central to interrupting this cycle. A predictable environment that will make success possible provides an opportunity for the child to gain esteem and skills. The environment that will respond to these children's anger as a message that they are experiencing hurt communicates important acceptance and caring. This is a basis for growth, a condition for education, and a requirement for teaching these children.

The educational program should be designed to fit the child's specific needs. If the child is overly stimulated by space, the reduction of working space then becomes a part of the program. If the child is distracted by extraneous visual stimuli or has figure-background difficulty, the optical characteristics of materials and the physical space in which work on those materials occurs should minimize that difficulty. A precise and complete analysis of the child's learning apparatus and management of stimulation is required in order to design an appropriate educational environment. A full psychoeducational diagnosis would include an assessment of all the child's information-processing apparatus including his sensory (input), integrative, and motor (output) systems, which have been described in this chapter. It would also include the child's image of his own body and his self-concept. General normative information on the product or performance such as can be obtained from intelligence testing does not provide an adequate understanding for planning a program. Task performance, the process rather than the product, is usually of more benefit to the teacher. A summary of the performance over many subtests can be very misleading, since the child's profile is most often extremely variable and information about major deficiency as well as efficiency is lost in a single-product measure.

A full educational assessment of the child should include both formal and informal measures of the basic skill areas. Listening, reading, thinking, oral expression, form drawing, and spelling are a few of the areas about which specific information must be obtained.

One of the more useful procedures for obtaining information, relevant to planning an educational program, is to engage in diagnostic teaching—involving the child in more or less standardized educational situations and observing his responses.

Interdisciplinary diagnosis is a complete and, of course, an expensive procedure requiring the services of professionals who are very often not available. Even if such a sophisticated diagnostic battery were available to all children, there would still be major hurdles to a complete understanding of the child from a programming perspective. The professional groups involved are far from a mutually acceptable understanding of how they can most effectively collaborate as a diagnostic team. Further, the various types of information generated by the different examinations do not necessarily constitute a consistent body of knowledge from which a treatment program can be logically derived (Knoblock, 1966; Gallagher, 1966).

If a child fails to learn it should be understood that there are errors in the arrangement of the educational environment. The professional cannot be relieved of responsibility by relying on a concept of error in the child to explain failure of the intervention or treatment. Frequently the typical environments, such as the regular classroom, relax when a difficult child has been identified as brain-injured. Since the problem is so "obviously" inside the child's head, the logic goes, the environment cannot be responsible. This logic is futile for the child since environments that experience no responsibility for the child fail to make any adjustment in his interest. In these instances changes are most often defensive to protect the environment and frequently to exclude the child.

The technical dimensions of the educational task are certainly many and complex. The teacher must know at all times where the child is and where he or she expects the child to be with reference to specific areas. When the current structure, which includes the teacher, environment, and program, fails, immediate correction is essential. This assumes that the teacher is aware of and can explore alternatives. In this sense, the teacher is a monitor and a manager.

Another aspect of the task has to do with knowing when the child has reached an objective and is ready to move to another. For the teacher to perseverate at one level when the child is already beyond it leads to boredom, irritation, and eventually conflict. There should be an ongoing process of evaluation with a capability of change, based on feedback of how well the structure is accommodating the child with reference to the goals that have been established.

Teaching materials per se have been examined in terms of specific contributions to learning situations. Cruickshank and his colleagues have described some relationships between certain teaching materials and psychological and motor functions (see Table 4-1).

Wallace and Kauffman (1973) have pointed out that the typical school curriculum offers little assistance to the child who has difficulty developing social skills. They described two programs

TABLE 4-1. Relationships Between Teaching Materials and Psychological and Motor Functions

	Parquetry	Block Design	Peg Board	Sorting	Matching	Sequence Patterns	Stencils	Cutting	Pasting	Coloring	Geometric Form Copying	Coding	Tracing	Puzzles
Eye-Hand Coordination	X	X	X	X	X	X	X	X	X	X	X	X	X	X
Seeing Design or Pattern as a Whole	X	X	X					X			X	X	X	X
Fine Muscle Development	X	X	X	X		X	X	X	X	X	X	X		
Establishing Handedness	X	X	X		X	X	X	X	X	X	X	X		X
Concept of Spatial Relationships		X	X			X	X	X			X	X		X
Depth Perception		X												
Left-to-right Progression		X	X		X	X					X	X		
Organization of Approach to Task	X	X	X	X	X	X	X		X	X	X	X		X
Color Discrimination	X	X	X	X	X	X	X			X	X	X	X	X
Form Discrimination	X	X	X	X	X	X	X	X	X	X	X			X
Relation of Figure to Background	X	X	X		X		X			X				X
Increased Attention Span	X	X	X	X	X	X	X	X	X	X	X	X	X	X
Control and Limitation of Perseveration		X	X	X	X	X	X	X	X		X			
Temporal-Spatial Relationships	X	X	X		X	X	X			X				X
Size Discrimination				X	X		X	X		X				X
Classification and Grouping				X	X	X								
Laterality		X	X	X	X	X	X	X						X
Directionality		X	X	X	X	X	X	X	X		X	X		X

From: Cruickshank, W. M. *The Brain Injured Child in Home, School, and Community.* Syracuse, N.Y.: Syracuse University Press, 1967, pp. 156–157.

113

developed to teach skills to children with social learning deficits. Fagan, Long, and Stevens developed a curriculum with activities for sequencing and ordering, anticipating consequences, appreciating feelings, managing frustrations, inhibitions and delay, and relaxation. Goldstein (1965) developed a social learning curriculum to teach children to think critically and act independently to the end that they can ultimately manage their own lives and achieve success socially and occupationally.

A considerable body of literature has been developed on motor training for brain-injured children to correct problems in body image and control. Since poor body image constitutes one of the major aspects of psychopathology in these children, it is a very important part of a treatment program.

Kephart (1960) has suggested techniques for helping children gain knowledge and control of their body parts, which include, for example, identification of body parts from verbal cues and the imitation of movement based on visual cues. Barsch (1965) has developed a curriculum based on movigenics—"the study of the origin and development of movement patterns leading to learning efficiency. . . ."

Getman (Getman & Hendrickson, 1966) has made significant contributions to the area of visuo-motor training. He has developed procedures for training in eye movement patterns, eye teaming skills, eye-hand coordination, and visual form perception.

The familiar sensory-motor and perceptual training methods suggested by Montessori (1965) and the tactile-kinesthetic procedures such as those of Fernald (1943) have also been used with these children. Many aspects of perceptual motor training have been questioned in terms of the consequences for educational achievement (Hammill, 1972; Goodman & Hammill, 1973; Sullivan, 1972; Saphier, 1973; Pryzwansky, 1972; Wallace & McLaughlin, 1975). Ross (1976) has pointed out that training in a subskill only provides that skill, not direct help with subject matter. The further study and examination of the conceptual base for this area of programming will be of interest to the theoretition and the practitioner over the next several years.

In summary, the brain-injured child, like all children, may be viewed as an adapting member of a group. Adaptation, the satisfying mutual accommodation of the organism and its environment, is dependent in large part on the integrity of the neurological system of the organism. The complex and elaborate neurological equipment provides these children with the capability of receiving and processing all kinds of information about their environment and, simultaneously, about their actions within that environment. Their integration of the information about the environment and themselves provides the basis for their response to both. Unlike other children, their adaptation has not been satisfying either to themselves or to their environment. Their linkages have been aberrant in the presence of faulty equipment; their maladaptation is understood in terms of behavioral and/or learning difficulties due to central nervous system dysfunction.

The teacher or therapist, while unable to directly access the faulty system in the child, can control the various aspects of the environment to support the child's positive learning and successful adaptation. Getman (1970) has stated:

Hopefully, in the effort to become true teachers of children, we will once again realize that we actually teach children nothing—we can only so arrange situations and conditions that each child can bring what he already knows to the learning opportunity and thus become a learner. (p. 39)

The job of teaching—of helping children learn to learn, to adopt a satisfying internal locus of control, to adapt to a wide range of settings, and to develop skills for a variety of task demands—has just begun.

Learning disabilities, which has categorically subsumed much of the professional area of study and intervention discussed here, has become a major focus of attention in educational legislation. The Education for All Handicapped Children Act (PL 94-142), passed in 1975, makes specific provision for these children to be served in the least restrictive appropriate educational environment. While learning disabilities is a categorical area in its own right, having substantially replaced other labels such as brain-injured or brain-damaged, it brings together and focuses the psychoneurological perspective on behavioral variance. Much of the applied educational treatment area reflects an integration of behavioral and psychoneurological views.

References

ADAMSON, W. C. The needs of teachers for specialized information in the area of pediatric psychiatry. In W. M.

Cruickshank (Ed.), *The teacher of brain-injured children*. Syracuse, N.Y.: Syracuse University Press, 1966, pp. 269-290.

AYRES, A. J. Sensory integrative processes and neuropsychological learning disabilities. In J. Hellmuth (Ed.), *Learning disorders* (Vol. 3). Seattle, Washington: Special Child Publications, 1968, pp. 41-58.

BARSCH, R. H. *A movigenic curriculum*. Bulletin No. 25. Madison, Wisconsin: State Department of Public Instruction, 1965.

BATEMAN, B. Learning disabilities: yesterday, today and tomorrow. *Exceptional Children*, 1964, *31*, 167-178.

BATEMAN, B. Three approaches to diagnosis and educational planning for children with learning disabilities. *Proceedings: 1967 International Convocation on Children and Young Adults with Learning Disabilities*. Pittsburgh, Pa.: Home for Crippled Children, 1967, pp. 120-130.

BELMONT, I., BIRCH, H. G., & KARP, E. The disordering of intersensory and intrasensory integration by brain damage. *The Journal of Nervous and Mental Disease*, 1965, *141*, 410-418.

BENDER, L. Psychological problems of children with organic brain disease. *American Journal of Orthopsychiatry*, 1949, *19*, 404-414.

BENDER, L. *Psychopathology of children with organic brain disorders*. Springfield, Ill.: Charles C Thomas, 1956.

BENDER, L. The brain and child behavior. *Archives of General Psychiatry*, 1961, *4*, 531-547.

BENDER, L., & SILVER, A. Body image problems of the brain-damaged child. *Journal of Social Issues*, 1948, *4*(4), 84-89.

BENSBURG, G. J. Performance of brain-injured and familial mental defectives on the Bender Gestalt Test. *Journal of Consulting Psychology*, 1952, *16*, 61-64.

BIRCH, H. G., (Ed.) *Brain damage in children: The biological and social aspects*. Baltimore, Md.: Williams & Wilkins, 1964.

BIRCH, H. G., THOMAS, A., & CHESS, S. Behavioral development in brain-injured children. *Archives of General Psychiatry*, 1964, *11*, 596-603.

BIRCH, H. G., & LEFFORD, A. Two strategies for studying perception in "brain-damaged" children. In H. G. Birch (Ed.), *Brain damage in children*. Baltimore, Md.: Williams & Wilkins, 1964, pp. 46-60.

BLACK, F. W. Neurological dysfunction and reading disorders. *Journal of Learning Disabilities*, 1973, *6*(5), 313-316.

BOSHES, B., & MYKLEBUST, H. R. A neurological and behavioral study of children with learning disorders. *Neurology*, 1964, *14*, 7-12.

BROCA, A. Sur le siege de la faculte du language articule avec deux observations d'aphemie (perte de la parole). *Bull. Soc. Anat.*, (Aout), T. VI: 1861.

BURKS, H. F. The hyperkinetic child. *Exceptional Children*, 1960, *27*, 18-26.

CLEMENTS, S. D. Minimal brain dysfunction in children. NINDB Monograph No. 3. U. S. Department of Health, Education, and Welfare. Washington, D.C.: Government Printing Office, 1966.

COBRINIK, L. The performance of brain-injured children on hidden-figure tasks. *American Journal of Psychology*, 1959, *72*, 566-571.

COTT, A. Orthomolecular approach to the treatment of learning disabilities. Reprinted by the Huxley Institute for Biosocial Research, New York, 1971, pp. 1-11.

CRITCHELY, M. *The parietal lobes*. London: Arnold, 1953, pp. 406-412.

CRITCHELY, M. *Developmental dyslexia*. London: Heinemann, 1964.

CRUICKSHANK, W. M. (Ed.). *The teacher of brain-injured children: A discussion of the bases for competency*. Syracuse, N.Y.: Syracuse University Press, 1966.

CRUICKSHANK, W. M. *The brain-injured child in home, school and community*. Syracuse, N.Y.: Syracuse University Press, 1967a.

CRUICKSHANK, W. M. The education of the child with brain injury. In W. M. Cruickshank and G. O. Johnson (Eds.), *Education of exceptional children and youth* (2nd ed.). Englewood Cliffs, N.J.: Prentice-Hall, 1967b, pp. 238-283.

CRUICKSHANK, W. M. *The learning disabled child in school, home and community*. Rev. ed. Syracuse, N.Y.: Syracuse University Press, 1977.

CRUICKSHANK, W. M., BENTZEN, F. A., RATZEBURG, F. H., & TANNHAUSER, M. T. *A teaching method for brain-injured and hyperactive children*. Syracuse, N.Y.: Syracuse University Press, 1961.

CRUICKSHANK, W. M., BICE, H. V., & WALLEN, N. E. *Perception and cerebral palsy: A study in figure background relationship.* Syracuse, N.Y.: Syracuse University Press, 1957.

CRUICKSHANK, W. M., BICE, H. V., WALLEN, N. E., & LYNCH, K. S. *Perception and cerebral palsy: Studies in figure-background relationship* (2nd ed.). Syracuse, N.Y.: Syracuse University Press, 1965.

CRUICKSHANK, W. M., & PAUL, J. L. The psychological characteristics of brain-injured children. In W. M. Cruickshank (Ed.), *Psychology of exceptional children* (3rd ed.). Englewood Cliffs, N.J.: Prentice-Hall, 1971.

DAVIDSON, H., & LANG, G. Children's perceptions of their teacher's feelings toward them related to self-perception, school achievement and behavior. *Journal of Experimental Education,* 1960, *29*, 107-118.

DEUTSCH, C. Auditory discrimination and learning: Social factors. *Merrill-Palmer Quarterly,* 1964, *4*, 277-296.

DOLPHIN, J. E., & CRUICKSHANK, W. M. The figure-background relationships in children with cerebral palsy. *Journal of Clinical Psychology,* 1951a, *7*, 228-231.

DOLPHIN, J. E., & CRUICKSHANK, W. M. Pathology of concept formation in children with cerebral palsy. *American Journal of Mental Deficiency,* 1951b, *56*, 386-392.

DOLPHIN, J. E., & CRUICKSHANK, W. M. Tactual motor perception of children with cerebral palsy. *Journal of Personality,* 1952, *20*, 466-471.

DUNN, L. M. Minimal brain dysfunction: a dilemma for educators. In E. C. Frierson and W. B. Barbe (Eds.), *Educating children with learning disabilities: Selected readings.* New York: Appleton-Century-Crofts, 1967, pp. 117-132.

EISENBERG, L. Psychiatric implications of brain damage in children. *Psychiatric Quarterly,* 1957, *31*, 72-92.

EISENBERG, L. Brain and behavior: Session I. Symposium, 1959. Conceptual problems in relating brain and behavior. *American Journal of Orthopsychiatry,* 1960, *30*, 37-48.

EISENBERG, L. Behavioral manifestations of cerebral damage in childhood. In H. G. Birch (Ed.), *Brain damage in children.* Baltimore, Md.: Williams & Wilkins, 1964, pp. 61-73.

FARNHAM-DIGGORY, S. Self, future, and time. *Monographs of the Society for Research in Child Development,* 1966, *31*.

FENNIMORE, F. Reading and the self-concept. *Journal of Reading,* 1968, *11*, 447-451.

FERNALD, GRACE M. *Remedial techniques in basic school subjects.* New York: McGraw-Hill, 1943.

FISICHELLI, V. R., COXE, M., ROSEFELD, L., HOBER, A., DAVIS, J., & KARELITZ, S. The phonetic content of the cries of normal infants and those with brain damage. *The Journal of Psychology,* 1966, *64,* 119-126.

FOURACRE, M. H. Learning characteristics of brain-injured children. *Exceptional Children,* 1958, *24,* 210-212.

FREUD, S. *The ego and the id.* Trans. by J. Strachley (Ed.). New York: Norton, 1960.

FROSTIG, M. The needs of teachers for specialized information on reading. In W. M. Cruickshank (Ed.), *The teacher of brain-injured children.* Syracuse, N.Y.: Syracuse University Press, 1966.

FROSTIG, M., & HORNE, D. *The Frostig program for the development of visual perception: Teacher's guide.* Chicago: Follett Publishing, 1964.

FROSTIG, M., LEFEVER, D. W., & WHITTLESEY, J. R. B. A developmental test of visual perception for evaluating normal and neurologically handicapped children. *Perceptual and Motor Skills,* 1961, *12,* 383-394.

GALLAGHER, J. J. A comparison of brain-injured and non-brain-injured mentally retarded children on several psychological variables. *Monograph of the Society for Research in Child Development,* 1957, *22.*

GALLAGHER, J. J. Children with developmental imbalances: a psycho-educational definition. In W. M. Cruickshank (Ed.), *The teacher of brain-injured children.* Syracuse, N.Y.: Syracuse University Press, 1966, pp. 21-43.

GARDNER, R. W. The needs of teachers for specialized information on the development of cognitive structures. In W. M. Cruickshank (Ed.), *The teacher of brain-injured children.* Syracuse, N.Y.: Syracuse University Press, 1966.

GESELL, A., & ARMATRUDA, C. S. *Developmental diagnosis. Normal and abnormal child development.* New York: Paul B. Hoeber, 1941.

GETMAN, G. N. *How to develop your child's intelligence.* Luverne, Minn.: Announcer Press, 1962.

GETMAN, G. N. The primary visual abilities essential to academic achievement. *Child vision care.* Duncan, Okla.: Optometric Extension Program, 1964.

GETMAN, G. N. The visuomotor complex in the acquisition of

learning skills. In J. Hellmuth (Ed.), *Learning disorders,* *Vol. 1.* Seattle, Wa.: Special Child Publications, 1965, pp. 49-76.

GETMAN, G. N. Recipient or participant? *Journal of Learning Disabilities,* 1970, *3*(1), 38-39.

GETMAN, G. N. & HENDRICKSON, H. H. The needs of teachers for specialized information on the development of visuomotor skills in relation to academic performance. In W. M. Cruickshank (Ed.), *The teacher of brain-injured children.* Syracuse, N.Y.: Syracuse University Press, 1966, pp. 153-168.

GETMAN, G. N., & KANE, E. R. *The physiology of readiness.* Minneapolis, Minn.: Programs to Accelerate School Success, 1964.

GOLDSTEIN, H., Moss, J. W., & JORDAN, L. J. The efficacy of special class training on the development of mentally retarded children. Summary Report, USOE, Cooperative Research Project 619, Urbana, Ill.: University of Illinois, 1965.

GOLDSTEIN, K. *The organism.* New York: American Book, 1939.

GOLDSTEIN, K., & SHEERER, M. Abstract and concrete behavior: An experimental study with special tests. *Psychological Monograph,* 1941, *53*(2).

GOODLAD, J. I. Understanding the self in the school setting. *Childhood Education,* 1964, *41*, 9-14.

GOODMAN, L., & HAMMILL, D. The effectiveness of the Kephart-Getman activities in developing perceptual-motor and cognitive skills. *Focus on Exceptional Children,* February, 1973, *5*.

HALLAHAN, D., & CRUICKSHANK, W. *Psychoeducational foundations of learning disabilities.* Englewood Cliffs, N.J.: Prentice-Hall, Inc., 1973, pp. 15-40.

HALLAHAN, D., & KAUFFMAN, J. *Introduction to learning disabilities.* Englewood Cliffs, N.J.: Prentice-Hall, 1976.

HALSTEAD, W. C. *Brain and intelligence.* Chicago, Ill.: University of Chicago Press, 1947.

HAMMILL, D. Training visual perceptual processes. *Journal of Learning Disabilities,* 1972, *5*(9), 552-559.

HARDY, W. G. On language disorders in young children: A reorganization of thinking. In E. C. Frierson and W. B. Barbe (Eds.), *Educating children with learning disabilities: Selected readings*. New York: Appleton-Century-Crofts, 1967, pp. 36-51.

HARING, N. G., & PHILLIPS, E. L. *Analysis and modification of classroom behavior*. Englewood Cliffs, N.J.: Prentice-Hall, 1972.

HARING, N. G., & SCHIEFELBUSCH, R. O. (Eds.). *Methods in special education*. New York: McGraw-Hill, 1967.

HEAD, H. *Aphasia and kindred disorders of speech*. Cambridge, Mass.: Cambridge University Press, 1926, 2 vols.

HEBB, D. O. The innate organization of visual activity: I. Perception of figures by rats reared in total darkness. *Journal of Genetic Psychology*, 1937, *51*, 101-126.

HEBB, D. O. *The organization of behavior*. New York: John Wiley, 1949.

HELD, R., & WHITE, D. Sensory deprivation and visual speed: An analysis. *Science*, 1959, *80*, 860.

HEWETT, F. M. *The emotionally disturbed child in the classroom*. Boston: Allyn & Bacon, 1968.

HIRT, J. B. Manifestations of the brain damage syndrome in school. In S. R. Rappaport, (Ed.), *Childhood aphasia and brain damage*. Narberth, Pa.: Livingston Publishing, 1964, pp. 45-51.

HOBBS, N. *The futures of children*. San Francisco, Cal.: Jossey Bass, 1975.

JACOBS, J. F., & PIERCE, M. L. The social position of retardates with brain damage associated characteristics. *Exceptional Children*, 1968, *34*, 677-681.

Journal of Learning Disabilities, Chicago, Ill.: Educational Press Association of America.

KAHN, E., & COHN, L. H. Organic driveness, a brain-stem syndrome and an experience. *New England Journal of Medicine*, 1934, *210*, 748-752.

KARELITZ, S., KARELITZ, R., & ROSENFELD, L. S. Infants' vocalizations and their significance. In P. W. Bowman and H. V. Mautner (Eds.), *Mental retardation: Proceedings of the First International Medical Conference*. New York: Grune & Stratton, 1960, pp. 439-446.

KENNY, T., CLEMMENS, R., CICCI, R., LENTZ, G., NAIK, P., & HUD-
SON, B. The medical evaluation of children with reading problems. *Journal of Pediatrics*, 1972, *49*(3), 438-442.

KEPHART, N. C. *The slow learner in the classroom*. Columbus, Ohio:
Charles E. Merrill, 1960.

KIRK, S. A., & BATEMAN, B. Diagnosis and remediation of learning
disabilities. *Exceptional Children*, 1962, *29*, 73-78.

KIRK, S. A., MCCARTHY, J. J., & KIRK, W. *Illinois Test of Psycholinguistic Abilities* (Rev. ed.). Urbana, Ill.: University of Illinois, 1968.

KNOBLOCK, P. The needs of teachers for specialized information
regarding their role in interdisciplinary teams. In W. M.
Cruickshank (Ed.), *The teacher of brain-injured children*.
Syracuse, N.Y.: Syracuse University Press, 1966, pp.
291-308.

KRONICK, D. Some thoughts on group identification: Social needs.
Journal of Learning Disabilities, 1974, *7*(3), 144-147.

LEWIS, R. S., STRAUSS, A. A., & LEHTINEN, L. E. *The other child* (2nd
ed.). New York: Grune & Stratton, 1960.

LEWIS, P. A. Implications of visual problems in learning disability.
Paper presented to the American Optometric Associa-
tion, February 26, 1961. Mimeographed.

LURIA, A. R. *The role of speech in the regulation of normal and abnormal
behavior*, J. Tizard (Ed.). New York: Liveright, 1961.

LURIA, A. R. *Higher cortical functions in man*. New York: Basic
Books, 1966.

MCCARTHY, J. J., & KIRK, S. A. *Illinois Test of Psycholinguistic
Abilities: Experimental edition*. Urbana, Ill.: Institute for
Research on Exceptional Children, University of Illinois
Press, 1961.

MCCARTNEY, L. D. Helping mentally deficient children of the
exogenous type showing central nervous system impairment to make better social adjustment. *American
Journal of Mental Deficiency*, 1956, *61*, 121-126.

MCGINNIS, M. *Aphasic children*. Washington, D.C.: Alexander
Graham Bell Association for the Deaf, 1963.

MAIER, N. R. F., & SCHNEIRLA, T. C. *Principles of Animal Psychology*.
New York: McGraw-Hill, 1935.

MARTIN, P. Mentally ill children respond to nutrition. *Prevention*,
February, 1974, pp. 95-101.

MONEY, J. (Ed.). *Reading disability: Progress and research needs in dyslexia.* Baltimore, Md.: Johns Hopkins, 1962.

MONEY, J. (Ed.). *The disabled reader: Education of the dyslexic child.* Baltimore, Md.: Johns Hopkins, 1966.

MONTESSORI, M. *Dr. Montessori's own handbook.* New York: Schocken Books, 1965.

MYERS, P., & HAMMILL, D. *Methods for learning disorders.* New York: John Wiley, 1976.

ORTON, S. *Reading, writing and speech problems in children.* New York: Norton, 1937.

PAINE, R. S. Neurological grand rounds: Minimal chronic brain syndromes. *Clinical Proceedings of the Children's Hospital.* Washington, D.C.: 1966, *22*, 21-40.

PENFIELD, W., & ROBERTS, L. *Speech and brain mechanisms.* Princeton, N.J.: Princeton University Press, 1959.

PIAGET, J. *The origins of intelligence in children.* Trans. by Margaret Cook. New York: Norton, 1952a.

PIAGET, J. *Judgment and reasoning in the child.* Trans. by Marjorie Warden. New York: Humanities Press, 1952b.

PIAGET, J., & INHELDER, B. *The psychology of the child.* Trans. by Helen Weaver. New York: Basic Books, 1969.

PRIBRAM, KARL H. Neurological notes on the art of educating. In Ernest R. Hilgard (Ed.), *Theories of learning and instruction: The Sixty-Third Yearbook of the National Society for the Study of Education.* Chicago, Ill.: The University of Chicago Press, 1964, pp. 78-110.

PRYZWANSKY, W. B. Effects of perceptual-motor training and manuscript writing on reading readiness skills in kindergarten. *Journal of Educational Psychology*, 1972, *63*(2), 113-115.

QUALTERE, T. J. *An investigation of the relation between visual figure-background disturbance and performance on Raven's progressive matric test in cerebral palsy children.* Unpublished doctoral dissertation. Syracuse University, 1957.

RAPPAPORT, S. R. Behavior disorder and ego development in a brain-injured child. *The psychoanalytic study of the child*, Vol. 16. New York: International Universities Press, 1961, 423-450.

RAPPAPORT, S. R. (Ed.). *Childhood aphasia and brain damage: A definition.* Narberth, Pa.: Livingston Publishing, 1964.

RAPPAPORT, S. R. (Ed.). *Childhood aphasia and brain damage: Volume II: Differential diagnosis.* Narberth, Pa.: Livingston Publishing, 1965.

RAPPAPORT, S. R. Personality factors teachers need for relationship structure. In W. M. Cruickshank (Ed.), *The teacher of brain-injured children.* Syracuse, N.Y.: Syracuse University Press, 1966, pp. 45-55.

RAPPAPORT, S. R. *Public education for children with brain dysfunction.* Syracuse, N.Y.: Syracuse University Press, 1969.

REED, J. C., & REED, H. C., JR. Concept formation ability and non-verbal abstract thinking among older children with chronic cerebral dysfunction. *Journal of Special Education*, 1967, *1*, 157-161.

REGER, R. "Brain injury" and brain injury. *Psychology in the Schools*, 1969, *6*(2), 158-161.

REITAN, R. M. Psychological deficit. *Annual Review of Psychology*, 1962, *13*, 415-444.

REITAN, R. M. *The effects of brain lesions on adaptive abilities in human beings.* Indianapolis: Department of Neurosurgery, Indiana University Medical Center, 1959.

REITAN, R. M. A research program on the psychological effects of brain lesions in human beings. In N. R. Ellis (Ed.), *International review of research in mental retardation (Vol. 1).* New York: Academic Press, 1966, pp. 153-218.

REITAN, R. M., & HEINEMAN, C. E. Interactions of neurological deficits and emotional disturbances in children with learning disorders: Methods for differential assessment. In J. Hellmuth (Ed.), *Learning disorders* (Vol. 3). Seattle: Special Child Publications, 1968, pp. 93-135.

RIESEN, A. H. The development of visual perception in man and chimpanzee. *Science*, 1947, *56*, 107-108.

ROGERS, C. R. *Client-centered therapy.* Boston: Houghton Mifflin, 1951.

ROSENBLITH, J. F., & ALLINSMITH, W. (Eds.). *The causes of behavior: Readings in child development and educational psychology.* Boston: Allyn & Bacon, 1962.

ROSS, A. *Psychological aspects of learning disabilities and reading disorders.* New York: McGraw-Hill, 1976.

SABATINO, D. A. The construction and assessment of an experimental test of auditory perception. *Exceptional Children*, 1969a, *35*, 729-737.

SABATINO, D. A. Identifying neurologically impaired children through a test of auditory perception. *Journal of Consulting and Clinical Psychology*, 1969b, *33*(2), 184-188.

SAPHIER, J. D. The relation of perceptual motor skills to learning and school success. *Journal of Learning Disabilities*, 1973, *6*(9), 583-592.

SARASON, S. B. *Psychological problems in mental deficiency* (3rd ed.). New York: Harper & Row, 1959.

SCHILDER, P. *The image and appearance of the human body*. New York: John Wiley, 1950.

SCHILDER, P. *Contributions to developmental neuropsychiatry*. L. Bender (Ed.). New York: International Universities Press, 1964.

SCHULMAN, J. L., KASPAR, J. C., & THRONE, F. M. *Brain damage and behavior: A clinical experimental study.* Springfield, Ill.: Charles C Thomas, 1965.

SEARS, P. S., & SHERMAN, V. *In pursuit of self-esteem: Case studies of eight elementary school children*. Belmont, Cal.: Wadsworth, 1964.

SHAW, M. C. *A study of certain aspects of perception and conceptual thinking in idiopathic epileptic children*. Unpublished doctoral dissertation. Syracuse University, 1955.

SHAW, M. C., & CRUICKSHANK, W. M. The use of the Bender-Gestalt Test with epileptic children. *Journal of Clinical Psychology*, 1956, *12*, 192-199.

SHERRINGTON, D. S. *Man on his nature*. Cambridge: Cambridge University Press, 1955.

SMITH, K. U., & SMITH, W. M. *Perception and motion: An analysis of space-structured behavior*. Philadelphia, Pa.: W. B. Saunders, 1962.

STEVENS, G. D., & BIRCH, J. W. A proposal for clarification of the terminology used to describe brain-injured children. *Exceptional Children*, 1957, *23*, 346-349.

STRAUSS, A. A., & KEPHART, N. C. Behavior differences in mentally retarded children measured by a new behavior rating scale. *American Journal of Psychiatry*, 1940, *96*, 1117-1123.

STRAUSS, A. A., & KEPHART, N. C. *Psychopathology and education of the brain-injured child. Vol. II. Progress in theory and clinic.* New York: Grune & Stratton, 1955.

STRAUSS, A. A., & LEHTINEN, L. E. *Psychopathology and education of the brain-injured child.* New York: Grune & Stratton, 1947.

STRAUSS, A. A., & WERNER, H. Disorders of conceptual thinking in the brain-injured child. *Journal of Nervous and Mental Disease*, 1942, *96*, 153-172.

STRONG, R. T. *The identification of primary school age children with learning handicaps associated with minimal brain disorder.* Unpublished doctoral dissertation. University of Utah, 1964.

SULLIVAN, J. The effects of Kephart's perceptual-motor training on a reading clinic sample. *Journal of Learning Disabilities*, 1972, *5*(9), 545-551.

TALBOT, M. E. *Edouard Seguin: A study of an educational approach to the treatment of mentally defective children.* New York: Teachers College, Columbia University, 1964.

TEUBER, H. L., & WEINSTEIN, S. Ability to discover hidden figures after cerebral lesions. *A.M.A. Archives of Neurology and Psychiatry*, 1956, *76*, 369-379.

THOMPSON, L. J. Reading disability: *Developmental dyslexia.* Springfield, Ill.: Charles C Thomas, 1966.

VALENTINE, M. A hyperactive child needs nutrients, not drugs. *Prevention*, April, 1971, pp. 169-176.

VEGAS, O. V., & FRYE, R. L. Effect of brain damage on perceptual performance. *Perceptual and Motor Skills*, 1963, *17*, 662.

WALLACE, G., & KAUFFMAN, J. *Teaching children with learning problems.* Columbus, Ohio: Charles E. Merrill, 1973.

WALLACE, G., & McLAUGHLIN, J. *Learning disabilities.* Columbus, Ohio: Charles E. Merrill, 1975.

WEPMAN, J. *Recovery from aphasia.* New York: Ronald Press, 1951.

WERNER, H. Abnormal and subnormal rigidity. *Journal of Abnormal and Social Psychology*, 1946, *41*, 15.

WERNER, H., & STRAUSS, A. Types of visuomotor activity in their relation to low and high performance ages. *Proceedings of the American Association of Mental Deficiency*, 1939, *44*(1), 163.

WERNER, H., & STRAUSS, A. A. Pathology of figure-background relation in the child. *Journal of Abnormal and Social Psychology*, 1941, *36*, 236-248.

WIEDERHOLT, J. L. Historical perspectives on the education of the learning disabled. In L. Mann and D. Sabatino, (Eds.), *The second review of special education*. Philadelphia: JSE Publisher, 1974.

WYLIE, R. C. *The self-concept: A critical survey of pertinent research literature*. Lincoln: University of Nebraska Press, 1961.

ZIGMOND, N. K., & CICCI, R. *Auditory learning*. San Rafael, Cal.: Dimensions Publishing, 1968.

PART THREE

Philosophies of Deviance and Science

The next two chapters address themselves to the more basic philosophical issues of deviance and science. Most theories fail to make explicit the underlying base of their assumptions and views of human existence and human experience.

It seems important, therefore, in a book on new views and processes in the area of deviance and disability to examine some of their philosophical bases.

CHAPTER FIVE

Philosophy
of Deviance

Introduction

One of the most significant discrepancies in the American dream is that between the hopes for children as expressed in creeds and the purposes of institutions, and the accelerating incidence of psychological and social morbidity in children. The hope is to optimize the development of children, accepting only their genetic potential as a valid constraint. The theoretical, technological, and social concepts that would allow programming of such an opportunity for children have not been developed. Knowledge of child development, the technologies of education, concepts of child rearing, our understanding of environment and its impact on children, and knowledge of the contingencies of the physical health of children have been increased. In recent years significant social changes have even made in, for example, expanding the boundaries of acceptable behaviors and beliefs. The paradox, however, is

131

that children continue to be extruded from public institutions, such as the public school, for their failure to comply with the behavioral standards of that institution. There is an apparent momentum in the direction of better understanding and more positive interventions in the lives of children and an inertia in the systems to implement those interventions.

Social deviance is a phenomenon that provides unique perspective on the human characteristics of a culture. To understand the human values in a culture, it is instructive to examine what the culture rejects. To understand the cultural process for managing significant difference, it is useful to understand the institutionalized procedures for responding to deviance. Disturbance is a special case of deviance or, more broadly, the social registration of deviance.

In this chapter on philosophy of deviance the reader will find a discussion of some issues that the authors consider salient to the examination of theories of disturbance. The general arguments are outlined below:

1. Emotional disturbance takes its meaning from the social system in which it occurs.
2. The dynamic interplay of the history and philosophy of science and society is viewed as an important determinant of theories of disturbance.
3. Theories of disturbance are products of the behavioral and social sciences.
4. Two major streams of philosophical influences are identified in these sciences and their development of theories of disturbance: (a) positivism, and (b) existentialism.
5. An appeal is made for a transcendence of the epistemological constraints of traditional science and of the stale social stereotype of the problem of disturbance.
6. An appreciation of the view of man as unique and the human experience as the primary source of knowledge about man is considered central to the development of a sound theory of human deviance or disturbance.

Systems for or of Disturbance?

In this section the following general points are made: (1) disturbance is embedded in social institutions and administrative systems; (2) it has meaning(s) in those institutions and systems which may or may not fit the meaning it is given in theoretical explanation; and (3) the discontinuity of theory and practice must be understood in part as a function of the additional meaning assigned to disturbance by the system in which "it" is treated. Some have suggested, as will be noted later, that this "additional meaning" is the total meaning. There are several systems that could illustrate these three general points: mental health, social welfare, legal-correctional, educational, and so on (Rhodes, 1972). Special education, actually a subsystem of the educational system, will be used as an illustrative example.

Special education is a formal, public, professionalized system for responding to children who, for whatever reasons, cannot be included in the normal socializing systems—in this instance, the regular educational system—without assistance. The responsibilities of special educators interact not only with the products of the extrusion processes of the normal system, i.e., children with special labels, but also with the processes that identify, label, and move children away from normal child life. Some have argued that special education maintains the labeling and extrusion processes.

Historically, special education has assumed instructional responsibility for children who, as a result of significant physical or intellectual variance, were not able to successfully adapt to the regular or "normal" curriculum. The response has been either to circumvent the disability with prosthetic devices, or to alter the normal curriculum (Trippe, 1963).

In the last decade, special education has assumed responsibility for the education of emotionally disturbed children. The educational mandate has been to alter the child's performance relative to the normal curriculum (Trippe, 1963). The social mandate has been to reduce the behavioral variance in the classroom, that is, to normalize the child to fit the value structure of a particular social system.

The special education of emotionally disturbed children has generated an extremely complex interaction of social and psychological theories and interventions. The interaction has been complex because of the status of theory in the social sciences and the deep cultural entanglement of the basic issue, that is, child variance. There is considerable support for the position, as is pointed out in this volume, that isolation of the variant behavior from the environment in which it occurs, either conceptually or for the purpose of changing it, is to deny or change the phenomenal nature of the behavior.

There has been understandable unevenness and confusion in knowing what to do, how, or why. One cannot be reassured, at this point, that the professional, scientific, social, or ethical issues that have emerged are substantially understood or are in the process of being effectively sorted and analyzed. Theories and practices in the mental health field have merged into thinking and professional practices of special education. This was not a systematic process and could hardly be considered a credit to the scientific integrity of any of the professional fields involved. Confusion, ambiguity, and vagueness in language, definitions, assumptions and, more generically, in theory have compounded the problems of the social and philosophical roots and contexts of currently competing frames of reference.

The "specialness" of special education as a professional area has been examined many times. The need for examining special education has not derived primarily from accumulated knowledge and, therefore, the reordering of an area of science. Rather, it has most often been forced to reexamine the way it orders the world, and the particular ordering to which it responds, as a result of social, legal, and ethical issues. While this is not independent of accumulating knowledge, neither is it a function of that knowledge.

Special education has preseverated on questions of homogeneity, the appropriate parameters for grouping, the most effective methodology and materials, the efficacy of arrangements, etc. The "answers" to these questions remain generally inconclusive or inconsistent. On points of general consensus, such as the data generated by studies of the efficacy of special classes, there remains a deep discontinuity with practices (Kirk, 1964).

The traditional lag between theory and practice, between accumulated knowledge and public action, is well known and documented. How does a society and the knowledge it formally accumulates in its scientific community get together? How does knowledge about children, about what we do to children, and about what we should do for children get brought into some reasonable alignment? Obviously a serious response to these questions goes deep into political, ethical, and legal issues as well as into questions of science. The questions do, however, suggest a general frame of reference for judging the limited scope of questions that commonly ally the professional and the scientist.

Children have a genetic mandate to grow up and a cultural mandate to confine their behavioral development within certain limits. The environments in which the child grows up (home, school, community) must meet physical survival needs and fulfill a cultural mandate to perpetuate the behaviors that support cultural life. It is the interaction between the relative fulfillment of these mandates that produces man qua man, be he good, bad, disturbed, retarded, criminal, etc. Childhood is that time in the life span in which this interaction is formulated (although the rules for that formulation already exist) and opportunity is maximal for altering that interaction.

The perpetuation needs of the environment are met with social processes that are relatively inflexible. For example, relatively little has changed in the administration of public systems of education. The child, on the other hand, survives by inherent adaptability and learning. Children change rapidly as their dynamic psychobiological momentum interacts with the social structure designed to channel that momentum into meeting environmental perpetuation goals. That is, the child-environmental exchange will be most acceptable when the growth energy of the child and the maintenance energy of the environment flow in a single direction.

Handicapped children are those children who either conflict with or fail to contribute to the perpetuation needs of the environment over a sufficiently long period of time and with sufficient intensity as to cause the environment alarm over its own welfare or that of the individual or both. The environment then takes action in terms of two referent points: preservation of its integrity and a value of individual welfare. These two often conflict in terms of the public action that is taken. Hence, a child who threatens the integrity of a regular classroom will be removed to a "special" place where a supposedly more suitable program, such as a special class or special school is available.

Society has assured itself that it will not abdicate responsibility for the welfare of the individual by the social legislation it has passed. The problem comes when the special program in a special place is not demonstrably better for the child than the regular classroom, as has been suggested by efficacy studies. That the "objective" decision based on individual welfare criteria does not prevail—that is, children are moved into arrangements that can be demonstrated to be in *their* best interests—should not surprise us. The highest priorities are those having to do with environmental integrity and stability, which probably have Darwinian philosophical roots. Activities such as labeling children, a significant product of the professional diagnostic process, and stigma, the cultural byproduct, serve to maintain the primary direction of accountability to the environment.

Special education has developed as an attempt to mediate between the needs of institutions and the needs of individuals. Special education is a specific instance of the more general cases of mental health, welfare, and corrections. In the more general cases the mediation is between individuals and society or social institutions. So then, the special class, like the psychiatric hospital or the correctional center, is both a place of deterrence and remediation or rehabilitation. That is, it serves both to remove the individual from society and, supposedly, to alter the condition of the child that made this removal necessary.

The definition of the problem, then, be it psychiatric, welfare, special educational, or other, has been in terms of the individual in society. This basic paradigm of the one in relation to the many permeates our thinking about deviance and intervention. The person who cannot adapt to society, or a child who cannot learn in or adjust to the regular classroom are examples. There are problems inherent in this view.

First, there is considerable reason to believe that our special systems of mediation, including special education, have not themselves been entirely satisfactory for the minority or the different. The questions about what is special about special education are not unlike the questions of what is therapeutic about a psychiatric hospital or what is corrective about correction settings. Part of the problem in defining the special case is that there is no clear boundary for, or definition of, the general case in education. If, indeed, education is for life (Pestalozzi, 1969), how then do we understand special education?

Another problem is in the assumptions we make about the people involved. We have yet to define a truly homogeneous group. The problem may well be that homogeneity is more a social concept used as a tool for legitimizing extrusion than a technical concept related to the characteristics of children per se (Farber, 1968). In retrospect, the concept has been successfully used for segregating children. It has not particularly aided in our understanding and, therefore, our restorative and rehabilitative management of children.

The third problem is that of justification or accountability. These children are not only "treated" in a special place, they are removed from the nonspecial place. We have developed an elaborate technology in support of the technical functions and left ourselves without a way to understand or justify the exile function.

Finally, perhaps one of the most difficult and illusory problems is the definition of the problem itself. It is often assumed that disturbance, retardation, disability, etc., are generic quantifiable phenomena. Yet it is difficult to define these concepts apart from the context in which they exist. This has been known for a long time with deprived children, for example, but that knowledge has not been incorporated into the way in which "special" children are understood and taught. The problem of a disturbed child in a regular classroom changes in a special classroom. It also changes in another regular classroom. It is different at home. That is, the migration of a child from one environment to another is not independent of the problem the child is said to have. Professionals often act as though the problem were a constant, and it is simply moved to another environment where the tools are available and the conditions exist that will help us do better work on the problem. This might be thought of as analogous to the medical model of diagnosis and surgical treatment. Fortunately for the patient, and for the surgeon, appendicitis experienced at home is appendicitis diagnosed at the clinic, is appendicitis in the operating room. This assumption of constancy across environments does not necessarily obtain with behavioral variance of disturbance.

The epiphenomenal problem of deviance is complex and the definitions that exist are many. Each time a group of special children gain social and professional attention, a plethora of definitions of the problems of those children follow. The inconstancy is not, as is typically thought, simply in the definitions, but rather in the primary view of the world from which the definition is derived.

Consolidation vs Synthesis of Theory

A single unifier, organizer, or grid for the various theories is probably not possible. Some theoretical conceptions are primarily descriptive in nature, while others are much more directed at the explanations of phenomena. Another distinction may be drawn in terms of the focus of inquiry. Some theoreticians are primarily interested in the collective, the way things "hang together," or the system. These would include areas such as social systems theory. Others are interested in more discrete phenomena. The focus on behavior in behavioral psychology would be an example. Some theoreticians are concerned about the relationship between the individual phenomenon and the collective, between the molecular and the molar. Ecological theory would be an example. These distinctions are relative to emphasis and not absolute focus.

Another distinction is based on the utility of the work. Some are primarily concerned about an intervention, that is, what can be done to change an existing situation. Others are more interested in theory construction per se. The most divisive issues in theory, however, have to do with the epistemological assumptions and the interaction of those assumptions with the social context of the theory.

It is not surprising that in a pluralistic society multiple theories of deviance exist. It is further not surprising that in a logical positivistic orientation to science and to knowledge that there should be efforts to focus on rationality and order, to make sense out of it all. That is, in a pluralistic society monolistic assumptions are made about knowledge and science. Scientific investigations proceed with the assumption of one, lawful and ultimately discoverable, reality. Socially, on the other hand, many realities are acknowledged and considered appropriate. These realities are distributed multivariately. The variables include, for example, age, sex, social class, and culture. There are several reality dichotomies, such as subjective and objective, or spiritual and material. Each reality affirmed has its own value as is suggested by adjectives, such as "merely" when applied to subjective or "materialistic" when applied to a person.

In recent years the revival of mysticism, of increased awareness and sensitivity, and of "mind expansion" through various means has led to questioning by some of the adequacy of the formal boundaries of reality specified by traditional science. If science is not to be pluralized, then certainly the role of science, its boundaries and its authority, in the larger social system requires continuous scrutiny and definition. The dynamic relationship between science and society has, of course, been acknowledged as a major topic of study. Such study cannot be kept in a single department or even within the university because the implications for the entire social system are immense. Nowhere is this juncture more critical than in the scientific study of deviance.

Logical Positivism, History,
and Mental Health
(Disturbance in Science and Society)

In this section on positivism an attempt will be made to generally:

1. Define the concerns of logical positivism.
2. Trace the adoption (institutionalization) in science and society of certain assumptions and rules of the positivistic position.
3. Describe some of the implications of that process whereby certain theories of disturbance based on positivistic premises got imbedded, for example, in the mental health movement and later assimilated into the attitudes of people and institutionalized as areas of science as well as in the bricks and mortar of social forms.
4. Define the nature and properties of theory as the intellectual framework in which the positivistic assumptions are articulated and the phenomenon of disturbance defined and conceptually manipulated as a part of the scientific process.

These topics will be discussed in two sections. (a) The mental health movement—Some theoretical and philosophical foundations, and (b) The nature of theory.

Obviously the traditional science framework is not limited to nor bounded by positivism. Neither is positivism limited to logical positivism. The traditional science framework, however, in its limited treatment here is discussed primarily with reference to the philosophical position of logical positivism. While logical positivism is not a popular contemporary philosophy, "many of its ideas live on" (Ayer, 1957, p. 73). Certainly many of its assumptions characterize the behavioral sciences and are objects of attack from the left in psychology and education.

This section is included because some theories of disturbance have been developed based on these assumptions. More importantly, the authors would suggest that the maturity of these theories must be understood relative to the areas of study they are able to handle, given their assumptions.

The history of science in the United States is an evolution of a particular empiricism fashioned out of philosophical developments both in this country and Europe. It is important, in retrospect, to note the relative absence of an impact of Eastern

139

philosophies of knowledge on the philosophy of science that evolved. Intellectual events such as the Vienna Circle's articulation of logical positivism in 1912 had an important impact on science and, at that time, the separation of the scientific enterprise from areas of mysticism, metaphysics, and values took place. The logical positivistic position acknowledged one reality and one set of criteria for validation. What is real can be observed, measured, and described. The observable characteristic of reality established its nature as that directly available, or potentially available, to the sensory equipment of the observer. The characteristic of measurability gave it some structural form that had a correspondence to the structure and processes of logic and mathematics. That reality could be described presumed its essential publicness and universality.

A significant aspect of logical positivism was the basic concern with the structure of language. The cultural basis of the structure of sentences and meanings of words obscured the reality referent of the intended communication. The meaning of a statement was determined by the way in which it could be verified, and verification was a matter of testing by empirical observation.

There were many constraints imposed by this orientation in areas of observation, measurement, and description. In addition to the methodological constraints, there was a boundary imposed on the phenomena that could be considered for "scientific" study. This boundary was a function of the philosophical position itself. While this position has undergone substantial revision since 1912, many of the basic assumptions in the current epistemology of science are included in this basic view of the world.

In a sense, Ayer suggests, philosophy later merged with science to become the logic of science, the intellectual policeman, freeing scientists from metaphysics. As Schlick and Wittgenstein argued, philosophy was to be more an activity to clarify propositions rather than a body of doctrine.

The Mental Health Movement: Theoretical and Philosophical Foundations

In the late eighteenth and early nineteenth century many of the speculative "arm chair" disciplines at that time, such as anthropology, adopted an empirical orientation. They went to the field to observe, measure, and describe the phenomena that they had previously thought about from a distance.

At the same time, an interesting development was occurring from a philosophy of science point of view. A neurologist in Vienna by the name of Freud was ushering in a social revolution with fundamental implications for the human sciences. Freud resisted the eighteenth-century assumptions that the brain and its mechanical and chemical functions could be sufficiently understood to explain mental illness (Hart, 1931).

In the enthusiasm created by these discoveries (anatomy and physiology of the brain including, for example, cerebral topography) it was confidently anticipated that the nature and causes of mental disorder would speedily be laid bare. These hopes have not been realized, however, and the opinion is rapidly gaining ground that, although the value of the physiological method cannot be disputed, there is ample room for some other mode of approaching the problem. This other mode has now been furnished by the development of the "psychological conception." (pp. 27-28)

Freud developed a model of personality, an abstraction of reality, to be used as the basis for explaining behavior. His procedure, mostly case study, has become a primary methodology in the behavioral sciences that followed him.

This conception treated mental disorder as a phenomenon that could be studied and understood without being bound to organic brain function. Hart points out that the development of a psychology of insanity had to overcome the early confusion that existed between this area and ethics, metaphysics, and theology. "Finally, however, psychology succeeded in freeing itself from its alien companions, and the way was clear for its application to the study of insanity" (p. 28). Janet, Freud, Kraepelin, Jung, and others led this conceptual battle.

The coming of age of a science of behavior has had growth pains reminiscent of the trauma of its birth. It is significant here to note that the logical positivist move to free philosophy from metaphysics was designed to point out the factual meaninglessness of metaphysical statements of truth that could not be empirically verified. As Ayer (1957) points out, language has important functions other than reporting facts, including, for example, metaphysical statements that express attitudes to life. "All that is claimed is that they are not capable of stating facts" (p. 74). Recent developments have questioned the relevance of contemporary psychological theories that are so conceptually dislodged from their original roots such as ethics.

Hart (1931) pointed out methodological issues that, from an epistemological point of view, may be ghosts haunting our laboratories.

At the present day,[1] therefore, there are two dominating "conceptions," the physiological and the psychological, differing widely in their mode of dealing with the subject, but both alike founded upon the employment of the scientific method. (p. 28)

The scientific method to which Hart made reference included the observation and recording of data and the classification of that data into groups or series and "the discovery of a formula which will enable us to resume these series in the most comprehensive and convenient manner" (p. 34). Freud's conceptions "... have profoundly affected the course of nearly all modern psychopathological investigation" (p. 16).

It was several decades later that Maslow (1966) pointed out the unfortunate limitations placed on the intellectual genius of Freud's work by epistemological traditions of science that prevailed in his time. Importantly, Freud, along with Charcot and others, had activated another revolution that was basically social (Trippe, 1963). This is an excellent example of the dynamic interplay between science and society. As a result of their work on hysteria, physical illness with psychological etiology as opposed to demonstrable physical etiology, psychological phenomena became a legitimate concern of the medical sciences.

This came at a time of debate over the philosophical questions of who speaks for the purpose and describes the place of man in the universe, who is the authority on issues of good and evil or right and wrong. The church had lost much of its traditional position as such an authority, creating a power vacuum. An important article comparing the language, structure, and roles of the church has been written by Seeley (1953).

In this country the seeds of the mental health movement were germinating. Beers wrote his important book on human abuse in asylums (1908). In 1912 Salman, a physician, was hired as the first director of the National Association for Mental Hygiene.

[1]This was first published in 1912.

He and Beers, along with others like Dorothea Dix, activated public support for a revolution in the case of the mentally ill. There was an important interaction between the ethical issues of human welfare and the medical science of treatment that emerged. The important social and moral questions related to deviance and the ethical dimensions of the phenomenon of mental illness were to be significantly raised a half century later.

In the meantime social structures have emerged to use and perpetuate the methods, data, and attitudes about psychological "reality." The evaluation of "real data" must be understood as a function of the epistemological foundation of the science that generated it. This interacts, as suggested above, with the nature of the social institutions that preserved and perpetuated that science.

Several problems are suggested by this analysis. Two will be mentioned here. First, the interaction of the science and society of man requires some reciprocal influence. What is known about man and society must change since neither man nor society is static. What seems to happen, however, is that the inertia of institutions tends to adopt and "lock in" certain conclusions about man. Those conclusions are frequently defended on the basis of "scientific" support.

Second, the methods of science achieve a high level of value. The means by which information is obtained judge that information and thereby become a higher value than the information itself. The perpetuation of a methodology becomes a social institutional responsibility. Scientific knowledge, then, becomes a product of the systems that nourish and perpetuate it as well as the methods that produce it. The interactions of social and epistemological issues are important and complex. How much we know and the social value and use of that knowledge are especially important dimensions of the behavioral and social sciences. Theories of disturbance are particularly sensitive to the interaction of the methods and values of science and the nature and behavior of social institutions. What we know about disturbance is of the order of knowledge of what we know about ourselves. Some have questioned whether there is a phenomenal division between the disturbed and the disturbing. Some have further questioned the existence of disturbance apart from the experience of it. Whether it exists or not must be understood with reference to the methods used in answering the question, how do we know?

The "fact" of the existence of disturbance and the "facts" of its nature(s) have been integrated at various levels into the behavioral and social sciences. There are theories of disturbance. In this present analysis of theories of disturbance from a positivistic framework, the nature of theory must be examined along with the structure of the language in which the scientific characteristics of disturbance are expressed. It is hoped this will provide an expanded basis for analyzing the nature of bodies of behavioral and social knowledge about disturbance.

The Nature of Theory

The structure of scientific knowledge and the processes by which that knowledge is obtained are described in many other writings. For a thorough discussion of the nature of theory construction the reader is referred to Braithwaite (1953), Nagel (1961), or Kaplan (1964). While a thorough review of these and other writings is not necessary here, it is necessary to outline the nature of the basic principles, or theories, of science, which Madsen (1968) has described as "the most complex products of the most complex organisms on the earth" (p. 12). There are several ways to view and define theories as intellectual tools. Deutsch and Krauss (1965) describe physical science theories in terms of the following components: an abstract calculus, theoretical constructs, and rules of correspondence. The view briefly outlined here is that suggested by Rapoport (1969). Rapoport divides theory into three aspects, all of which are present in scientific theories. They are deductive, predictive, and heuristic.

Deductive theory deals with things or events that have only a conceptual existence. It does not deal with objects in the world of sensory experience. It is a collection of theorems and propositions established by the use of deductive techniques of formal logic as in mathematics. The truth or proof of a proposition is established by the validity of the logical deductions, not by correspondence with experienced reality. The basic propositions (axioms or postulates) are assumed to be true. The logical system of mathematics or deductive theory is context free. Rapoport, paraphrasing Bertrand Russell, pointed out that ". . . in mathematics we never know what we are talking about nor whether what we are saying is true" (p. 3).

Predictive theory is empirically or content oriented. It is concerned with the best fit of idealized conceptions to the real world. The content of the physical sciences is based on models of parts of the real world. Physical laws are basic propositions, analogues of mathematical postulates. The truth of assertions is determined by observable data. The predictive power of physical science theories comes from the connection between theoretically deduced proposition and observation.

Predictive theory has two epistemological by-products that are relevant to understanding certain assumptions of theories of deviance. The first byproduct is in the understanding that the physical world is governed by laws, and knowledge of those laws endows one with power to control and manipulate that world. The second is the understanding that the source of knowledge is not authority or pure reason but direct contact with nature.

Knowledge is acquired by asking the right questions formulated out of theory and actively eliciting the answers from nature. Answers come from controlled experimentation, not from passive waiting.

Given the commitment to a formal methodology for the discovery of basic properties of reality, what is "known," or the existing conceptions, are always subject to revision based on new data appropriately obtained. Knowledge is therefore always tentative. Rapoport illustrates this process with the impact of quantum theory on classical electrodynamics. These by-products of the predictive theory basis of physical science constitute the epistemological foundation of the philosophy of science.

Heuristic theory is another aspect of scientific theory. This aspect is based on explanatory appeal and intuitive understanding. Explanation in this sense may be independent of prediction. "Freudian theory 'makes sense' to Freudians, and this feeling of having understood the sources of compulsion in the human psyche and in human conduct gives the theory its explanatory appeal, regardless of its predictive power, which is anything but impressive" (Rapoport, 1970, p. 7). The structural theory of linguistics is another example. It makes no prediction but makes possible the description of language in a systematic way.

Heuristic theory is especially important in areas where we are still looking for new paths to new kinds of knowledge. Here there is more chance for error and less agreement on the rules for assessing validity and thereby determining error.

The forces that encourage conceptual invention, the creative potential for making personal and subjective experience objective and for aligning private ordering of the world with public ordering include charlatans as well as heroes, sometimes with vague distinctions between the two. Here there is opportunity for the convergence of persuasion, social values, attitudes, and power. The same social climate that supports heroes with hero worshippers honors the dynamics of commitment, conviction, trust, and vested authority. This is how an idea "comes in its own time." The existentialists have suggested that the nature of truth is such that reconciliation of the private and public, subjective and objective is not possible. The implication of a reconciling methodology is an affirmation of the supremacy of empirical and rational values.

Some current debates that illustrate the problems that arise in a society in which the logical positivistic values of science collide with the quasi-empirical heuristic traditions in the behavioral sciences include, for example, program evaluation, efficacy studies, and the appropriateness of behavioral objectives.

Rapoport points out, " . . . all science began as a dawning of an intuitive understanding of how 'things hang together' " (p. 8). While, as he further states, heuristic theory provides "intellectual points of leverage for investigation" (p. 8), there is still the problem of how things seem to "hang together" for one man, for all men, and beyond the experience of man.

If disturbance exists, as postulated by theories described in this volume, does it exist as a lawful phenomenon which can be observed and validated by experience? Or does it exist as a function of the "way we look at it," where the explanatory appeal rather than the empirical support may be the basis for accepting the position? Neither is necessarily "better," but they are different and have different implications for the approach to studying the phenomenon. The use of heuristic theory does not suggest that the phenomenon does not exist in some lawful, potentially verifiable, form. Similarly, it does not assure any reality beyond the immediate "fit" of the heuristic with experience and a particular utility. This issue must be understood with reference to the question, what is the nature of reality? As noted elsewhere in this writing, some argue that experience *is the* reality.

References

AYER, A. J. The Vienna circle. In A. J. Ayer, W. C. Kneale, G. A. Paul, D. F. Pears, P. F. Strawson, G. J. Warnock, & R. A. Wellheim, *The revolution in philosophy*. London: Macmillan, 1957, pp. 70-87.

BEERS, C. W. *A mind that found itself.* New York: Longmans, Green, 1908.

BRAITHWAITE, R. B. *Scientific explanation.* Cambridge: Cambridge University Press, 1953.

DEUTSCH, M., & KRAUSE, R. M. *Theories in social psychology.* New York: Basic Books, 1965.

FARBER, B. *Mental retardation: Its social context and social consequences.* Boston: Houghton Mifflin, 1968.

HART, BERNARD. *The psychology of insanity* (4th ed.). New York: Macmillan, 1931.

KAPLAN, A. *The conduct of inquiry.* San Francisco, Cal.: Chandler, 1964.

KIRK, S. A. Research in education. In H. A. Stevent & R. Heber, *Mental retardation.* Chicago, Ill.: University of Chicago Press, 1964, pp. 57-99.

MADSEN, K. B. *Theories of motivation.* Kent, Ohio: Kent State University Press, 1968.

MASLOW, A. H. *The psychology of science.* New York: Harper & Row, 1966.

NAGEL, E. *The structure of science: Problems in the logic of scientific explanation.* New York: Harcourt, Brace, Jovanovich, 1961.

PESTALOZZI, J. H. *The education of man.* New York: Greenwood Press, 1969.

RAPOPORT, A. Modern systems theory: An outlook for coping with change. Paper delivered at the John Umstead Lectures, North Carolina Department of Mental Health, February, 1970.

RHODES, W. C. *Behavioral threat and community response.* New York: Behavioral Publications, 1972.

SEELEY, J. R. Social values, the mental health movement and mental health. *Annals of the American Academy of Political and Social Science*, Vol. 286, March 1953, 15-24.

TRIPPE, M. J. Conceptual problems in research on educational provisions for disturbed children. *Exceptional Children*, 1963, *29*, 400-406.

CHAPTER SIX

Human Experience and Human Science

Introduction

In a previous chapter on philosophy of deviance, the development of logical positivism and its impact upon the mental health movement was considered. Further, the nature of theory—including the various aspects of deductive, predictive, and heuristic theory—was discussed. In this chapter the focus is on a critique of these traditional scientific frameworks and the limitations these frameworks have placed on the study of man and the study of deviance. Finally, existentialism is examined as an emerging perspective to understanding man and deviance.

A Critique of Traditional Science

One of the most eloquent attacks on the classical scientific position has been leveled by Maslow (1966). His critique is pertinent as a bridge between the old and the new sciences of behavior and will be used as the basis for the following discussion.

Maslow criticized from within the value system of science, wishing to expand its relevance to human problems, not to destroy or replace it.

In principle, at least, science should be capable of generating normative psychologies of psychotherapy, of personal development, of eupsychian or utopian social psychology, of religion, of work, play, and leisure, of esthetics, of economics, and politics, and who knows what else? (p. xiv)

The change in the nature of science was overdue in Maslow's view and, except for accidents of history, should have come out of the psychoanalytic movement. The determinism, reductionism, and causality of nineteenth-century science, in which Freud was raised, were intellectual barnacles he never shed.

Even though he spent his whole life and unwittingly cutting the ground out from under this version of science and, in fact, destroying it, along with all pure rationalisms, Freud remained loyal to its *Weltanschauung* so far as I can tell. Unfortunately, none of the other great contributors to the development of modern psychodynamics—Adler, Jung, Reich, Rank, Horney, Fromm—were scientists and so did not address themselves directly to this problem. (p. xiv)

Wirth, in the foreword of Maslow's important writing on the psychology of science, points out that Maslow "challenges the dominant *Weltanschauung* that governs the definition of problems and methodologies in the sciences concerned with human personality and behavior" (p. ix). Maslow argues that our limited knowledge of human personality is the result of the methodology of psychological research that has been modeled after the "mechanomorphic tradition" of the physical sciences. Wirth, summarizing Maslow's position, states that psychological researchers, employing mechanistic techniques that work so effectively in studying animal behavior and some aspects of human behavior, come to regard these methods as the only means for obtaining scientific knowledge about personality. "Such adherents are guilty of attempting to define the whole phenomenon of the human being in terms of the parts they can manipulate well" (p. ix).

He [Maslow] notes that an ethnocentric attachment to the scientific *Weltanschauung* of the West can bar us from ideas from other intellectual frameworks that may advance our knowledge about dimensions of human experience. He is bold to offer "Taoistic science" as one such possibility. (p. x)

The availability of limited methodological alternatives for creditable inquiry is dangerous in that it not only limits the knowledge that can be obtained, but it also interacts with the human potential of the scientist to lose perspective on the limits of his practices. "If the only tool you have is a hammer it is tempting to treat everything as if it were a nail" (p. x).

The Study of Man's Nature

Where does the behavior come from? What is there of being that exists outside man's experience of being? Does it matter? Is it all that matters? What constraint does language place on understanding? How can the culture be transcended?

Scientific knowledge is developed primarily to enable man to predict and control, that is, to do something. However, the knowledge that has increased his power in acting on his environment has not substantially contributed to his knowledge about himself, his nature and destiny, beyond the cognitive boundaries of time and space or his experience. He has not gained the power in becoming or in being that he has obtained in doing.

Historically, the concepts and rules of one concern (doing) have tended to govern, judge, and frequently subvert the other concern (being). The early study of human anatomy, for example, was conducted in secret because of religious attitudes about, and concern for, the body. Now the scientific study of the body is accorded a higher value than religious attitudes about it. Obviously those attitudes have changed over time, and there is some reciprocal influence. They are, however, different sets of questions and their reconciliation has been the source of some conflict. An example is the controversy surrounding the appropriate incisions in autopsies. Some procedures reflect more "respect" for the body than others. This controversy existed between European and American pathologists—attitudes toward the body being different in the two countries.

There have been many attempts at syntheses of the values of science and the philosophical and religious values of man.

The issues have been divided according to questions of art and science, of schools of philosophy such as logical positivism and existentialism, of mind, body and spirit, and countless other presumed polarities. This has frequently resulted in co-option of one area by another rather than synthesis. An example is provided in the history of psychiatry. Why were problems in living, in adjustment and adaptation, moved into the province of medicine? What is the source of medical authority in these areas? Again, what is the relationship between what is known about man and his identity or his essence? Mammoth institutions and major social systems and interventions have been developed based on the presumption that the questions are equivalent. Elaborate rules and procedures and well articulated social sanctions have been developed out of the medical science framework. The assumption is that one set of questions can be answered in the same way as the other set of questions. The real world of behavioral values has stood up and it is understood in medical terms: deviance is pathological; abnormality is sick.

Questions of value, of purpose, of love, of man became "scientific" concerns in that they were dealt with in professional and technical settings. The authority and procedures of science became the governing principles. This situation has been observed and questioned most eloquently by Szasz (1961). In the sixties there was a large scale attack on the "medical model."

Limitations in the Study of Deviance

The reality of deviance, from this frame of reference, is understood in terms of the assumptions and the methods available for studying and treating the deviance. That is, deviance is defined with reference to the value system of the framework in which it is understood. This reality and the values assigned to it do not necessarily have to match experienced realities. Neither does it acknowledge the alternative realities it is possible to experience. The goodness-badness and appropriateness-inappropriateness judgments imposed by any one reality on all other realities have been questioned by Laing (1967).

A predominant reality is a socialized, "agreed upon" way of perceiving the world. What is agreed upon, however, is culturally variable. Beauty is real. Keats called it truth and all that we know or need to know. What is beautiful and what is morally true, however, depends on the culture in which the judgment of beauty is made (Laing, 1967). There is considerable cross-cultural research indicating that people learn to view their physical as well as their social and moral worlds differently (Benedict, 1934). This becomes a particularly difficult and relevant issue in a pluralistic culture, such as that in the United States.

When our experience, that is, our own reality, does not match the constructs available for it, we feel alien and must either adapt to our alienation or invent constructs to make community possible. Alienation feels like loneliness out of control, and we seek relief from it.

Laing argues that the "condition of alienation, of being asleep, of being unconscious, of being out of one's mind is the condition of a normal man" (p. 28). If our inventions of constructs and behavior for relief significantly offend the environment in which we live, we are likely to be extruded. The environment seeks its own relief from intolerable deviation. Here extrusion is secondary, a social action taken in response to our alienation. Tiryakian (1962) has pointed out that society "treats alienation from society as wrong doing" (p. 96). If, on the other hand, our articulation of our alienation "fits" the alien experience of enough others we become leaders and revolutionaries. The environment then must adopt the inventions and thereby make its own adaptations. This is the nature of a social movement. The social and moral roots are the same for what society banishes and what it eventually relies on for renewal.

The last decade has been interesting in this regard. There has been more report of deviation and indeed a fascination with it. This is obviously not totally the result of exclusive concern with "scientific" realities of deviance. The drug scene, for example, was a direct confrontation of and challenge to the conventional experience. The commune structure has challenged the conventional social and political systems of judging behavior and experience.

There is currently a dissonance over who man experiences himself to be and the concepts available for understanding that experience. One way to examine this dissonance is in terms of the primitive instinct or the tribal nature of man versus the culturally nurtured and therefore the "understood" nature of man. Part of the man-culture rebellion can be understood as, "I am not who I am understood to be," or "Who I am and who you say I am are different," or "Who I am and who I understand myself to be are not the same."

As we become more sophisticated in our scientific understandings of man and more elaborate in our cultural definitions of rules for man, we have more difficulty rationalizing the most primitive genetic and biological heritage of man. Basic drives and aggression come primarily out of our primitive tribal heritage. Values, rules, and understanding or patterns of thinking come primarily out of our culture. Purpose is an acceptable negotiated adaptation of the two. If we are more responsive to our primitive instinct we are likely to exceed the acceptable cultural boundaries of behavior and be labeled and treated as irresponsible or crazy. We are likely to experience such responses as confusion or abuse. If we are more responsive to the cultural imperatives, our behavior is more likely to be viewed as appropriate but may also be viewed as cold and impersonal. We are likely to experience it as meaningless or "playing the game." Man must be able to both feel good and survive. He must experience personal meaning in the pain of surviving. He must find a space for his passion.

Who is man that science has been unmindful of him? What is science that it has given man power but comforted only his body? While it is true that science cannot be all things to all people, the point here is that the values and rules of science have come to pervade all things.

Obviously both religion and psychology have to account for both purpose and problems. What we have failed to do is effectively integrate the concerns of both the religious heritage and the heritage of psychology in our analysis of basic questions. In our attempts at integration, as has been suggested, each area has largely co-opted the interests of the other so that religion is left without a God or psychology is left without a science. While the very important area of psychology of religion has worked on this area, it has been kept too much in the church and in the divinity school.

Psychology did not start this way. Its earliest intellectual kinship was more with philosophy and theology. The scientific revolution, however, with the decline of the political role of the church, captured much of the momentum of the development of psychology. How one obtained information became more important than the information itself. This necessarily shifted the attention of the empirically oriented psychologist to topics that could be studied within the constraints of available methodology.

There have been other tracks in the development of psychology that have maintained a more philosophical orientation and methodology. These tracks have resisted the epistemology of traditional science. Existential psychology is one example. These tracks have been limited in their dispersion and impact because of the empirically oriented value system of society.

As a result of our shift to the rules and realities of empirical science, we have looked for moral leadership in places that have no moral heritage. We have moral victories on battlefields that have been amoral. We have lost the sense of the good, the unnegotiable and inalienable right. We have substituted arguable evidence. The former was in ethics and religion; the latter is in science and law.

The truth that was the province of religion and mediated in prophecy, song, and poetry has been replaced by a thrust that is the province of science and is mediated by equations, objectives, precision, and correct method. A concern with the supernatural has been replaced by an analysis of the natural. What was once the province of revelation is now the province of research. The moral defense of behavior has been largely replaced by the psychological defense of behavior. Metaphysics has been overcome by theory.

The value is predominantly on the empirical world, *the* reality. Man's speculations, dreams, and fantasies are considered data to be understood and processed with reference to a particular theoretical conception. What we know about subsumes and judges what we dream about.

The work on the nature of man and his goals has been separated from work on understanding the problems of man. The work on problems is public, professionalized, and scientific. It proceeds with little attention to the existential nature of man, which is studied more with reference to personal experience and religious rules such as those governing meditation or prayer. These primary areas are divided by a basic conflict in value systems.

In a day when statistical prediction has replaced prophecy, when Skinner has replaced Socrates in education, how do we deal with alienation and death, with personal purpose and life? While we can deal with comparative theory, how do we deal with comparative reality? Perceptual theory deals with differential processing, not with differential reality.

One of the major themes of history has been the problem of evil. Evil has been satanized, personalized, psychologized, and socialized. We have made it a part of our nature and we have made it unnatural. We have found ways to overcome it and have simultaneously accepted it as always with us. Having found other concepts and languages for evil, have we come closer to its solution? Do we no longer need a demonology if we have an adequate psychology?

Many recent innovations in thinking and behaving have forced a reconsideration of the adequacy of our beliefs about man.

The absurd has gained legitimacy. The paradox has obtained credibility in its own right. The revolution against convention, including the conventions of science as well as of aesthetics and ethics, has considerable momentum. Innovations in dress as well as in thinking, in behavior, and perhaps in feeling have become commonplace. Concern with personal being, with community, and with being "straight" has increased substantially in the last decade. Man gets concerned about what he feels is important and does not have. The concern with mysticism, drugs, and alternative living arrangements can be viewed as man's serious, and perhaps desperate, attempt to rediscover himself and his place in the world. Alternative structures, reactivated sensitivities, and new realities are goals of people who still will to be in spite of a devastation of their experience.

Perhaps as a result of discontinuities and paradoxes such as those suggested here, man more than ever needs a relevant myth to organize and make sense out of his own experience. Perhaps more than ever he needs a ritual to help him with forgiveness and reconciliation. Perhaps more than ever he needs commitments that engage his deepest passions and purposes that challenge his most ultimate concerns. Perhaps more than ever man needs to reinstitute the place of the martyr as a legitimate alternative to the twentieth-century group process corollary, the scapegoat. Perhaps more than ever before man needs a place where it is expected and acceptable that reason does not reign. Perhaps more than ever before man needs to expect and honor instinctive "learning" that transcends his own language and prior experience. Perhaps man needs to institutionalize personal renewal, to know and fill both the space that is his own uniquely and that is all man's to share.

These are not the functions of science. As suggested earlier there is no scientific model that fits man. Yet science provides the intellectual substructure that has permeated most thinking about life.

Theories of emotional disturbance, discussed in this volume, are basic to the evolving science of human difference. They must be judged on the scientific grounds in terms of their own merit. But they must also be judged for the nature of the phenomenon of disturbance they describe as a property or characteristic of man. That is, what is man if a characteristic or condition of man can be that he is "disturbed"? Finally, they must be judged for their social consequences in terms of how man gets treated as a result of the particular theory or point of view. The pervasion of the thinking and values and practices of the theory into the culture must be a part of its assessment.

The theories are only reviewed in this volume. The human questions are not dealt with systematically. Rather, the reader should be sensitized to questions the authors have learned to ask in studying theories of disturbance. In some places the authors' responses to some of those questions are a part of the manuscript. We have tried to indicate clearly those instances since one of the major purposes of this writing is to persuade readers of the personal importance of the questions and their own response, not to convert readers to a particular position.

Existentialism: Another Perspective

Mounier pointed out that existential thought "refuses to hand the monopoly of revealing reality over to the system of classification demanded by rationalism" (Tiryakian, p. 73). Existentialism represents an orientation to reality, to truth, and to knowing that is fundamentlaly different from the logical positivistic orientation described earlier.

Tiryakian summarized existentialism as "an attempt to reaffirm the importance of the individual by a rigorous and in many respects radically new analysis of the nature of man" (p. 77). The traditional philosophy of science, already discussed, did not deal with the problem of existence or the problem of man. It focused more on the nature and structure of knowledge. Existentialism is more concerned with man as subject than man as object, more oriented to subjective knowledge than a logical structuring of data. Reality is personal and private, it cannot be judged by criteria of publicness or universality. It is enough that it is now—it does not have to apply at other times or places or for other people.

Existence, in Kierkegaard's view, is affirmed by passionate choice made in the context of despair, anxiety, and faith (Tiryakian, p. 89). It is outside the structures of reason or abstractions. Truth is what it is experienced to be. The interpretation or response *is* the reality. The only real duality is that between the authentic and the nonauthentic.

We judge ourselves and our neighbors in the light of a few particular tracts and events, rather than in terms of the integral whole. In judging ourselves we are mainly influenced by the opinion of others: it is their opinion which first comes to mind, for our own private opinion seldom floats on the surface. (pp. 95-96)

Allport (1960), in a symposium on existential psychology, points out that, while European existentialism has been preoccupied with dread, anguish, despair and nausea, with the courage to be being the only essential resolution or adaptation, the American "quasi-existential order" (client-centered, growth, self-actualization, and ego therapies) is more optimistic. He also notes the inclination in American psychology to "recast existential dogma into testable propositions" (p. 95).

Tiryakian, reviewing Jasper's work, asserts that there is no Science; only a variety of scientific disciplines, each perceiving the world or reality in different ways. Further, the various sciences rest upon assumptions which by definition are not subject to proof. "The realm of science is the realm of objectivity, but this does not exhaust all of being" (p. 115).

Continuing to review Jasper's position, Tiryakian goes on to say:

The physical sciences are not always aware of their intrinsic limitations, but the social sciences (in particular, psychology and sociology) are always confronted with their limitations in studying man. Man's freedom in choosing his actions is a foremost limit to the scientific pursuit of absolute knowledge about human behavior. Just as the sciences *in toto* can only explore and explain "objects" in the world and never the world itself, so the social sciences can only study aspects of man, but never integral man himself. Man as a whole has a nonobjective side which is impervious to scientific research. (pp. 115-116)

Laing (1967) states, "physics and the other sciences of things must accord the science of persons the right to be unbiased in a way that is true to its own field of study" (p. 240). To be objective in the sense of depersonalizing is as much a mistake and yields as much false knowledge as personalizing things. "In contrast to the reputable 'objective' or 'scientific,' we have the disreputable 'subjective,' 'intuitive,' or, worst of all, 'mystical'."

He ... [Freud] ... descended to the "underworld" and met there stark terrors. He carried with him his theory as a Medusa's head which turned these terrors to stone. We who follow Freud have the benefit of the knowledge he brought back with him and conveyed to us. ... He survived. We must see if we now can survive without using a theory that is in some measure an instrument of defense. (p. 25)

Gendlin (1962), analyzing the extreme positions of logical positivism and existentialism in the debate regarding the science of psychology, notes that they both agree that humanly important areas cannot be investigated scientifically. The logical positivists are concerned that the integrity of science will be compromised in such an attempt. The existentialists are concerned that the integrity of human experience will be sacrificed. The largest group, he contends, is in the middle, calling for a new methodology in all sciences of human behavior.

Gendlin argues that the concept of experiencing is useful as a basis for beginning such a development. Experiencing is involved in all thought and behavior and is affected by behavior, thought and situations. He symbolized and defined experiencing with reference to empirical criteria without altering its direct access to the person, thus answering the concerns of both groups. Gendlin argues that "prescientific" work must be done, namely, the definition of new variables. "It is not at all permissible to omit this portion of the labor from the total endeavor of science" (p. 20). To require one to be scientific before one has devised variables is "deadly." He points out that theory, which can refer to experiencing, must *lead to* testable hypotheses. Observational categories must be fashioned with a language and carefully defined concepts before orthodox scientific methodology can be used. Gendlin therefore suggests a method for the existentialists and an extension of logical and empirical definitions of variables for the positivists.

Most would argue that the basic rational-empirical positions of traditional science and the phenomenological orientation to the subjective domain of experience have not been reconciled. Even the large group in the middle seeking a new methodology for the human sciences has mixed views regarding the value system that will be most pervasive.

The subsequent portions of this chapter will deal with a very limited discussion of selected topics that are important concerns in the embryonic human science emerging within the philosophical framework of existentialism.

Experience and Human Science

The existential position affirms the importance of man's experience as the nature of what is real for him. Experience is not "noise" to be reduced or systematically controlled by design in order to make possible the exposure of the more basic, less personal, objective "facts." Philosophically it is not only acceptable truth, it is all the personal knowledge of life that man ever has. It is his experience of his life that is the basis of his knowing that he lives. The uncertainty of experience is the agony of his existence. He is most alive when he is most uncertain, according to one existential proposition. In his alien state man is free to be, to decide, to act on his own private convictions—a leap of faith, since he has no external validation of the rightness of his decision.

In his experience man has all of life he will ever know. He makes passionate choices that rule over his responses to and interpretations of the world. He is paradoxically always free, yet always exiled to his own experience.

It is here that some have looked for the material out of which to fashion a psychology of man. It is here the abnormal deviance hypothesis has been in conflict with the normal alienation hypothesis. In the analysis of experience, the dread and despair of existential anxiety must be understood apart from psychopathology, such as neurotic anxiety. It is in the personal theater of experience that the mask of consensus is removed from social deviance and disturbance. Here delight may replace the registration of social distaste and disapproval. Acts of celebration may replace acts of oppression.

In his experience man bears both the burden of social meanings and conventional patterns and the potential for fresh, open, direct encounter with himself and his unique meanings. While nailed to both genetic and social crosses of reason and propriety, man always has the potential for being the gull in flight. Rarely does he transcend the anguish of his dying. Yet, this resurrection of spirit is always his hope and a spontaneous possibility.

Laing, in *The Politics of Experience*, views all men as " . . . murderers and prostitutes—no matter to what culture, society, class, nation we belong, no matter how normal, moral, or mature we take ourselves to be" (1967, p. xiv). We have become estranged, Laing argues, from our authentic possibilities, alienated to the roots. "We are bemused and crazed creatures, strangers to our true selves, to one another, and to the spiritual and material world. . . ." (p. xv).

Laing contends that what must be claimed or discovered is not so much theory as authentic experience. Social phenomenology is the science of experience, the study of the relation between experience and experience. In fact, experience is the only evidence. Behavior, in a science of persons, is a function of experience, and both experience and behavior are always in relation to something other than self. Natural science does not deal with the phenomenon of the interaction of behavior and experience. It has no logic to express it and no method to analyze it. Theory is the "articulated vision of experience."

Laing describes many domains and modes of experience that are alien. "Many who are aware of fantasy believe that fantasy is the farthest that experience goes under 'normal' circumstances. Beyond that are simply 'pathological' zones of hallucinations, phantasmagoric mirages, delusions" (p. 11).

He calls this human condition an almost "unbelievable devastation of our experience. Then there is empty chatter about maturity, love, joy and peace" (p. 11). This further divorces experience from behavior. What is "normal" then becomes a condition that is anti-experience. The condition of alienation, of being asleep, of being unconscious, of being out of one's mind, is the condition of normal man (p. 12). Society educates children to " . . . lose themselves and become absurd and thus be normal" (p. 12). Freud, Laing contends, demonstrated that " . . . the *ordinary* person is a shriveled, desiccated fragment of what a person can be" (p. 10).

Regarding theory, Laing maintains that it can be viewed relative to the emphasis it places on experience or behavior, or the relationship between experience and behavior. He points out that experience oriented theory that neglects behavior is misleading, while theory focusing on behavior to the neglect of experience is unbalanced. "Any *theory* not founded on the nature of being human is a lie and a betrayal of man. An inhuman theory will inevitably lead to inhuman consequences . . . " (p. 32).

When we do rediscover ourselves, Laing says, we are confronted with a shambles,

Bodies half dead; genitals dissociated from heart; heart severed from head; head dissociated from genitals. Without inner unity, with just enough sense of continuity to clutch at identity—the current idolatry. Torn—body, mind and spirit—by inner contradictions, pulled in different directions. Man cut off from his own mind, cut off from equally his own body—a half crazed creature in a mad world. (p. 33).

We are all implicated. Such has become the nature of current human existence. Therein lies the Achilles heel of modern science and the potential for developing a truly human science. "Existence is a flame which constantly melts and recasts our theories" (p. 34). Much of current social science deepens the mystification of experience. Violence, Laing states, "cannot be seen through the sights of positivism" (p. 37).

We must then repudiate a positivism that achieves its "reliability" by successfully masking what is and what is not, by serializing the world of the observer, by turning the truly given into *capta* which are *taken as given* by denuding the world of being and relegating the ghost of being to a shadow land of subjective values. (pp. 38-39)

Watts (1961) too has substantially expanded the image of man as the focus of study. Differences between individuals and their social contexts lead to many different attempts to obtain relief from the conflicts generated by those differences. The escapes range from neurotic and even psychotic states to "socially permissible orgies of mass entertainment, religious fanaticism, chronic sexual titillation, alcoholism, war—the whole sad list of tedious and barbarous escapes" (pp. 21-22).

Watts goes on to state that if we are serious about understanding the integration and disintegration of personality we must understand depersonalization, "those experiences in which individual self awareness is abrogated and the individual melts into an awareness which is no longer anchored upon selfhood" (p. 31). This transcendence of self is described in Hindu literature as unification of the individual with the cosmic being, *atman*, which transcends selfhood and materiality.

Some men desire such experiences; others dread them. Our problem here is not their desirability, but the light which they throw on the relativity of our present-day psychology of personality.... Some other mode of personality configuration, in which self-awareness is less emphasized or even lacking, may prove to be the general (or the fundamental). (p. 31)

Watts argued that the western idea of the ego trapped man between loneliness and death. He viewed Vedanta, Taoism, and the western sciences of sociology and ecology as sources of knowledge and philosophy from which man could develop an identity that transcends the concept of the ego. "Our mistake has been to suppose that the individual is honored and his uniqueness enhanced by emphasizing his separation from the surrounding world, or his eternal difference in essence from his Creator. As well honor the hand by lopping it from the arm" (p. 32).

Consistent with the spirit of these developments, Lilly (1972) has talked about the development of a "new natural science," that focuses on the inner subjective space. Bakan (1972) has described psychology as ready to "kick the science habit."

Man As Mystery: A Part and Apart

Man senses his incalculable attachment. He belongs to and is a part of all he can see, hear, taste, smell, and feel. He can see himself as a part of nature or at the center of it. He has considerable freedom to alter the nature of his relationships, his attachments.

Since his wonder of why he was, and who, he has dealt with himself in terms of comparison and contrast, his uniqueness and his universal nature. Man has been most clever in his construction of concepts, a language, and a process of thinking. On what is there, he has laid his understanding and knowledge. For the attachment between things, he has created the concept of relationship and a rather elaborate language to describe it. He has studied relationships in terms of the concepts he generated. He has gone further and fashioned a science out of the concepts, language, and data he has collected. There is the dialectic, the experience of relatedness or attachment, and the science or quasi science that has developed around theories of relationship.

The artifacts of science do not inspire the spirit of man to effect essential connections with other men. The social, behavioral, and physical sciences do, however, give man processes for obtaining, ordering, and sharing data about the basic connectedness of things. The pursuit of the suspicion that things are connected and do indeed "hang together" and the later development of a formal science has given man power to predict and, therefore, to control events, including the behavior of other men. Psychology includes the scientific study of relationships.

Science has provided a framework and rules for thinking about structures, relationships, and systems. It has provided him with a basis for heuristic understanding of occurrences and a predictive basis for understanding what has and what probably will occur again. That is, science has provided conceptual systems for understanding the controlling both within a time-space and across time. What it has not done and, indeed, could not be expected to do, is provide him with similar powers relative to his human experience. If man can predict and control the processes of his intuitive life, then he has reached the outer limits of his creativity.

Man has sensed the relatedness of many things: the wind, trees, seeds, rain, soil, seasons. These awoke poetry, art, and music in some, while arousing the sounds of science in others. The ecologists have generated a body of knowledge about the reciprocity of forces in a specified field. General systems theory has identified methods for establishing a boundary and identifying interactive components which, if sufficiently specified, can provide advantage in power to understand the products or outputs in terms of the available energy and the relationships between the components.

While to some extent the boundary is essentially arbitrary, the language and concepts of systems would lead us to conclude that "systemness" is inherent in the nature of things. We fix limited boundaries for utility; that is, we bound a system in terms of what we have interest in understanding for a purpose. We do not have the concepts or capability to manage the enormity of certain larger systems.

Time has been used as a boundary, a dependable structure to help order and understand events. It is not a boundary for the experience of men. Time is the basic structure and organization of man's ontogenetic history. It moves in the direction of increasing complexity in relating. Man's language and gestures are increasingly complex as they become embedded in the time-place fixtures of the culture. What is subtle in one place and time may be quite overt at another. Children are maturing when they become more astute in making these distinctions.

Art forms—music, dance, painting, literature, poetry, etc.—are relied upon more and more for man's cultural transcendence, that is, his escape from his cultural time-space imprisonment. Transcendence is essential for man to renew his attachment to himself, his sense of being alive, and to affirm that he is more than any cultural boundaries would suggest. Emptiness is the experience of no escape from the cultural quarantine of man's spirit. If man's essence is more than he knows himself to be and more than others know him to be (and it is or there would be no philosophy, no religion, no art), then he must have been one with it, else creation would indeed be a surrealistic joke.

As he joins culture man integrates what he has made with himself, what God has made. It is this integration that makes power, love, man, and God mysterious. Time, aging, is the ally of culture, not of man. The child that will "lead them" is a young child.

The most deceitful seduction is that which convinces a child that joy is the promised land of the culturally "mature," a condition of the future. The most unforgiveable sin may be the cultural conspiracy against the child which makes that seduction work. It takes time to con a child out of his spirit, to "channel his energies" and "develop his potential." Is it possible that human development is a process of deteriorating essence?

Time is also phylogenetic. All of time tells the same story. Man is a socialized angel. His mystery is his angelness, not his socialization. We work on his socialization—that is what education, mental health, welfare, corrections, etc., are about. We relegate work on knowing his essence, the angel, to places of mystery—that's what prayer and meditation are about.

Just as man is not bounded by time, so space does not contain his full meaning. The body is but a point of reference—or what are dreams, ideas, visions and memories about? We reside in fixed structure yet we are those structures or why do we discover physical space, objects, angles and relationships that have been there all along? We do not look at what we see or listen to what we hear, because we are not simply receivers and processers of information; the sound and sight sources are part of us or we would never have seen or heard.

My skin is but the boundary I use in relating myself to the culture man has created. Without the artificial time and space points for reference, culture would not work. Man's handiwork, culture, would be impossible.

Man cannot get his words around his experience. The poets have found the most words to portray the essential intimacy and privacy of experience. Love, beauty, God, pain, hate—these are the potential of all men to experience but of few to mediate with words. The painter, the sculptor, and occasionally the architect have coined images to "speak the thousand words." The dance has a literature of movement for similar meanings.

Yet art does not propose a boundary for man's experience. It proposes rather a celebration of the union it engenders. Art affirms the ability of man to get his "mind around the medium" and his inability to get the medium around his mind.

Neither paint, poetry, design, dance nor the sum of all man's symbols can do more than signal where any one man may be. The most spiritual of symbols cannot be greater than the spirit that gave it structure. Man who has connected his symbols and his myths shifts from mastered to master and back again.

A painting is limited in time and place. It begins and ends with the paint and canvas. Yet if that were all, there would be no art to painting. Time and place are blurred by the intimate experience of the painter and his success in making it public.

Unlike painting, music involves both the architect of the signals, the composer, and the builder, the musician who brings that structure into the field of the experience of others.

It is significant to observe that these basic art forms are experienced by two different sensory modes, viz. auditory and visual. While it is true that a beautiful painting will frequently create associations that engage other sense systems not activated directly by the painting, the primary stimulus, the painting, is not a multiple medium. Man's experience of the sense data goes above, below, and beyond the data provided.

The question of man qua man has had more attention than the question of social man or the collect. We are now riding on the wake of two fundamental issues: man must now deal with his proximity to other men, if you prefer, social man and community; and, our understanding must extend beyond our recent and relatively short-lived logical positivistic epistemology.

Man, a part of the larger order, has stationed himself at the center of knowing since it is his concepts and language out of which that knowledge is fashioned. Yet since the Psalmists and before, man has known that he was beyond his knowledge about himself. His sense of wonder and awe was in *who* he was and the modest experience of himself as a part of creation that included the stars (Psalm 8).

The question of what is man, of the genus what is matter, came rather recently in history. Man is a definable system of organic parts, a particular molecular structure, susceptible to microbial hazards, genetic accidents, etc. The sin of science may be its seduction of man into equating the two questions.

Review

Theories of emotional disturbance have been generated which reflect quite dissimilar conceptions of man and of science. Some of the views are primarily committed to the basic structures, processes, and values of positivism and, therefore, maintain more alliance with the rules of formal science. Other views are more interested in the phenomenon of disturbance and in understanding, systematically if possible, the experience of being disturbed and of disturbing. Different assumptions about the nature of man, the nature of deviance, the structure of knowledge, and the methods of knowing are involved. In this and a previous chapter an attempt has been made to explore some of these issues in consideration of the presentation of theories of disturbance set forth in this volume.

In the other chapters these issues are not neatly sorted by theory. The formal theoretical work on disturbance has not been systematic in dealing with these issues. Consequently, to present them so here would be misleading. The assumptions about man, deviance, and knowledge are mixed, within as well as between theories.

The division into sections on logical positivism and existentialism, while not entirely arbitrary, should not be considered too absolute. The distinction made in the divisions of the book are more of relative emphasis than of absolute position. Frankly, much of the work reviewed here is more in the mixed or middle area. In some of the chapters the division is made within the chapter itself.

References

ALLPORT, G. W. Comment on earlier chapters. In Rollo May, *Existential psychology*. New York: Random House, 1960.

BAKAN, DAVID. Psychology can now kick the science habit. *Psychology Today*, 1972, 5(10), 26-28, 86-88.

BENEDICT, R. *Patterns of culture*. Boston: Houghton Mifflin, 1934.

GENDLIN, E. T. Experience and the creation of meaning. New York: Free Press, 1962.

LAING, R. D. *The divided self*. New York: Pantheon Books, 1969.

LAING, R. D. *The politics of experience*. New York: Pantheon Books, 1967. Copyright © R. D. Laing, 1967. Reprinted by permission of Penguin Books Ltd.

LILLY, JOHN C. *The center of the cyclone*. New York: Julian Press, 1972.

MASLOW, A. H. *Motivation and personality*. New York: Harper & Row, 1954.

MASLOW, A. H. *The psychology of science*. New York: Harper & Row, 1966.

SzASZ, T. S. *The myth of mental illness.* New York: Dell, 1961.
TIRYAKIAN, E. A. *Sociologism and existentialism.* Englewood Cliffs, N.J.: Prentice-Hall, 1962.
WATTS, A. W. *Psychotherapy, east and west.* New York: Pantheon Books, 1961.

PART FOUR

Phenomenological Views and Approaches

Phenomenological views are based on direct investigation and description of the phenomena of deviance and disturbance consciously experienced as free as possible from unexamined preconceptions and presuppositions. Edmund Husserl developed the outlines of twentieth-century phenomenology. His was a descriptive psychology. He systematically examined and repudiated empirical psychology as the ultimate basis of logic. He made a systematic attempt to purify the phenomena of all merely factual ingredients as studied by the empirical sciences. He called for the suspension of belief in the reality of what seems to be the immediately given. He then tried to isolate the field of pure phenomena given with absolute certainty. The field includes each experiencer's own ego, his acts of viewing, and the phenomena itself in all its modes of givenness.

Beginning in 1916, Heidegger used the phenomenological approach as the most promising way of uncovering the categories of human existence. He saw the meaning of "being" as the supreme question, which could be approached by analysis of the beings that we ourselves are. He introduced a phenomenological approach to interpreting the ontological meaning of such human conditions as being in the world, anxiety, and care.

Jean Paul Sartre used the phenomenological method for descriptive explorations of the imagination and the emotions.

Phenomenology has probably had its strongest influence on Gestalt psychology and on the study of human psychopathology where Karl Jaspers stressed the subjective exploration of the patients' subjective experience.

Among the views presented under the category of phenomenology, ecological views seem to incorporate the more logical positivistic views of behavioral theories and psychoneurological theories. However, ecological views of human conditions of deviance and disturbance fall much more strongly into the category of pheonomenology.

CHAPTER SEVEN

Labeling Theory: Sociological Views and Approaches

The term "deviance," defined as the breaking of social rules, is new in sociology. Many older sociological theories of deviation used other terms—crime, social disorganization, or social problems. All the theories, however, focus on social rule breaking.

During the 1960s, a theory of deviance was developed which has come to be identified as symbolic interactionist, social reaction, or labeling theory. The term symbolic interaction reflects the contributions of George Herbert Mead (1934). Mead theorized that the human self is a creation of communication with others. The process involves "taking the role of the other" in social communication. When two persons in communication are mutually taking the role of the other, they are able to assign isomorphic (mirror-image) meanings to the messages sent between them. A

This chapter was written by Professor Don Des Jarlais, School of Education, New York University, and James Paul.

171

sender must be able to take the role of the other (the receiver) to know what meanings the receiver is giving to the symbols used by the sender. The social self arises through the process of repeatedly taking the role of the other and having others take one's own role.

Labeling refers to the public designation of a person as deviant. This process sets powerful social expectations in motion. A known deviant is expected to break rules. Labeling theorists emphasize the effects of social expectations about known deviants and their opposites, known conformists.

Labeling theorists postulate that one does not become a deviant by breaking rules. One must be labeled a deviant before the social expectations that define the deviant role are activated. Examples of the labeling process are criminal conviction, commitment to a mental institution, and placement in a self-contained special education class. Note that it is possible to be labeled without having broken a rule. Labeling theorists are particularly interested in the formation of deviant identities and find that deviant identities are formed in the same manner as nondeviant identities. In both cases, individuals conform to the expectations of others. The deviant role is conferred upon a rule breaker by the audience that directly or indirectly witnesses the rule breaking. The role usually has a specific name—prostitute, thief, drug addict, problem child. Since the rule is functional for the social system as a whole, there are social pressures on the individual to play it fully. There are covert rewards for skillful performance, e.g., money, attention, control over group actions, forbidden pleasures; and obstacles are erected to prevent individuals from abandoning the role.

The labeling process does not always follow rule breaking. Probably in most cases a deviant label is not conferred upon the rule breaker. Everyone breaks social rules, many do so consistently. Yet few are chosen to be labeled as deviants.

Some individuals are not labeled merely because their rule breaking is not discovered. In many cases, however, known instances of rule breaking escape the labeling process (Becker, 1963, Scheff, 1966). There are a number of factors that influence whether or not deviance will be attributed to the rule breaker. These factors include the extent to which the system needs to have a deviant role filled, the frequency and visibility of the rule breaking, the tolerance level for rule breaking, the social distance between the rule breaker and agents of social control, the relative power of the rule breaker in the system, the amount of conflict between the rule breakers and agents of social control, and whether or not anyone has a special interest in enforcing penalties against the rule breaker.

Labeling theory stresses the role of agents of social control. Agents of social control are those with the responsibility for enforcing social rules. They include the police, the court system, psychiatrists, teachers, and parents. It is the agents of control who invoke the labeling process. They are responsible for selecting, from among a number of rule breakers, those who will play deviant roles. This process is often carried out under the rubric of treatment or rehabilitation.

Cultural transmission theory emphasizes the psychological similarities between deviants and conformists. Both have the same set of motives and psychological characteristics. Deviants are socialized into a nonconforming value system. Labeling theory goes one step further. It emphasizes the behavioral similarities between deviants and conformists. Both groups break social rules often, and both groups conform to most social rules, e.g., the thief may be a good parent. The differences between deviants and conformists are only apparent in their behaviors and are actually a result of the social reactions to their behaviors.

Because labeling theory is dominant theory of social deviance, and because it is gaining acceptance in fields outside of academic sociology, it is worth discussing the criticisms and revisions that have appeared since the initial development of the theory. Several sociologists (e.g., Matza, 1969, Gove, 1970) have criticized the lack of emphasis in labeling theory on the contributions of the rule breaker in the process of becoming deviant. Labeling theory emphasizes the contributions of the agents of social control, but tends to ignore any contributions by the rule breaker. Matza (1969) focuses on the self-determination of the person becoming deviant and argues that his active cooperation is necessary to the process.

The second major criticism of labeling theory concerns the relationship between the labeling process and the adoption of a deviant role by the person labeled. Critics of labeling theory (see the volume edited by Gove, 1975b) maintain that the labeling process often prevents deviant acts by either leading to providing effective therapy for the labeled person or through a deterrence effect.

Proponents of the theory have responded (Becker, 1963, Kitsuse, 1975; Schur, 1975) by maintaining that labeling theory is *not* a theory of the etiology of deviant acts, but rather it is a perspective that forces social scientists to examine the actions of *all* the actors involved in the processes through which certain acts and persons come to be perceived as in violation of social norms. To understand deviance in the context of labeling theory, it is as important to study the actions of rule creators and rule enforcers as it is to study the actions of the rule breakers.

Since theories of deviance tend to have a life span of ten to fifteen years, one may expect the criticisms of labeling theory to continue, and a new theory to arise in the early 1980s.

In a curious way, labeling theory reintroduced the idea of social pathology into the study of deviance. Previous theories had mostly emphasized the social harm done by agents of social control. Pathology was identified in the theory, but it was located in the rule enforcers rather than in the rule breakers.

Labeling theory is clearly a phenomenological theory. Labeling theorists explicitly realized (e.g., Becker, 1963) that the nature of a theory is significantly influenced by the perspective and values that the theorists employ. Labeling theorists deliberately chose the perspective of the deviant himself to investigate the phenomenon of deviance. This perspective has produced insights, particularly into the effects of social control, that were not available to the "neutral observer" perspective.

Scheff (1966) has systematically applied labeling theory to mental illness as a form of social deviance. The theory is developed entirely in sociological terms. Mental illness is explained in terms of social rules and the reaction to the breaking of social rules. There is *no* reference to individual differences, either psychological or physiological. To be mentally ill is to play a certain role in society. The major points of Scheff's theory are summarized below.

(1) A stereotype of mental illness exists in American culture. This stereotype defines the social role of being mentally ill. It is easily learned by most individuals.

(2) Residual rule breaking, the breaking of implicit (implied, not explicitly stated) social rules, is widespread in society.

(3) Some acts of residual rule breaking come to the attention of the authorities. The authorities presume mental illness and proceed to label the rule breaker.

(4) The rule breaker then adopts the role of being mentally ill. The stress involved in the labeling process facilitates the adoption of the role. Once in the role, the person is punished for not correctly playing the role and rewarded for correctly playing the role.

Scheff concludes that the labeling process is the most important determinant of the behaviors associated with the term mental illness.

Gove (1970, 1975a) argues that the individual contributes to the process of mental illness. The psychiatric symptom is the most important part of the individual's contribution.

There is also considerable evidence that when residual rule breaking comes to the attention of the psychiatric authorities, it is a result of conflict rather than accident. The conflict may be with the police (Hollingshead & Redlich, 1958) or within the work setting (Lemert, 1962) or within the family (Yarrow, et al., 1955, Sampson, et al., 1962). Admission into a mental hospital may be seen as extrusion from a social system or escape from conflict within a social system.

Given the emphasis on the actions of social control, the concept of social power runs throughout labeling theory.* The thoery emphasizes the relative power of agents of control over deviants, and the psychological effects of this state upon the deviants. The interventions using labeling theory have thus been as much political as they have been therapeutic. The civil rights movement, in its efforts to remove discrimination against minorities in the labeling processes, is an example of an intervention based on labeling theory. Mercer (1973) has noted how labeling works against blacks and Spanish-speaking persons in the application of the label "mentally retarded."

Deviance in Children

Sociologists have not studied deviance in children to the same extent that they have studied deviance in adults. There is a voluminous literature on juvenile delinquency, but sociologists and social psychologists have tended to treat adolescence as a period distinct from both childhood and adulthood (Gold & Douvan, 1969).

Given that the study of deviance is concerned with rule breaking and social control, there are important conceptual differences in the study of deviance in children and the study of deviance in adults and adolescents.

*Lofland (1969) has explicitly restated deviance theory in social power concepts.

Adults and adolescents are expected to both know the rules of their society and have developed the appropriate motives to follow the rules. Neither knowledge nor appropriate motives are attributed to children. Given this difference, the study of deviance in children tends to focus on how children learn rules and develop motives toward conformity to rules.

Erikson (1964) believes that one of the functions of labeling deviance is in teaching social rules. Most social rules, such as the rule against lying, are not absolutes. It is often difficult for the child to distinguish between the acceptable, white lie and the unacceptable punishable lie. Varied forms of testing behavior helps identify the situations in which the rule against lying either is or is not applicable. When the label "liar" is involved, it is obvious that the rule holds. The public designation of a "liar" also helps clarify the rule. Lying becomes what a liar does in situations to which the rule is relevant.

The study of how children develop motivation to conform has often been the study of *impulse control*, that is, how motives to break rules are limited.

Socialization is the term used to describe the various social learnings discussed above. Generally, socialization includes the learning of attitudes, skills (both motor and cognitive), and motives (Gold & Douvan, 1969). The overlapping purposes of socialization are to prepare the child for participation in the society and to permit the society to continue itself over generations.

By definition, then, the "correctly" socialized child will not be a deviant in his society. An "incorrectly" socialized child will be at least a rule breaker. If he is caught and labeled, he will be a full deviant.

Various specific failures in a child's socialization can lead to various specific types of deviance. Clausen (1968), however, presents reasons why socialization failure may lead the child to mental illness as a type of deviance.

1. Mental illness acts as a residual category for nonspecifiable rule breaking.
2. Considerable anxiety is involved in the socialization of children by parents.
3. Interpersonal conflict is usually present.
4. The greatly unequal distribution of power in the family may lead the child to internalize the anxiety and conflict produced.

One of the reasons to expect socialization failures in American children is the wide variety of socialization agents, who often make contradictory demands on children. Lippitt (1968) defines the *socialization community** as those members of the total community wih an interest in influencing the growth and development of the young. There are ten clusters within the socialization community:

1. the formal education system;
2. the churches;
3. the leisure time agencies with recreational, cultural, and character education programs;
4. the social control and protection agencies, such as the police and courts;
5. the therapeutic, special correction, and resocialization services, such as social workers, counselors, programs for the handicapped;
6. employment offices and work supervisors of the young;
7. political leaders who have an investment in involving the young in political activities;
8. parents;
9. like-age and older peers;
10. the mass media.

To some extent, there will be conflicting definitions of appropriate conduct within each cluster, and among the different clusters. Each conflicting group proposes its own set of rules for the young. In such a conflict situation, the distribution of power, that is, who can enforce his version of the rules, is of critical importance.

Conflicting demands from different socialization agents produce a stressful situation for the person being socialized.

SOCIOLOGICAL INTERVENTION

Sociological-social deviance interventions are significantly different from physiological and psychological interventions

---

*The socialization community is a community of interest. It is not necessarily a community in the sense of common values, consistency, coordination, and frequent communication.

along a number of dimensions. It will be useful to clarify some of these differences before examining specific interventions in detail. The first of these differences is simply one of scale. Sociological-social deviance interventions are typically larger and more complex than other interventions aimed at the reduction and/or prevention of mental illness. An attempt to reduce the level of disorganization within a community is on a different order of magnitude than trying a new drug or undergoing psychotherapy within a doctor's office.

A second difference is that sociological-social deviance interventions require change in the behavior of the "nonmentally ill" as part of any intervention. All sociological theories posit a strong relationship between deviant and nondeviant behavior. It is sociologically impossible to have large-scale changes in the behavior of deviants without large-scale changes in the behavior of non-deviants. A sociological intervention would therefore be aimed at changing the behavior of nonemotionally disturbed as much as it would be aimed at changing the behavior of the emotionally disturbed.*

A third difference is in the application of theory to intervention. Sociological-social deviance interventions are likely to be much less consistent with their theoretical bases than other types of interventions are with their respective theoretical basis. All interventions occur within the context of what is politically possible at a given time and place, and all mental illness interventions have political implications. For sociological-social deviance interventions, however, the politics of an intervention are usually more intense and more likely to cause subtle sabotages of the purpose of the intervention. All of the sociological theories discussed relate social deviance to the distribution of resources and power within the society. Any intervention that involves redistribution of resources and power will be subject to strong political considerations. One of the effects of these political considerations will be severe compromising between what the social deviance theory states should be done and what actually is done. A sociological intervention is typically based on both sociological theory and political ideology.

Sociological interventions are sufficiently different from physiological and psychological interventions to require different

---

*This is one point at which the overlap between sociological and ecological interventions is complete. The distinction between sociological and ecological interventions on one side, and chemotherapy and psychotherapy on the other is quite clear.

concepts in assessing them. Physiological and psychological interventions are typically assessed in terms of the *behavior change on an individual*, or the behavior change in a set of similar individuals. Sociological interventions should be assessed in terms of *social change*—change in the basic social conditions that affect all members of the society. Typically this change involves a new social meaning for the particular behavior in question.

The most frequently made distinction in the study of social change is between the reform level of change and the revolutionary level. Some sociological writers make a distinction between reform movements, which aim for change in a limited area of the existing social order, and revolutionary movements, which aim at a fundamental reconstruction of the entire social order. Smelser (1962) makes a distinction between norm oriented change and value oriented change. Norm oriented change is focused on the social rules of the society, with the intent of making the rules more consistent with the existing value system. Value oriented change is focused on the value system of the society, with the intent of replacing the old value system with a new one. The replacement of one coherent value system with a new coherent value system describes a revolution. Adoption of a new value system requires new norms and institutions to symbolize and express the new values.

In the area of mental illness, a reform sociological-social deviance intervention would modify social conditions to "*help*" the deviants "*adjust*" to the existing social order, and the nondeviants to "*adjust*" to the deviants. Thus occurrence and intensity of mental illness would be reduced, and the existing social order strengthened. A revolutionary sociological-social deviance intervention would ask both deviants and nondeviants to *convert* to a new system of values and establish a new social order. Under this new order, occurrence and intensity of mental illness would be greatly reduced.

Using the distinction between reform and revolutionary social change, and the previous distinction between logical positivist and phenomenological theories, four types of sociological-social deviance interventions will be discussed:

1. Reform interventions based on logical positivist theories
2. Revolutionary interventions based on logical positivist theories
3. Reform interventions based on phenomenological theories
4. Revolutionary interventions based on phenomenological theories.

Logical Positivist-Reform Interventions

The best example of a large-scale logical positivist-reform intervention is the community mental health centers program. Development of the concept of community mental health centers occurred during the 1950s, but it was the 1963 Community Mental Health and Mental Retardation legislation that produced a nation wide system. The mental health centers were to provide additional resources, interagency cooperation, and consultative services from professionals to the entire population on a sufficiently broad basis that the mental health of that population would be improved.

The reform scope of the community mental health centers was to enhance the ability of the existing sociopolitical system to alleviate mental illness. Community mental health centers were clearly not intended to be revolutionary in the sense of creating new political structures or new family structures. The initial focus in the community mental health centers was toward expanding clinical services in the community (Bloom, 1971, p. 8).

The assumption was also made that "the repository of wisdom regarding community mental health needs was the mental health professional and his colleagues in other social agencies" (Bloom, p. 8). This is not the type of assumption that leads to revolutionary changes.

The assumptions and aims of the initial community mental health centers also imply a logical positivist theory of mental illness. An individual pathology model is assumed to be the best orientation to mental illness rather than the more phenomenologically oriented model such as the ecological or social deviance models. To the extent that social deviance theory was used, it was primarily the social disorganization theory of deviance. Social disorganization theory described high rates of deviance as the result of inadequate community resources.

The available resources were not capable of meeting the physical, psychological, and social needs of persons living in disorganized areas. The lack of adequate mental health services thus leads to high rates of mental illness. The method to reduce rates of mental illness is then to expand services, particularly to those community areas where the services are most inadequate to the needs.

The theory implicit in the Community Mental Health and Mental Retardation legislation is different from social disorganization theory mainly in the estimate of the cause of the social

180

disorganization. The early Chicago sociologists saw social disorganization as the temporary result of immigrants adjusting to a radically different culture. This cause of social disorganization was also seen in the fifties and sixties in the form of migration within the country but was not considered the prime cause of high rates of deviance in the disorganized areas. The prime cause of high rates of deviance in these areas was structural strain within the social system. Merton's formulation of *anomie* may be taken as a prototype of the contradictions within society that resulted in high rates of deviance. The theory implicit in the Community Mental Health Centers' legislation thus combined the more logical positivist parts of functionalist theory with its basic social disorganization premises.

The legislative mandate establishing the community mental health centers also envisioned prevention of mental disorders as a coequal goal with treatment. The theoretical bases for the prevention efforts have been considerably more diffuse than the theory implicit in the greater provision of therapeutic services. The major idea is that psychological stress contributes to mental illness. This concept is part of Durkheimian anomie theory, social disorganization theory, and functionalist theory, as well as numerous psychological theories of mental illness.

Several strategies (Bloom, 1971) were developed from this concept for the prevention of mental illness. The first of these strategies is crisis intervention. Successful crisis intervention requires the identification of individuals in extreme stress, and then the provision of short-term services toward the resolution of the crisis. Crisis walk-in centers and suicide-prevention centers are typical examples of the crisis intervention strategy.

A second, earlier prevention strategy may be termed anticipatory guidance. This is an attempt toward presolution of anticipated crises. The typical form of anticipatory guidance is a group meeting, for example, with expectant parents. Drug education programs would also be considered efforts at anticipatory guidance.

These prevention strategies, particularly the consultation strategy, involve mental health professionals working with a wide variety of community members, rather than just with the mentally ill. This has had several important effects on the community mental health professionals. The first is a certain political sophistication from attempting to produce change in communities rather than change in individuals. The professional stance of the disinterested scientist-expert is not particularly effective in influencing community processes. More frequently an activist-reformer stance is required.

A second development resulting from community mental health work is a move toward new theory. A body of theory and data has developed. New disciplinary hybrid areas such as community psychology and community psychiatry are emerging. It appears that these fields will include elements of ecological, socialization, and deviance theories.

Logical Positivist-Revolutionary Interventions

It is difficult to identify successful revolutions based on logical positivist theories of mental illness as social deviance. Even if one develops a revolutionary theory and precipitates a revolution, events usually do not coincide with the predictions derived from the theory (see Brinton, 1965). In addition, theories of mental illness as social deviance do not seem to fit the ideological conditions for successful revolutions (see Smelser, 1962, for a description of those conditions).

The Russian revolution is probably the best example of a successful revolution based on a logical positivist theory that conceptualized "mental illness" as social deviance. Clearly Marxism is a logical positivist theory, and Marx tied the "alienation of labor" to the oppression of the working class by the bourgeoisie. While the "alienation of labor" should not be considered synonymous with mental illness, it clearly would include much of the mental suffering among the working class. The results of this formulation can be seen in the current Soviet tendency to treat psychiatric illness as either physiologically based (and thus not "mental") or as attributable to the counterrevolutionary attitudes of the patient (Medvedev and Medvedev, 1971).

When one examines revolutionary movements that have been partially successful, i.e., they have managed to survive but have not had a major effect upon their surrounding culture, then there are numerous examples of logical positivist-revolutionary interventions. The Synanon drug treatment organization would be one of these partially successful movements. It has managed to survive within American culture, but has not been able to get large numbers of persons (either drug users or nonusers) to adopt its radical lifestyle.

The theory of deviance behind the Synanon organization is clearly a logical positivist theory. In what has come to be called Synanon's Manifesto the causes of drug addiction and the preferred methods of treatment are described (see Yablonsky, 1965, pp. 56-59). The "addictive personality" is considered to be essentially a self-centered child. This child is placed in an "autocratic family structure" in which his behavior is subject to strict control. Concomitant with the behavior control are the brutally honest Synanon group sessions and the inculcation of an eclectic philosophy stressing the virtues of self-reliance. The "successful" Synanon member gradually acquires status and responsibility within the system and eventually becomes a truly "inner-directed person."*

Synanon theory is thus clearly related to Durkheim's anomie theory. Durkheim postulated that man requires strict social regulation of his needs. Synanon communities provide such strict social regulation. Synanon theory is also clearly related to Freudian theory (control over the childish, self-centered id) and neo-Freudian ego psychology, e.g., the development of "controls from within" (Redl and Wineman, 1952).

Synanon's ability to keep addicts from returning to heroin use has become well known. This has led a number of other organizations working the drug addiction field to adopt many of Synanon's methods. In addition, Synanon's influence can be seen in the various psychotherapies that can loosely be called "attack" therapy (see Yablonsky, 1965; Bach, 1968). Synanon has become something of a social movement in addition to a drug addiction treatment.

There are, however, two recurring criticisms that must be considered in assessing the Synanon intervention. Coincidentally, it is these criticisms that most clearly show Synanon as a revolutionary reform intervention. The first and most important criticism is that Synanon does not "return" the cured addict "to the community." Once a person becomes a full member of Synanon, he rarely becomes a conventional member of the community. He usually remains a permanent member of the organization. This is in sharp contrast to the other drug abuse treatment programs that set

---

*Charles Dederich, the founder of Synanon and primary developer of the Synanon method and philosophy, points out that the classic nineteenth-century inner-directed personalities did originate in authoritative family environments (Yablonsky, 1965).

the goal of functioning in the larger society as the ultimate goal of the treatment process.

In contrast, Synanon is a "life style" that the person adopts after discarding his "dope fiend" life style (Yablonsky, 1965). Given that this new life style permits full development of the person according to his own (newly adopted) values, why should he give up this life style for one of the life styles of conventional society?

The rationale for not leaving Synanon is most easily understood in reference to revolutionary ideology. If a "troubled" person converts to a revolutionary ideology that gives him the experienced ability to control those troubles, no one would expect him to abandon that revolutionary ideology and start to support the status quo. A more reasonable expectation is a permanent commitment to the ideology accompanied by proselytizing. The second expectation is independent of the ultimate validity of the "experienced ability" or the ultimate validity of the ideology in identifying the causes of the "troubles."

The second criticism of Synanon is that a relatively low percentage of drug addicts are sufficiently motivated to become cured by Synanon or by Synanon-like programs (National Clearinghouse for Drug Abuse Information, 1975). A reform treatment program would not have difficulty in recruiting patients. In contrast, even a very successful revolutionary ideology finds few persons willing to adopt the strict discipline of the party.

Phenomenological-Reform Interventions

There are many different types of programs and activities that could be discussed within the phenomenological-reform framework. The open classroom, attempts at humanistic education approaches in revised curricula, normalization procedures with handicapped populations, and new approaches to family therapy are examples.

The intervention to be described here is child advocacy. It may be useful to first indicate what child advocacy is not. It is neither a well-developed systematic intervention, a set of procedures, nor a service or treatment system. Rather, child advocacy is a social movement manifested in several different action modes and located in different social systems. While any one child advocacy program will have its own particular style and structure, for the most part they are involved in monitoring the activities of children in different social settings and intervening in those situations where they believe the children's needs are ignored or children's rights violated. The interventions range from providing feedback to the responsible adults in the setting where the unmet needs are identified, through policy development and reformulation, to the courts where the legal issues are confronted directly.

Various advocacy programs relate to one or more of the following aspects of the rights of children: 1) their rights as learners to have an educational program that responds to their particular learning style and needs, 2) their rights as human beings to have a warm environment that regards them with dignity and responds to their needs, and provides reasonable opportunities for them to experience themselves as worthy and adequate, and 3) their rights as citizens with constitutional protections.

While there are many issues of concern to child advocates, the labeling of children is a central concern in almost all child advocacy programs. Here child advocates borrow directly from the social deviance theory of labeling. Child advocates maintain that the labeling of children, e.g., as "mentally retarded," or "emotionally disturbed," is too frequently done on bases that are irrelevant to the child's social functioning (Mercer, 1968).

A second central concern of child advocates is the harm done to children under the guise of bureaucratic rules. Such rules are seen as having a logic of their own that is contrary to the inner logic of the child's experience. This concern is very similar to Merton's concept of "ritualism" and other dysfunctional aspects of bureaucracy.

The child advocacy movement is clearly a reform movement in that it is in agreement with the expressed ideals of American society, but wishes to bring the experiences of children closer to those ideals.

Phenomenological-Revolutionary Interventions

There are probably revolutionary interventions based on phenomenological theories of social deviance. Labeling theory, with its basis in symbolic interactions, is the most phenomenological of the theories, and is oriented towards continual reform rather than revolution. Labeling theory takes a critical stance towards all groups possessing social power and thus is not appropriate for advocating the replacement of dominant power group by a new dominant power group (Becker, 1973; Lofland, 1966).

Phenomenological-revolutionary movements tend to be based on mixtures of theology and political ideology as well as sociology. They are based on a view of the universe rather than a view of social rule breaking. The psychedelic movement of the middle 1960s can be used as an example (see Leary, 1968; Rubin, 1967). This social movement can clearly be considered revolutionary in its advocacy of new values, rituals, styles of interpersonal interaction, and modes of personal expression. It is also clearly phenomenological in its emphasis on the primacy of mystical experience and the value of altered states of consciousness.

This social movement questioned the concept of "mental illness" and emphasized the need to have a wider range of tolerance for the behavior of individuals. Psychological difficulties experienced by individuals were likely to be seen as resulting from attempting to follow an artificially restrictive set of behavioral rules rather than from any psychopathology within the individual.

The Unification Church, founded by Sun Myung Moon, is another example of a phenomenological revolutionary intervention. The revolutionary aspects of this movement can be seen in its emphasis on preparing for the millennium (see Lofland, 1966) and its communal lifestyle (Batson, 1976). Within the belief system of the movement, psychological problems are not defined as "mental illness," rather they are seen as the result of not living according to the "Divine Principles." Thus a behavior change to live in accord with the Divine Principles will relieve the psychological problems of the individual.

The two examples cited here are of phenomenological-revolutionary movements that at best can be termed partially successful. This is not meant to imply that all such movements will have limited success; Christianity, Islam, and Buddhism could be cited as very successful phenomenological revolutions. Nor is it meant to imply that partially successful movements do not have an effect on rates of "mental illness." It should be noted that such phenomenological-revolutionary movements typically arise during periods of rapid social change (Smelser, 1962; Lang and Lang, 1961), when one would expect higher rates of deviance in general and mental illness in particular (cf. Durkheim, 1951). Whether such movements "treat" or "mistreat" the mentally ill may be primarily a question of how one wishes to define mental illness. It is clear that these movements do meet many of the social and psychological needs of their members.

Summary

From a sociological perspective, "mental illness" behavior involves the breaking of social rules. Thus mental illness will always involve questions of moral judgments and conflict between those enforcing social rules and those seen as violating the rules.

Mental illness must also be seen as a social production. Social factors may hinder or facilitate the performance of "mentally ill" behavior, influence the public recognition of the behavior as "mental illness," and affect the provision of treatment for the behavior. The various deviance theories emphasize different social factors in these processes.

Sociological interventions are focused on altering the rates of occurrence of mental illness rather than upon treating individual cases. Thus they require social changes—at least in the distribution of resources and power among groups within society, if not in basic values and institutions.

References

BACH, G. R. & WYDEN, P. *The intimate enemy.* New York: Avon Press, 1968.

BATSON, D. Moon Madness: Greed or Creed? *APA Monitor*, 1976, 7(6), 1, 32.

BECKER, H. Labeling theory reconsidered. In Howard Becker, *Outsiders: Studies in the sociology of deviance.* New York: Free Press, 1963.

BLOOM, B. L. Strategies for the prevention of mental disorders. In Gershen Rosenblum (Ed.). *Issues in community psychology and preventive mental health.* New York: Behavioral Publications, 1971.

BRINTON, C. *The anatomy of revolution.* New York: Vintage Books, 1965.

CLAUSEN, J. (Ed.). *Socialization and society.* Boston: Little, Brown, 1968.

DURKHEIM, E. *Suicide*. New York: Free Press, 1951.

ERIKSON, K. Notes on the sociology of deviance. *Social Problems*, 1964, *1*, 307-314.

GOLD, M. & DOUVAN, E. (Eds.). *Adolescent development*. Englewood Cliffs, N.J.: Prentice-Hall, 1969.

GOVE, W. Labeling and mental illness: A critique. In Walter Gove (Ed.). *The labeling of deviance: Evaluating a perspective*. New York: Halstead Press, 1975a.

GOVE, W. (Ed.). *The labeling of deviance: Evaluating a perspective*. New York: Halstead Press, 1975b.

GOVE, W. Societal reaction as an explanation of mental illness: An evaluation, *American Sociological Review*, 1970, *35*(5), 873-888.

HOLLINGSHEAD, A. B. & REDLICH, F. C. *Social class and mental illness: A community study*. New York: John Wiley, 1958.

KITSUSE, J. The new conception of deviance and its critics. In Walter Gove (Ed.). *The labeling of deviance: Evaluating a perspective*. New York: Halstead Press, 1975.

KUHN, T. *The structure of scientific revolutions*. Chicago, Ill.: University of Chicago Press, 1970.

LANG, K. & LANG, G. *Collective dynamics*. New York: Crowell, 1961.

LEARY, T. *The politics of ecstasy*. New York: Putman, 1968.

LEMERT, E. Paranoia and the dynamics of exclusion. *Sociometry*, 1962, *25*, 2-20.

LIPPITT, R. Improving the socialization process. In J. Clausen (Ed.). *Socialization & Society*. Boston: Little, Brown, 1968, pp. 321-374.

LOFLAND, J. *Deviance and identity*. Englewood Cliffs, N.J.: Prentice-Hall, 1969.

LOFLAND, J. *Doomsday cult*. Englewood Cliffs, N.J.: Prentice-Hall, 1966.

MATZA, D. *Becoming deviant*. Englewood Cliffs, N.J.: Prentice-Hall, 1969.

MEAD, G. *Self and society*. Chicago, Ill.: The University of Chicago Press, 1934.

MEDVEDEV, Z. & MEDVEDEV, R. *A question of madness: Repression by psychiatry in the Soviet Union*. New York: Vintage Books, 1971.

MERCER, J. R. Labeling the mentally retarded. In Earl Rubington and Martin J. Weinberg (Eds.). *Deviance: The interactionist perspective.* New York: Macmillan, 1968.

MERCER, J. R. Racial differences in I.Q.: Fact or artifact? In C. Senna (Ed.). *The fallacy of I.Q.* New York: Third Press, 1973.

NATIONAL CLEARINGHOUSE FOR DRUG ABUSE INFORMATION. *Report Series, Series 34.* No. 1. "Treatment of Drug Abuse: an Overview." Washington, D.C.: Department of Health, Education, and Welfare, 1975.

REDL, F. & WINEMAN, D. *Controls from within: Techniques for the treatment of the aggressive child.* New York: Free Press, 1952.

RUBIN, JERRY. *Do it!* New York: Simon & Schuster, 1967.

SAMPSON, H., MESSINGER, S. L. & TOWNE, R. D. Family processes and becoming a mental patient. *American Journal of Sociology,* 1962, *68*, 88-96.

SCHEFF, T. *Being mentally ill.* Chicago, Ill.: Aldine, 1966.

SCHUR, E. Comments. In Walter Gove (Ed.). *The labeling of deviance: Evaluating a perspective.* New York: Halstead Press, 1975.

SMELSER, N. *The theory of collective behavior.* New York: Free Press, 1962.

YABLONSKY, L. *Synanon: The tunnel back.* Baltimore, Md.: Penguin, 1965.

YARROW, M. R., SCHWARTZ, C. G., MURPHY, H. S., & DEASY, L. C. The psychological meaning of mental illness in the family. *Journal of Social Issues,* 1955, *11*(4), 12-24.

CHAPTER EIGHT

Ecological Views and Approaches

Ecology has only recently come into existence as a significant term in the field of child variance. Therefore, it does not yet
have a strong identity as a "school" of thought and a coded
change-technology associated with it. The logical extension of this
perspective into human care practices in the current period has
recently led to social, professional, and legal activities such as
mainstreaming, deinstitutionalization, declassification, litigation,
due-process procedures, attacks on psychological tests, and child-
advocacy programs.

On the level of the individual, it has led to environmental manipulation in the home, the school, and the community.
Ecology has also become a significant theoretical influence in family therapy, awareness expansion, sexual therapy, gestalt therapy,
open classrooms, free schools, deschooling efforts, and development of counterinstitutions.

From the point of view of the ecological perspective there is no denial that some members of a collective unit may find it difficult to follow prescribed social pathways in daily living. There is no denial that some individuals experience psychic pain. There is no denial that some have physical anomalies. However, the social, physical, and psychic process by which these factors become a disability is a collective process. It is a holistic phenomena in which the factors mentioned above are transformed into deviance. This deviance transformation can occur against a background of cultural avoidances peculiar to the society or collective unit in which it occurs. Human factors avoided by one society may be idealized and cultivated in another. Visions can be hallucinations or divine realizations depending on the culture and the period of time in which they occur. A hunchback can be an orthopedic disability or a gift of God, depending on time and place. Homoerotic male behavior was manly love in the soldiers in Plato's Republic, but homosexuality is pathology or sin in Boise, Idaho.

Ecology and Variance in Children

The ecological point of view is oriented to adaptation. It is concerned with the adaptation between the organism and his environment. The term environment has a much broader connotation than its current usage. Helm (1972) suggests that in ecology, environment is treated as "oecumene," thus comprehending not only space and habitat but the sociocultural resources and groups beyond the society. It implies the "known world" of any particular people. Ecology is from the Greek word *ekos* or house. Its precise origin is not known, although it is attributed to the German naturalist and Darwinian Ernst Heinrich Haeckel (1834-1919). Paul B. Sears, in his book *Charles Darwin: The Naturalist as a Cultural Force* (1950) writes:

Haeckel's grasp of the problems of living nature is suggested by the fact that he coined the word "oecology," now ecology, to cover the study of the broad configurations which exist within and among communities of organisms. (p. 42)

Dictionary definitions of ecology currently consider it in two ways:

1. a branch of science concerned with the interrelationship of organisms and their environments; and

2. the totality or pattern of relationships between organisms and their environment (*Webster's Seventh New Collegiate Dictionary*, 1969).

As applied in the field of child variance, the ecological point of view shifts the focus from the child and his personality, psychic make-up, and behavior, to the problem of mutual adaptation between the child and his "community." It is concerned with the broad configuration independent of the individual child in that configuration.

John Calhoun (1962) has extensively demonstrated this phenomenon with lower animals. He has investigated the patterning of relationships between certain features of environmental manipulation and behavioral abnormalities. He has demonstrated that he can engineer environments to produce multiple "pathologies" in life patterns, physical organs, and behaviors in rats and that these noxious outcomes interact with each other as well as certain designed features of the environment. In focusing upon the behavioral anomalies that appear in his engineered conditions, Calhoun defines pathology as the inability to adapt to ongoing conditions.

Behavior becomes incompatible with these conditions, at least to the extent that the individual fails to fulfill that role which contributes to the success of the biological or cultural system of which he is, or should be, a component part. (p. 1)

He sees individuals who fail to adapt as having become enmeshed or trapped by circumstances with which they are unable to cope successfully. Such unusual circumstances, he terms "ecological traps." The task of the intervener is to devise better ways of recognizing and avoiding ecological traps (Calhoun, 1962).

Calhoun (1967) has been successful in devising such ecological traps for animals to demonstrate not only their influence in creating pathological individual behavior, but also in influencing collective behavior and creating total pathological communities. He showed how "pathological" engineering of the environment (control of space, sleeping arrangements, eating arrangements, pathways, etc.) could trigger interacting sequences of pathologies in astounding ways in (1) the individual and group, (2) the physical organism, the behavior, the life functions, and (3) back into the environment itself.

Calhoun has been particularly effective in controlling space. Under crowded conditions, behavioral pathology became extreme in rat colonies. The consequences of behavioral deviations were most apparent among the females who were unable to carry pregnancy to full term or to survive delivery of the litters if they did. An even greater number, after successfully giving birth, fell short in their maternal functions. In the males, behavior disturbances ranged from extreme sexual deviation to cannibalism and from frenetic overactivity or hyperactivity to a pathological withdrawal from which individuals would emerge to drink, eat, and move about only when other members of the community were asleep.

In other studies Calhoun was able to produce widely varying abnormal types within a single colony by designing ecological traps (Calhoun, 1967). Within the same colony he could produce abnormal aggression, abnormal withdrawal, extreme homosexuality, etc. Later, in physical pathology studies of these same animals, he was able to demonstrate gross physical changes and differences corresponding to the behavioral types. Both adrenal weight and heart (ventricle) weight were positively correlated with observed behavior. The more the animal withdrew from social interaction, the fewer the demands that seemed to be placed upon these vital organs.

These experiments dramatize the fact that although the organism somehow ingests his or her surroundings and gives back a reflection of it in behavior, organ-systems and lifestyle, the maladaptation is a composite of person and setting. The setting contributes its portion of the pathology. It also indicates that altering the environment in "pathological" directions can have multiple effects on multiple individuals.

Habitat, Setting, Environment

Ecologists always consider the individual, group, and behavior as components of the environment or habitat. They are convinced that it is only through social convention that our mental structures separate these components from the whole. The following extract about behavior and settings is representative (Barker, 1969).

Our data show that people and other entities are components of the environmental units they inhabit in the same way that a generator is a component of an engine and a bat of a ball game. Real-life settings are eco-behavioral entities, and the concepts and principles which explicate them are utterly alien to those that explicate their component parts, the behavior of individual persons among others. (p. 36)

Barker and his associates (Barker, 1963, 1968; Barker & Schoggen, 1973) have studied behavior in one midwestern community for many years. In comparing that community to a community in England called Yoredale, Barker says that transposing the children of midwest to Yoredale, and vice versa, would transform their behavior in various ways. He concludes that:

The force of a community's settings vis-a-vis children are examples of the power of environmental units over behavior, or of their superordinate position with respect to their human components.... (p. 8)

In the classic, and still relevant, study of mental disorders in urban areas by Faris and Dunham (1965) in which the natural areas of the city of Chicago were shown to be distinctively differentiated with respect to mental illness rates, the authors come to a conclusion similar to that of Barker. Each zone retained its characteristics through time whether its inhabitants were native-born, foreign-born, or Negro. Also, each racial or national group changed its character over the years as it moved from one zone to the next. The zones not only maintained their characteristics through the years in spite of the flow of various racial and national groups through them over different time periods, but they invariably impressed their effects on each of these groups.

Ecological Niche

When talking about specific human ecological predicaments such as "emotional disturbance" in the context of its occurrence, we are talking about alien niches, or functional roles in a habitat or setting. Such a niche is a nonviable life pattern consisting of a social place and occupation that exists in alienation within a particular sociocultural context.

The individual usually finds his way, or is shunted into, these contrived niches through a succession of ecological traps that are set up by the society and social system to defend against variation in its members. When the individual departs from the species stereotype of the community or the subsystem of the community, he sets into motion a progressive series of ecological traps. These ecological traps continue until the community or one of its subsystems has either extruded him or maneuvered him into a contrived and alien niche, a cul de sac in the ecosystem. The niche not only invites and interacts with certain patterns of behavior and activity, but it tends to fix and hold the relationship in that particular pattern.

The deviant categories themselves—mental deficiency, mental illness, delinquency—provide culturally created ecological niches that lead to a way of life that is alien, isolated, and socially without function. In addition to outright extrusion procedures that are formalized within organizational units such as schools, court systems, welfare systems, etc., these systems have developed socially or culturally created ecological traps that put the individual into an environmental bind. The track-system, and even some aspects of special classes within the educational system might be viewed in this light. The very processes and procedures of the legal, detention, probate, and policing patterns within the juvenile section of the social system of legal correction have been seen by many authors as creators of delinquency. The surveillance processes of this particular system can be viewed as a culturally created ecological trap.

The way in which social systems can process people into alien and spurious niches through ecological traps is evident in the Riverside, California, study by Jane Mercer (1968). In studying mental retardation and its variety of meanings, Mercer was interested in mental retardation as "an achieved social status." She says:

Mental retardation is an achieved status. It is a position in the group that is contingent upon the performance or, in this case, the lack of performance, of the individual. Thus, mental retardation is specific to a particular social system. A person may hold the status of a mental retardate in one social system yet participate in other social systems in which he is not regarded as mentally retarded and does not hold that status. (pp. 12-13)

Mercer found that the major definer in the community was the school system. If the school system assigned the status of mental retardate to a child, other agencies, such as welfare and corrections, were likely to accept the school label. In studying the mildly retarded in the school she discovered that not all children with low IQs achieved the status of retarded. It was found that in order to achieve such a status in the school system the child progressed through several rather clearly differentiated states as he moved from the status of "normal student" to the status of "EMR" student.

In Riverside, the first step to acquiring the status of EMR is to enroll in the public school system rather than the Catholic school system. The Catholic school system had no special classes, therefore none of its students were labeled mentally retarded.

The second step is to fail to meet the role expectations of the teacher. The student may be assigned a deviant status by being asked to repeat a grade and thus become a "retained student." Of the EMR children studied, 72 percent had repeated one or more grades at some time during their educational careers. (This did not happen to all children with low IQs.)

The third stage is attained if, after having been retained, the student still does not perform satisfactorily according to the teacher's expectations. Here, the teacher may choose to socially promote the child who will thus escape the EMR status and retain the status of a regular student. If not, he or she moves to stage four and becomes an "academic problem."

At this critical juncture there are several alternatives. The student may be defined as a "reading problem," "an underachiever," "a speech problem," or some other label that retains his or her status as a student in a regular class. The other alternative is to send the child to a psychologist. He or she thus moves to stage five as a "case-to-be-evaluated."

The psychologist may then render a clinical judgment and decide that this is "an emotionally disturbed child," "a situationally distressed child," or other categories than mental retardate. However, if the child is given an intelligence test and fails it, and the psychologist decides that this is due to mental retardation, the student moves to stage six—the official labeling.

California law requires that parents be notified before a child is placed in special education. The parents may be adamantly opposed to placement and this resistance may dissuade the psychologist from assigning the child to an EMR status. The "staff conference" may decide that although the child scored low on the IQ test, he or she is really emotionally disturbed rather than retarded, and thus, is not recommended for placement and returns to regular class status.

In comparing children who achieved the status of mental retardation with other children of the same intelligence quotient level who did not achieve such status, Mercer (1968) discovered that teachers' reactions and perceptions of the child played an important part in acquiring or failing to acquire the status. A child who was perceived by the teacher as having low academic competence, poor adjustment, poor work habits, low competence in English, and few friends was also perceived as having low mental ability and as "mentally retarded." A child of the same IQ level who was seen as having low academic competence and poor adjustment, but at the same time was seen as possessing good work habits, relative competence in English, and was easy to manage and liked by peers, was not seen as having low mental ability and was not perceived as mentally retarded.

Thus, it can be seen in this set of studies that a child may be shunted through a variety of binds into a superfluous or specially contrived alien niche. It is also apparent that the way in which the teacher, the psychologist, the parent, and peers respond to the child plays a part in ascribing deviation and in processing the child into a spurious niche outside the mainstream of life of the larger ecosystem.

The word "niche" comes from the French "nicher," to nest. *Webster's Seventh New Collegiate Dictionary* defines niche as "a) a place, employment, or activity for which a person is best fitted, and b) a habitat supplying the factors necessary for the existence of an organism or species" (p. 570).

In focusing on behavior, Sells (1966) says:

... it may be said that the response repertoire represents the natural way in which a species "makes its living" in the natural environment. (p. 134)

Duncan and Schnore (1959), in trying to define niche from the sociological point of view, say that one of the most important concepts in ecology is the pattern of activity. At the common sense level the closest approximation to the ecological use of "activity" is the notion employed by the term "occupation."

"Functionary" is a less frequently used term that carries a similar connotation and—within general ecology—the concept of "niche" designates practically the same thing. (p. 137)

Hawley (1950) says that a useful conception in studies of communities is the niche, or functional role, because this concept focuses attention upon what organisms do in the habitat rather than upon their morphological characteristics. From this perspective, a community may be viewed as an organization of niches, since the activities of each class of organism influence the activities of every other class in the association. In defining niche, Odum (1963) claims that ecologists use the term habitat to mean the place where the organism lives, and the term niche to mean the role that the organism plays in the ecosystem; the habitat is the "address," and the niche is the "profession."

From the organism's perspective, niche implies the place that the individual has found for himself (or a species or population has found for itself) within a constant set of circumstances in an ecological unit. From the point of view of the environment, it is a place that has been made for the organism (or population) by the environment and its collective.

Holism

Edward Rogers (1962) says that the most vital concept that ecology can bring to our thinking is that of holism, the idea that man is a part of a comprehensive system of dynamic interdependencies.

In recent years there seems to have developed a growing awareness of this comprehensive system of interdependencies. As a consequence a new interest has developed in physical ecology. There seems to be a new sense in our society that man is a very dependent part of a comprehensive system and by changing one part we change the whole.

However, we still treat the variant individual as distinctive, unique, and independent of the whole. We treat him or her as an isolated unit, without a function or place in the whole.

For all we know, the variant condition of the individual may be a very necessary part of our own psychological and physical balance and survival. Although we may not comprehend his or her part in the general scheme of things, we could be creating grave harm to our whole system by our extensive campaigns to change such individuals one by one. Perhaps there is a need to consider the whole social unit as maladapted and, instead of interfering with the processes of the single individual, perhaps we should try to examine and intervene in the comprehensive, holistic system. Ecological research has not given us enough information yet for pinpointed intervention methodology, but it has clearly shown how the whole can be changed by adventitious changes in a particular aspect of the whole.

For instance, rapid and violent social changes can influence infectious physical processes by disrupting established social relationships (Chapman, Hinkle, and Wolff, 1960). The occurrence of epidemics and increased morbidity from infections among human populations during periods of major change, readjustment, and mass dislocation is well known. Increased industrialization during the nineteenth and twentieth centuries and the resulting migrations from rural to urban life and from one country to another resulted in high morbidity from tuberculosis. The high mortality was usually considered the result of exposure to cold and rain, lack of food, excessive effort, crowding and contact of a migratory population with new and fresh sources of infections to which they have developed insufficient immunity. The explanation, however, is probably more complex. In a given society, mortality from tuberculosis has been found to be closely tied to the period in the history of a culture when the use of industrial machines becomes widespread. Mortality reaches its peak about ten or twenty years after industrialization and thereafter falls off rapidly.

The incidence of hyperthyroidism in Norway increased 100 percent during the first year of World War II, when the country was invaded. These, and other medical observations have led Dubos (1969) to conclude that there is reason to wonder whether any microorganism cannot become the cause of disease if suitable conditions are provided for it. There are many circumstances, some being of common occurence in human medicine, where the physical, chemical, physiological, and probably psychological factors that affect the host, play far more decisive parts in the causation of disease than does this or that microorganism.

In 1865, when Pettenkofer was appointed the first professor of hygiene at the University of Munich, health conditions in that city were very bad. The general death rate was 33 per 1,000 population, sanitary conditions and housing were appalling, and industrial expansion was making the situation worse. As a contrast, there was the city of London. England was the first country to experience the ill effects of industrialization and the first country to react against them. Her social reforms of the mid-nineteenth century put her far ahead of other countries in matters of health. In London, the general mortality had dropped to the then remarkably low level of 22 per 1,000 population.

Using this example, Pettenkofer decided to make Munich as healthy as London. Pettenkofer saw that the social environment, as well as the physical environment, was part of man's biota or ecosystem. He realized that customs and habits have a great influence on health and must be investigated just as carefully as physical factors.

Fortunately, Pettenkofer was acutely aware of the importance of the political power of the society in bringing about necessary reforms to transform Munich. With the cooperation of the political forces, clean water was brought from the mountains, a new sewage system was installed with outlets of carefully established safety, a new public slaughterhouse was built and food inspection was rigorously enforced, housing projects were launched, health commissioners functioned in every community, and it is supposed that there were other important changes in the manner of living.

Using London as his ecological model, he continued to push reforms; and by the end of the century he had reduced general mortality to the rate of 22 per 1,000 population. Munich was then one of the healthiest cities in Europe.

In citing the Munich experience, Rogers (1962) says:

This case study suggests that we might reduce the confusion and perhaps be more efficient as well as effective in our preventive programs if we could learn to see our ecosystem and its health problems in larger chunks rather than increasingly smaller ones. (p. 761)

He also says that this example suggests that ecological models might be employed effectively, now as they were then, even though the exact etiological factors remain unknown.

Early ecological studies of the relationship between "the spatial pattern and the moral order" of urban areas present other examples of the "holism" of the ecological frame of reference (Park, Burgess, & McKenzie, 1925). These studies of Chicago showed not only that population composition, literacy, dependency rates, and disease rates varied greatly in different sections of the city, but also that there were variations in mental life and behavior within the different sections. It was shown with reasonable certainty that the high rates of delinquency were products not of biological inferiority of the population stocks that inhabit the slum areas, nor of any racial or national peculiarity, but rather of the nature of the social life in the areas themselves (Shaw & McKay, 1931). The delinquency rates remained constantly high in certain urban areas that were inhabited by as many as six different national groups in succession. Each nationality suffered from the same disorganization in these areas and each nationality alike improved after moving away from the deteriorated areas.

Other studies in Chicago showed "natural areas" for high rates of suicide (Carvan, 1928), mental retardation (Jenkins & Brown, 1935), and "hobohemia" (Beck, 1956).

This review of classical concepts in ecology, along with the illustrative data on organismic variance, puts disturbance in a special perspective. Child variance is related to the ways of life in a particular place. Ways of life can be analyzed into such conceptual tools as occurrence, adaptation, habitat, niche, holism, etc. Nevertheless, it is the ways of life that create, energize, process, and maintain variance. The kind of variance (disturbance, retardation, delinquency) is not as dependent on the state of the organism as on the ways of life flowing through the organism in a particular place at a particular time.

If the place and time codes certain acts as disturbance, the child is processed through disturbance machinery into a disturbance niche. If the acts are coded as delinquent or retarded, the child is processed into a different alien niche. In any case, alienation is the state of his existence.

Many different organismic sciences can apprehend this particular plight of a child relegated to variance status by the ways of life in a particular place at a particular time. Sciences such as sociology, psychology, medicine, ethology, and anthropology have provided important data relative to disturbances in an ecosystem.

The next section will review representative studies from a variety of disciplines to show how the ecological perspective is applied in each science.

Sociology and Mental Disorder

In earlier ecological studies of the urban areas by the "Chicago School" of sociologists it had been shown that there was a distinctive pattern identifying natural areas of the city, what one might call different ways of life in a city. Such indices as the percentage of foreign-born, the percentage of homes owned, the sex ratio, and median rentals paid, the density of population, the rate of mobility, the educational rate, the percentage of rooming houses and hotels, and the percentage of condemned buildings, roughly tended to identify certain areas and to differentiate between them. These indices could be said to measure the extent of social disorganization between the different communities and the natural areas of the city. At the same time, other types of data, representing social problems such as juvenile delinquency, illegitimacy, suicide, crime, and family disorganization, might be considered as indices representing effects or results of certain types of social processes or ways of life. In all of these social problems of a city there was the concentration of high rates close to the center, with rates declining in magnitude as one travels in any direction toward the city's periphery.

Faris and Dunham (1965) used this same technique to study the problem of mental disorder. It was an attempt to examine the spatial character of the relations between persons who have different kinds of mental breakdowns. In general, they found that the highest rates were clustered about the center of the city, and the rates were progressively lower at greater distances from the center. There was a concentration of high rates in the rooming house districts. The Negro areas had high rates and the foreign-born slums also had high rates. The outlying residential sections and the lake front hotel and apartment-hotel subcommunities had the lowest rates, no matter what race or nationality inhabited that region.

In order to give a clearer understanding of the actual ecology of "insanity" in Chicago, Faris and Dunham divided the city into five concentric circles, each containing four or more zones within a two-mile radius of each other, with the exception of Zone 1, the central business district, constructed on a one mile radius. On their sectional map of the city it was clearly shown that by far the highest rate for "insanity" in the city occurred in the central business district, in the center circle or Zone 1. In every zone, in every section of the city, with the exception of the southwest side, there was a steady decline in rates as one traveled from the center of the city to the periphery.

Faris and Dunham (1965) concluded that:

This presentation definitely establishes the fact that insanity like other social problems, fits into the ecological structure of the city.

As such the distribution of insanity appears to be a function of the city's growth and expansion, and more specifically of certain undetermined types of social processes. (p. 37)

Many similar studies have been conducted in other cities, generally confirming the area or section distribution shown by the Faris and Dunham study (Schroeder, 1942; Green, 1939; Hyde & Kingsley, 1944; Hafner & Reimann, 1970; Levy & Rowitz, 1973). More recently, studies of this sort have turned toward the relationship between social class and mental illness rather than subcommunities and mental illness—e.g., the Midtown Manhattan study of total prevalence of mental illness (Srole et al., 1962; Langner & Michael, 1963) and a major study on social class and mental illness by Hollingshead and Redlich (1958). These studies propose to show a definite relationship between occupancy of a social class status and mental illness, with the lowest socioeconomic groups having the highest rates and the highest socioeconomic groups having the lower rates.

Much of the research on social class and mental illness has been reviewed by Petras and Curtis (1968). They note that the literature has shifted away from an emphasis upon conditions inherent within individuals and social groups to an emphasis upon explanations in terms of faulty interaction processes between the individual and the group. This emphasis is, according to Petras and Curtis, best incorporated in the phrase "social stress."

Medicine and Mental Illness

Medical studies in human ecology place an emphasis on the responding side of the adaptive relationship and look closely at the individual and his reactions to stress between himself and his environment.

The individual's perception of his environmental world can take on all aspects of a real external threat, and if he perceives threat his body reacts as though the threat was real. Under circumstances perceived as threatening, he may inappropriately evoke primitive metabolic or reproductive patterns that ordinarily serve to maintain the body and the stock. The individual's adaptive and protective patterns are limited in number, and the form of the reaction is shaped by the particular history of experiences of the individual rather than the particular noxious factors evoking the reaction. Bodily functions that are usually phasic become continuous. Involved tissues are pressed beyond their limits. Devices ordinarily serving to protect the body then destroy tissue.

A large-scale study of men and women in the context of their environment, and its relationship to their health was conducted by Chapman, Hinkle, and Wolff (1960). The life stories of more than 500 ostensibly healthy people were analyzed; shorter segments of the lives of approximately 3000 were observed. This sample not only included native Americans, but also homogeneous groups of foreign-born persons, with an entirely different cultural tradition.

These researchers found that illness was not spread evenly through these populations. During the prime of life only about one-quarter of the individuals accounted for more than one-half the episodes of illness. In some groups there were more than twenty times as many episodes of disabling illness in the "least healthy" members as there were in the "most healthy."

These individuals with the greatest number of illnesses also had the greatest variety of illnesses. Those with a great deal of illness not only had many minor, but often numerous major disorders of medical, surgical, and psychiatric nature, including infections, injuries, new growth, and serious disturbances of mood, thought, and behavior.

These researchers found that episodes of illness often clustered during particular, limited periods of time, contiguous with other periods during which few or no illnesses occurred. They found that the periods of high illness corresponded with the periods perceived by the individual as the most threatening. They found that those more often ill, in contrast to those least often ill, usually viewed their lives as having been difficult and unsatisfactory. These individuals were evaluated as being more inflexibly oriented toward goals, duties, responsibilities. Typically, they were in conflict over pursuing their own ends and ambitions on the one hand, and acting responsibly and according to early learned principles about wives, children, parents and friends, on the other hand. They "took things seriously" and were anxious, self-absorbed, "turned inward," and unduly sensitive.

In contrast, those who were rarely ill often viewed their lives as having been relatively satisfactory. In general, they viewed themselves as having had preferred sibling positions, good marriages, and rewarding careers.

Yet, within a given population when the most healthy were compared with those who experienced the greatest amount of

illness, it was evident that physical hardships, geographic dislocation, exposure to infection, rapid social change, and interpersonal
problems occurred with almost equal frequency in their lives.

Chapman, Hinkle, and Wolff (1960) interpret these
findings as evidence that the relationship between the occurrence
of illness and difficult life situations is not solely with the difficulty
of the situation as seen by a neutral observer—

... but is closely related to the amount of threat in the situation as
perceived by the person who experienced it. (p. 195)

They say that their studies indicate that not only psychosomatic
illnesses but symptomatic illnesses of all kinds arise in and are remarkably influenced by environmental circumstances *perceived by
the individual as threatening.*

Grace, Wolf, and Wolff (1951) observed that in those who
perceive themselves as threatened in a given way, the mucous mem-
branes of the large bowel become engorged and motility and secretion is augmented. This is the pattern of ejection used in ridding the
organism of materials inadvertently taken in. In this case, however,
it is being evoked inappropriately to help the individual rid himself
of an unattractive interpersonal problem that cannot be dealt with in
this way. Abnormal secretions and the byproducts of breakdown
may then destroy the lining of the bowel, resulting in ulcerative
colitis.

Chapman, Hinkle, and Wolff review many other studies
that have concentrated on a variety of the body's organs to demonstrate that these organs become more readily damaged during or
following periods perceived by the individual as threatening. They
claim that these changes could be induced or terminated rapidly by
appropriate alteration of the environment.

Fried (1964) suggests that higher rates of psychotic disorders appear among the lower status group either because low
status is stressful in and of itself, or because the limited resources
available to people of low status results in greater impact and/or
cumulation of other stresses and crises. He then discusses the findings of Jaco's (1960) study that psychiatric disorders are dispropor-
tionately high in the unemployed as distinguished from all other
occupational categories. Fried (1964) says:

Thus, the strong association of low socio-economic status and
treated psychiatric disorder could result from the fact that unem-

ployment is higher in the lowest status levels and is also markedly associated with psychiatric hospitalization or treatment. (p. 417)

There is a similarity in Fried's hypothesis that low status is itself stressful and the Chapman, Hinkle, and Wolff review of research that confirms the pathology of excessive adaptive or defensive reactions of the body to perceived threat. They point out that when a person feels his prestige endangered, the glands of internal secretion—the pituitary, the thyroid, and the adrenals—may respond as though his very existence were in jeopardy, as by starvation, or by the sudden unusual demands of low temperature or violent action.

Ethological Studies

As we turned to the medical literature and focused on the individual organism, we noted how human adaptation or excessive adaptation efforts also seemed to cluster together in individuals as part of the larger configuration of maladaptation. Various conditions of ill health, disturbed behavior, abnormal mental states, etc. seemed to congregate together in the same individual.

Let us turn now and examine another holistic phenomenon—the way in which a living collective or aggregate acts in unison within a circumscribed environmental area as a disturbed composite. First, we will review a few ethological studies of animal behavior in which an individual is singled out as a collective object of disturbance; and then we will attempt to demonstrate the progression of the same aggregate phenomenon into primitive human collectives.

This phenomenon is offered as a further instance of the holistic nature of maladaptation or disturbed relationship between individual and setting. In examining the relationships within the collective, disturbance can be viewed as a "community state" in which there is assembled participation. It might be described as an agitated energy state which suffuses a collective. In this state, the established system of exchanges occurring within a particular aggregate setting becomes arhythmical and inharmonious as a result of either a single event or a dissonant pattern of events that precipitate it.

In order to explain what is meant by an emotional disturbance as a community or collective phenomenon rather than a property of an individual, it is necessary to demonstrate a general living principle of the effect of a variant community member upon the collective. The hypothesis is that the general pattern of community response to disturbance in our current society is only a specific human instance of a collective phenomenon that has characterized the wide variety of living societies which have interacted with the environment across the history of evolution.

Let us take the example of an experimental project carried out by Jacques Cousteau (who became well-known through TV) and his group of oceanographic scientists. While studying undersea life at a coral atoll, the scientists deliberately created a deviant or variant within the collective biotic sphere to observe collective reaction of fish life around the deviant fish. They would either slightly drug a fish or a few fish, or they would place him in an underwater floating bowl so that behavior and image would present a distinctive difference or variation. The drugged or imprisoned fish then deviated from his own school in his swimming behavior and appearance, which became more erratic and obviously different. The transmitted effect of this deviation upon the underwater life collected in the vicinity was immediate and dramatic. Signals transmitted by the variant fish seemed to release responses in the immediately surrounding fish, and these responses swept across the aggregate sea life collected at the atoll. The variant's own shoal or school immediately darted away from the deviant one. Predator fish in the vicinity began immediately to lunge at him; and where possible, devoured him. It was as though the variant behavior immediately charged the biotic sphere with releasor signals that disturbed and disordered the collective state in the ecological unit located at the atoll.

Human deviation in a group or a community seems to have a somewhat similar effect upon the collective. Deviation produces a pattern of recoil and activities directed toward either bringing him into the group or isolating him from the group. A child who deviates in the classroom, the neighborhood, or the community will attract attention and effort to bring about changes in him. The child may be referred to a psychologist, a special class, a child-guidance agency, etc. If the deviant behavior persists, the child may be extruded into some type of institution.

In terms of responses of immediately surrounding members of the collective, behavior takes many excitable forms. There is an obvious release of charged emotions and moods in the observers—bearing marks of a medley of fear, anger, attraction, repulsion, etc. While one or the other of these mood-behavioral manifestations predominate in different observers of the collective, instances of all of them seem to appear. It is as though a variant individual releases a parliament of mood-behaviors in the collective.

The same collective response can be observed in various community forms from the simplest insect life, fish life, bird life, and animal groups from rats through chimpanzee, up to and including primitive human communities. When one of the community members deviates or when a stranger to the community stumbles into the collective, there is general consternation throughout the unit. In the anthill, in the beehive, and in the animal herd, in the bird flock, in the wolf pack, in the rat colony, in the chimpanzee colony, a species member who is different or strange has the same effect upon the collective. The one who differs upsets the living unit and brings on attack, flight, or extrusion. The same reaction is reported in simple and isolated human settlements.

The following rat-colony example is reported by Lorenz (1967):

Serious fights between members of the same big family occur in one situation only, which in many respects is significant and interesting: Such fights take place when a strange rat is present and has aroused intra-specific, inter-family aggression. (p. 155)

Lorenz reports that when the stranger comes close enough to one of the colony for that member to get wind of the intruder:

The information is transmitted like an electric shock through the resident rat, and at once the whole colony is alarmed by a process of mood transmission which is communicated in the Brown Rat by expression movements but in the House Rat by a sharp, shrill, satanic cry which is taken up by all members of the tribe within earshot. . . . With their eyes bulging from their sockets, their hair standing on end, the rats set out on a rat hunt. They are so angry that if two of them meet they bite each other . . . On the day of persecution of the strange rat all the members of the clan are irritable and suspicious. (pp. 155, 156)

The interesting thing about this set of intruder signals and respondent countersignals is that the deviation that sets it all off seems to lie in the smell of the stranger. If he is carefully saturated with the clan smell by mixing nesting materials and colony dirt in his hair, he is free to roam about within the colony with impunity. If an experimenter takes a rat out of the colony and cleanses him of the clan smell, he will be persecuted like a strange interloper.

A variant species member generally receives the same treatment from his own collective. Albinism in African mammalia produces such collective response (Marais, 1969). An albino springbok was solitary, but whenever she came in contact with a troop of her own kind, she was mercilessly attacked by male and female alike. A white klipspringer was also continually persecuted by others of its kind. A black wildebeest with a white blaze was thrust out of the herd.

Storks collect in a flock before migrating and kill all those who are lame, sick, or otherwise incapable of holding their own (Alverdes, 1927). Parrots who are wounded are ostracized and made to live alone outside the flock. A monkey who has been isolated since birth will show fear of other monkeys when he is first brought into the cage after isolation (Harlow, 1969). He may cower in a corner. This inevitably leads to vicious attacks by other normal monkeys. If he is left in the cage for any length of time he eventually will be killed. Chauvin (1968) reports that jays get agitated if a fellow jay is struggling. They will circle around if he lies still. Terns fly around a wounded bird—if he struggles they will scream as they circle; if he moves feebly, they will fly silently; if there is much blood they will kill him. Tinbergen (1960) reports that a struggling gull causes great agitation. Other birds gather together screaming loudly and swoop down in attack of the bird.

Anthropology and Abnormality

Somewhat similar behavior has been observed in primitive human collectives. The Chickimec Indians of Northeast Mexico killed strangers on sight by horrible means (Driver, 1961, p. 360). The Eskimo of Greenland does not allow a child to live who is sickly or without a mother (Meade, 1961). At other times of stress, children are killed before their parents. The Annassilah wall a man up and leave him to die when he is too old to hunt. If a man is sick and seems unable to recover he is thrown into the sea to die. In the primitive Kaonde tribe, children who do not walk by the proper time are killed (Melland, 1923). The author remembers infanticide cases where the child was not only a cripple, but an idiot and a mute (pp. 50-52). The aborigines in Polynesia speared a stranger who wandered into their area. "Anything strange is uncanny to the native who has a peculiar dread of magic from a distance" (p. 230). The Andaman Islanders often killed strangers, especially those who were not given any introduction to the people (Wood, 1934). They were thought to come from the Spirit World and their bodies were cut up in pieces and thrown into the ocean or burned (p. 64). The Australian aborigines feel strangers have evil magic. They are killed promptly. A stranger could not possibly fit into their tight kinship structure. There would be no place for him (p. 66). The Kayan of Borneo are very careful that no stranger shall handle a young child or gaze upon it too closely (Webster, 1942). The more influential the stranger the more his contact is feared, for any such contact or notice may attract to the infant the unwelcome and probably injurious attentions of the spirits.

These and other examples seem to establish a connection between the kind of reactive disturbance which is set up in an insect, fish, bird, or animal community and that which occurs in primitive human communities when a variant or strange species member attracts the attention of the collective. The only difference seems to be in the cultural ideologies and beliefs that become attached to the reactivity of human collectives.

Not only do human communities impose cultural content (taboos, values, etc.) upon departures from accustomed patterns of interaction between person and environment, but they also have created cultural definitions for normality and abnormality. Once having created these peculiar, contrived, cultural niches, the individual who is caught within them is treated in a particular way with either respect or disrespect.

Ruth Benedict (1961) has contributed an excellent review of anthropology and the abnormal in which she points out that what is abnormal in one civilization is an ideal type in another. Normality is culturally defined and is a socially elaborated term for that segment of behavior which has great usage in the culture; and abnormality is a term for the segment of behavior that a particular civilization does not use. According to Benedict, we no longer make the mistake of deriving the morality of our own locality and decade directly from the inevitable constitutions of human nature. We recognize that morality differs in every society, and is a convenient term for socially approved habits. Normality is in the same order of things. It is that which society has approved. A normal action is one which falls well within the limits of expected behavior for a particular society.

Each society takes its culturally approved and institutionalized types of behavior and works this type out to its ultimate potentialities. Insofar as a civilization is well integrated and consistent within itself, it will tend to carry its initial impulse toward particular patterns of actions or human types to an elaborate extent; and from the point of view of any other culture those elaborations will include more and more extreme and aberrant traits. Each of these traits, in proportion as it reinforces the chosen behavior patterns of that culture, is normal for that particular culture. Those individuals to whom it is congenial are accorded prestige in that culture. In another society, the same traits would receive social contempt, disapproval, and scorn if that society is differently organized. On the other hand, those individuals whose characteristics are not congenial to the selected type of behavior in that particular community, are the deviants, no matter how valued their personality traits may be in a contrasted civilization (Benedict, 1934).

Benedict illustrates her thesis with various types of behavior treated as abnormal in our society. Cataleptic and trance phenomena are highly valued in some cultures. Among the Shasta, an Indian tribe of California, a woman who passed through certain trance experiences was accorded the greatest prestige in the community.

The same behavior would be hallucinatory and acute psychoses in our society. Benedict also says that a tendency toward homosexuality in our culture creates all sorts of problems for the individual so inclined, whereas in many cultures it is highly regarded (for example, in Plato's Republic it is presented as one of the major means to the good life). A particular type, whose excess may be aberrant in one civilization, becomes the mode for another. Those individuals who exemplify the most extreme tendencies of that trait are treated as the most favored. In the Kwakiutl tribe of the North Pacific Coast of North America, paranoid behavior became the ideal model for behavior of all its members. These behaviors were carried out to extreme forms. There was uncensored self-glorification and megalomania, with extreme ridicule of opponents which is hard to find outside the monologues of abnormals within our own society. All of existence was seen in terms of insult. Not only derogatory acts performed by a neighbor or enemy, but all accidental events, like a cut when one's axe slipped, or a ducking when one's canoe overturned, were seen as insults that had to be wiped out. Among the Kwakiutl it did not matter whether a relative had died in bed of a disease or at the hands of an enemy, in either case the death was an affront to be wiped out by the death of another person.

In a study by Fortune (1963) of the Dobu on an island of northwest Melanesia, we also view a paranoid culture. Their polite phrase at the acceptance of a gift was, "And if you now poison me, how shall I repay you this present?" In this society, where no one may work with another and no one may share with another, Fortune describes the individual who was regarded as crazy by all his fellow members. He was not one of the community members who periodically ran amok, frothing at the mouth, and attacking anyone he could reach with a knife. Such behavior was within the pale. But there was one man of sunny, kindly disposition who liked work and liked to be helpful. The compulsion was so strong that he could not repress it in favor of the opposite tendencies of his culture. Men and women never spoke of him without laughing; he was silly and simple, and definitely crazy.

Thomas Szasz (1974) compares mental illness to other concepts such as deities and witches to which many different types of human misfortune were attributed. Faris (1969) demonstrated how the behavioral content of a psychotic was shaped by his environment. Becker (1964) studies deviant groups and demonstrates how one learns to be a deviant and measures that deviants take to isolate themselves from the approved cultural types.

All of these reports and studies point up the cultural content of deviance or differences. They show how the culture selects out certain behaviors as normative and good, and how it relegates others to aberrant and bad. In all of these cases, the behavior and life style is referred to a particular cultural composite, and derives its positive or negative connotations from that particular cultural pattern.

This is not to say that there are not constitutional factors that mold certain individuals in directions contrary to the culturally idealized type. The amazing thing however, is that for the vast majority of individuals the strength of the culture and the learning process of cultural transmission are so powerful that they can overcome internal constitutional tendencies. The fact that some individuals differ in spite of the power of the culture is an indication that there are bound to be variants in any culture. The human problems that a society makes for itself lie in its inability to cooperate with the environment in finding an authentic niche for such individuality. It is quite possible that the very difference of these individuals is the creative heart of the culture and society. Their difference could prevent the culture from continuing down an evolutionary path of more and more bizarreness in the preferred behavioral type it is pursuing. Their difference could provide the range of flexibility required in organisms for continued sequential adaptation to external changes in the ecosystem.

In a way, the combination of culture-creating ability, and phyletic reaction of the collective against the threat of group or individual deviance, aberrance, or variance, have come together to pose a major dilemma for modern society. Collective disturbance in reaction to "strangeness" or "difference" has become a social liability. It militates against adaptive flexibility, against creative cultural evolution, against behavioral mutation and behavioral metamorphism. It is possible in the long run that such cultural inflexibility could become a factor of species extinction if allowed to run its course. Behavior regulating institutions in our country such as education, corrections, mental health, and social services may, by permanently fixing the cultural standards for behavior and increasing their ability to remediate behavioral departures, be the accelerating force for such consequences. It is very possible that a growing or evolving society will have to find alternatives to such institutional fixing of cultural standards. Professional reaction against "labeling" and "treatment" may be a healthy antidote to rigid behavior shaping and regulating patterns and a balance against the dangerous path we may be traveling. School systems, business and industry, clubs and associations all seem to be combining to demand a narrower and narrower definition of prescribed behavioral types for their purposes. Further, there seems to be increasing convergence of agreement among these institutions with respect to the prescribed type. This draws a very tight band around acceptable or useful behaviors and relegates to extrasystemic and extrasocial a greater and greater array of individual differences both within the population and the individual.

Ways of life that lie outside this narrow band are responded to by these social institutions as being less than useful, and even unacceptable. Considering the United States as a melting pot nation, there are many patterned ways of life of many distinctive groups which fall outside this band. Recent history, such as the period of Nazi Germany, points out the danger of such cultural exclusiveness and argues for a careful look at the direction a nation may be unwittingly taking in relegating so many types of behavior and ways of life to the nonuseful category.

The Nature of the Problem

From the ecological perspective, then, we see that the nature of the problem of emotional disturbance becomes more complex than the view of behavioral, psychodynamic, or psychophysical theory. It differs from these other emphases particularly in its view of the problem as being "community-bound" and the product of a particular collective in a particular environment or place at a particular time in history. While it is quite possible to change an individual child's relationship to his living environment by operating upon his psychic world-view, his physical and constitutional make-up, or his behavior, such modifications leave untouched the ecological traps and the alien, community-functionless niches that are actively recruiting new vulnerables.

Furthermore, once a child has been firmly isolated and settled into a category and a spurious, alien niche that goes with that category, it is very difficult to reverse the procedure and change the living-out process that exists between the child and the community or subcommunity. Mercer found that within a particular school system it was very difficult to change a child's status once the child had traversed the various stages toward his special category and special class niche. The same thing is true for the mentally ill child who has gone through the ecological traps leading to a state mental hospital, or the delinquent child who has gone through the ecological traps in the social and legal-correctional machinery to be adjudicated and incarcerated. This is particularly true if the child's life-circumstances maintain him in an active attachment to a collective area or membership body which itself carries social taint, such as a "slum section" or a "black race."

In general, then, the problem of emotional disturbance is one of a field of activity or engagement as much as it is the problem of an individual. To resolve the problem, changes have to be made in the field-pattern immediately surrounding the child and even to adjacent patterns surrounding the child. Furthermore, to a significant degree, it is setting-bound. The child-setting itself, and its ecological procedures (as much, or more than the child's own characteristics) process the child into the condition of disturbance. As suggested by Mercer's study, a child may be retarded only as long as he remains in one setting or system—the school—and, for all practical purposes, he is not retarded outside of that system unless that system exerts direct influence on other settings or systems surrounding the child.

Even within a particular setting, there is a progression of ecological traps, which must successively direct the child into the emotional disturbance niche. Escaping these traps at any point along the way may prevent being locked into the niche itself. As Mercer has demonstrated, these ecological traps can be analyzed and mapped independent of a particular child.

The meaning given to the child's unique circumstances within a collective, particularly if these circumstances are a variant of the modal circumstances, is a profound determinant of what happens to the child in that setting. If we look at Benedict's contention that normality is culturally defined and is a socially elaborated term for that segment of behavior that has great usage in the culture, and abnormality is a term for that segment that a particular society does not use, we begin to see how "meaning" emerges within a particular habitat or ecosystem. For example, a member of the Dobu tribe was laughed at and seen as crazy because of his sunny, kindly disposition and because he liked to work and liked to be helpful.

The collective may also react excessively when a "strange" or "different" meaning is attributed to a species member. (The foreign Brown rat, lacking the colony smell, stumbled into a rat colony of which he was not a member and threw the colony into a state of total disturbance.)

Both of these characteristics of the collective (attributing meaning and excessive reactivity), are part of the active ongoing maladaptation between environment and child which is wrapped up in the term emotional disturbance.

Implications

There are numerous implications of this analysis of emotional disturbance. Among these are a variety of action or intervention implications.

First, it is a matter of strategy as to where one wishes to tackle the problem. There is the matter of convincing the community of its stance toward and involvement in the problem of disturbance (and related child categories and niches). If the community accepts and understands the possibility of its own contribution to the problem, ecological changes in the larger environment are much more feasible. There should be no claim, however that such understanding will do away with reactivity to strangeness or variation in species members. If this is truly a constitutional characteristic of insect, animal, and human collectives, as suggested in this chapter, it will not be eliminated. However, for particular categorical human problems, such as emotional disturbance, ecosystems might be modified so that reaction is ameliorated, and spurious niches might be reduced in number or made more viable parts of community life by finding a use for them within the community.

Furthermore, if there is an understanding of the contribution of the community and subparts or settings and systems within the community, there will be more cooperation given and more sanction awarded for analyzing the ecological traps within particular child settings.

For a particular child, the general frame of reference of ecological theory provides a different tactic for approaching the problem. Instead of concentrating all effort on changing the child, an analysis can be made of the adaptation difficulty between the child and the various behavioral settings within which he is functioning. Above all, an effort will be made to pry him loose from a useless, isolated, spurious niche within the living environment, with its functionless occupations and its unsatisfying human exchanges, so that he can be placed in the viable mainstream of the setting or system. If he has not already been locked into such a spurious niche (i.e., a special class or training school, etc.) efforts could be made to steer him clear of the progression of ecological traps, which can be discovered in a system's analysis such as that conducted by Jane Mercer.

If one is interested in a population of children or a group of children, one studies the population in the larger community or a subcommunity and looks for the succession of ecological traps to which this population is particularly vulnerable (the in-migrant white or black or Mexican American, or Puerto Rican, etc.) within their own area of habitat (the Barrio, black-town, little Appalachia, etc.). For such children there are numerous ecological traps lurking in the "service systems" that abound in such communities. There are ecological traps leading into the legal-correctional apparatus, into the social-welfare apparatus, into the educational apparatus, and so on. An analysis of these habitats as an ecosystem would be particularly useful in identifying the processing channels that can place a child in contrived or socially useless niche categories such as mental illness, mental retardation, delinquency, etc. It then might be possible to map out tactics for extricating the child from the progressive stream of events leading to an isolated, spurious niche.

In general, the principle implication of the ecological point of view is that modification or change requires entry into the living circumstances of the child, into his daily activities and associations within specific habitats and settings. This living complex must be approached as a unit and an attempt made to modify the unit, no matter what specific tactic is employed.

Gestalt Interventions

One of the major pattern of interventions consonant with ecological theory is the gestalt approach. Gestalt interventions aim at pattern changes in organism and environment as a unified field. The name most clearly associated with the gestalt approach is Fritz Perls (1973). His interventions are aimed at the contact boundary, the balance point, between the individual and his environment:

The environment and the organism stand in a relationship of mutuality to one another. Neither is the victim of the other. (p. 18)

He says that in considering the person as both an individual and a social creature, neither can be held responsible for the ills of the other. Man, being born with a sense of social and psychological balance, is constantly moving to establish equilibrium between his personal needs and the demands of society. Perls feels that when these movements bring him into a severe conflict with society because he has, in his search for the contact boundary overshot the mark and impinged too much on society, we call him criminal. When his search for balance results in his drawing back further and further and in society impinging too heavily on him, we call him neurotic.

Problem comes about according to Perls, when the individual and the group (family, classroom, co-worker, or social networks, etc.) experience differing needs and when the individual is incapable of distinguishing which one is dominant.

He says that intervention into this disequilibrium should deal with the here and now—here (in the classroom, therapy room, interacting network, etc.) and now (the immediate experiences of the present moment). There is no attempt to refer back in time or a different place except as those "realities" affect the immediate field. Students as patients are not invited to "talk about" traumas, they are encouraged to reexperience them in the here and now. They are taught to *concentrate* on the fullness of all their experiences as they are being experienced. They are taught not to censor or interrupt their experience and to live through and finish up unfinished experiences. A child who has a headache as a way of interrupting his anger is taught to experience both the headache (the interruption) and the anger (that which is interrupted) so that he/she can go on and experience his or her anger and thus discharge it: "Through making our patients aware, in the here and now, by concentration, of what these interruptions are, and how these interruptions affect them, we can bring them to real integration" (p. 73).

The major problems of contact boundaries between individuals and environment are

1. *introjection* (accepting, whole hog, externally imposed ways of acting, feeling, and evaluating)
2. *projection* (attaching our own feelings, wishes, desires onto people or objects in the environment)
3. *confluence* (demanding likeness, and refusing to tolerate any differences), and
4. *retroflection* (doing to oneself what one would like to do to another).

The basic orientation is that the individual (patient, client, student) can deal adequately with life problems if he/she knows what they are and can bring all their abilities into the here and now to solve them.

Among existing books on the subject, Fagan and Shepherd (1970, 1973) present a compendium of Gestalt theory, techniques, and applications in two edited books, and Pursglove (1968), Dye (1975), Smith (1976), Latner (1973), Parsons (1975) offer further methods and techniques.

Consultation

As an ecological procedure, consultation focuses upon configurations or interdependent patterns such as a family, a classroom, a school building, a service system, etc. When consultation does focus upon the targeted individual, it includes the niche that the individual occupies in the interacting configuration, as much as the properties and actions of the occupying individual. How does this niche serve the configuration? What are the mutually dissatisfying adaptation functions of this niche (learning, behavior, emotions, etc.) in this particular place or setting? How can the pattern be changed?

Consultation is the introduction of a new or extraneous force (through a person or group) into existing eco-active pattern. That is, the consultant functions outside the constellation of niches (i.e., outside the table-of-organization positions) in the existing configuration. For this reason, the unit frequently reacts within its own members and toward the consultant, as a hive, nest, colony, or tribe responds to the stranger (alarm, disturbance, excitement, confusion, hostility, extrusion, etc.). Nevertheless, as a nicheless stranger, the consultant is able to create a disequilibrium, which is necessary to interrupt the ongoing pattern (of attitudes, behaviors, perceptions, etc.) revolving around deviance. This makes it possible to bring about a different pattern in the configuration (classroom, family, systems, and so forth).

In this period of interruption, the consultant can be a catalytic agent for creative alteration of the existing configural elements; can introduce other elements (such as ideas, attitudes, perceptions, behaviors, structures, content, procedures) for assimilation into the configuration; or can help the configuration (system, family, classroom, organizational unit) dissolve and reconstitute itself in new form(s) or constellations.

When focusing upon the targeted individual the goal is to release him or her from the undesirable, spurious, or functionless niche he/she is occupying (through various inputs such as those in the immediately preceding paragraph). For maximum effectiveness, the consultant also aims to eliminate or change the niche which this unit member had been occupying so that it will not automatically be filled by another (i.e., the scapegoat niche, the clown niche) or so that it can be more functional and positive for the occupying member and the total configuration.

Networks and Covenants

Another current intervention procedure of an ecological nature is network intervention and self-help covenants. These two ecological approaches have much in common. The network interventions are usually directed by professionals. The self-help covenants are directed primarily by the "deviant" populations themselves.

Various approaches to, and types of, networks are being developed in the areas of deviance. Gatti and Coleman (1976) were hired to supply mental health services to a school district and to work with families and family subsystems of "troubled" children. Their basic work schema includes four basic principles:

1. Involving the whole family in a concrete, problem solving style.
2. Establishing and maintaining continuing contact with people and institutions affecting the child's life outside the family. (The intervenors see themselves as part of the network.)
3. They teach the constituents of the network to perceive the child's problems as "human and comprehensible even though troubled."
4. Offer a "cultural perspective on problems in living" to reassure, promote a sense of choice, and insure flexibility.

Speck and Attneave (1971) have developed elaborate and carefully conceptualized procedures of social network intervention to "retribalize" natural networks around the problem of "schizophrenic families." They view the symptomatic condition called schizophrenia as part of a constellation of disturbed role relationships such as "symbiosis—mutual binds of love and hate— and other abnormalities" (p. xiv) that are usually part of a total family, their relatives, and their friends and neighbors. Speck has also begun to work with "normal" families and networks.

Their primary goal is to demystify family and network secrets and collusions, to strengthen healing bonds, and to disrupt pathological ones. They mobilize forty to fifty people in a network around a family and its most obviously troubled member. They develop the extended kinship and friends network and arrange three or four total group meetings over a period of several months. They gather the group together, usually in the target family's home, explain the situation, attempt to present a demystified concept of the problem, invite a sharing of similar feelings, problems, etc. from the group, divide the group into an inner circle and outer circle, and use a variety of group techniques to focus upon the problem as part of the larger culture. They organize committees to actively work with the targeted individual around his or her real life problems and with the family around their active involvement in these problems.

They report regularity in phases that the network goes through in their effort to:

> ... utilize the power of the assembled network rapidly to shake up a rigidified system in order to allow changes to occur that the members of the system, with increased knowledge and insight into their predicaments, would wish to occur—and for which they are responsible. (p. 7)

In addition to limited focused networks, there are more comprehensive, permanent types of healing network structures which are springing up across the nation. These are networks of people who are mutually committed to each other in physical, mental, social and spiritual covenants. Among the more established covenant networks are Alcoholics Anonymous, Synanon, and the Camphill followers. More recent covenant networks are the Delancy Street Foundation for exconvicts, and the units established by Jean Vanier for "retarded" and "disturbed" populations.

These covenant networks organize themselves as subsystems and subcultures within the larger society. Each covenant network presents to their members a total way of life oriented to mutual support, healing, and care. They join in buffering each other against unhealthy forces in the larger society and live out a mutual commitment to a shared pattern of values. They are strongly motivated to self-awareness and development and to effecting the growth of fellow covenant members. They encourage a group consciousness of being an interdependent part of a distinct, differentiated healing ecosystem. Each covenant group has its own growth and healing rituals and each has an articulated picture of both the ills of the larger social system and ways of protecting oneself from such influences.

Usually, these covenant networks develop a distinctive, coherent culture, with a distinctive vocabulary, distinctive ways of behaving, distinctive customs, and sometimes, even distinctive habitats, foods, and manner of dressing. In a sense, they are niche-creating groups who carve out alternative niches to the deviant ones into which society has directed them. Some encourage permanent niche differentiation from the larger society; others encourage gradual total assimilation into the larger society and its general niches.

Summary

In summary, the ecological point of view treats emotional disturbance as a comprehensive problem of ongoing adaptation between organism and environment, with any maladaptation being conceptualized as residing as much in the environmental activity upon the child as the child's activity upon the environment. The disturbance is a pattern of maladaptive interactions whose effects are being created and experienced by a composite collective involved in a particular web of associations, revolving around a collective node—the child. The endpoint of this maladaptation, as a pseudosolution to maladaptation, is the extrusion of the variant individual to whom the problem is imputed, into a useless or functionless niche that has been contrived by the community to isolate that individual from vital community commerce.

The interruption of maladaptation patterns usually involves ecosystem interventions, that is, interventions that aim at the contact point between individual and environment. These include Gestalt procedures, consultation, and networks and covenants.

References

ALCOHOLICS ANONYMOUS. *Twelve steps and twelve traditions*. New York: A. A. World Services, 1953.

ALVERDES, I. *Social life in the animal world*. New York: Harcourt, Brace, 1927.

ANDERSON, N. *The hobo*. Chicago, Ill.: University of Chicago Press, 1923.

BARKER, R. *Stream of behavior*. New York: Appleton-Century-Crofts, 1963.

BARKER, R. *Ecological psychology*. Stanford, Cal.: Stanford University Press, 1968.

BARKER, R. Wanted: An eco-behavioral science. In E. P. Willems & H. L. Rausch (Eds.), *Naturalistic viewpoints in psychological research*. New York: Holt, Rinehart & Winston, 1969.

BARKER, R., & SCHOGGEN, P. *Qualities of community life*. San Francisco: Jossey-Bass, 1973.

BECK, F. *Hobohemia*. Rindge, New Hampshire: R. R. Smith, 1956.

BECKER, H. *The other side: Perspectives on deviance*. New York: Free Press, 1964.

BENEDICT, R. *Patterns of culture*. Boston: Houghton Mifflin, 1961.

BOTTS, E. *Family and social networks*. London: Tavistock Publications, 1971.

CALHOUN, J. B. Population density and social pathology. *Scientific American*, 1962, *206*, 3-10.

CALHOUN, J. B. Ecological factors in the development of behavioral anomalies. *Comparative Psychopathology*. New York: Grune & Stratton, 1967.

CARPENTER, J. R. *An ecological glossary*. New York: Hafner, 1962.

CAVAN, R. S. *Suicide*. Chicago, Ill.: University of Chicago Press, 1928.

CHAPMAN, L. F., HINKEL, L. E. & WOLFF, H. G. Human ecology, disease and schizophrenia. *American Journal of Psychiatry*, 1960, *117*, 193-204.

CHAUVIN, R. *Animal societies from the bee to the gorilla*. Trans. G. Ordish. New York: Hill & Wang, 1968.

DRIVER, H. E. *Indians of North America*. Chicago, Ill.: University of Chicago Press, 1961.

DUBOS, R. *Man adapting*. New Haven, Conn.: Yale University Press, 1969.

DUBOS, R. The germ theory revisited. Lectures delivered March 18, 1953 at Cornell University Medical College, New York.

DUNCAN, O. D., & SCHNORE, L. F. Cultural, behavioral and ecological perspectives in the study of social organizations. *American Journal of Sociology*, 1959, *65*, 132-147.

DYE, A., & HACKNEY, H. *Gestalt approaches to counseling*. Boston, Mass.: Houghton Mifflin, 1975.

FAGAN, J., & SHEPHERD, I. L. *Gestalt therapy now*. Palo Alto, Calif.: Science & Behavior Books, 1970.

FAGAN, J., & SHEPHERD, I. L. (Eds.) *Life techniques in Gestalt therapy*. New York: Harper & Row, 1973.

FARIS, R. Cultural isolation and schizophrenic personality. In A. H. Buss & E. H. Buss, *Theories of schizophrenia*. New York: Atherton Press, 1969.

FARIS, R., & DUNHAM, H. *Mental disorders in urban areas: An ecological study of schizophrenia and other psychoses*. Chicago, Ill.: University of Chicago Press, 1965.

FORTUNE, R. *Sorcerers of Dobu*. London: Routledge & Kegan Paul, 1963.

FRIED, M. Social problems and psychopathology. In Urban America and the planning of mental health services. *Group for the Advancement of Psychiatry Symposium*, 1964, *10*, 403-446.

GATTI, F., & COLEMAN, C. Community network therapy. *American Journal of Orthopsychiatry*, 1976, *46*, 4.

GRACE, W. J., WOLF, S., & WOLFF, H. G. *The human colon: An experimental study based on direct observation of four fistulous subjects*. New York: Paul B. Hoeber, 1951.

GREEN, H. W. *Persons admitted to the Cleveland State Hospital, 1928-1937*. Cleveland, Ohio: Cleveland Health Council, 1939.

HAFNER, H., & REIMANN, H. Spatial distribution of mental disorders in Mannheim, 1965. In E. Hare & J. Wing (Eds.), *Psychiatric epidiomology*. London: Oxford Press, 1970.

HALEY, J. *Changing families: A family therapy reader*. New York: Grune & Stratton, 1971.

HARLOW, H., & HARLOW, M. The young monkey. *Readings in Psychology Today*. Delmar, Cal.: C. R. M. Books, 1969.

HAWLEY, A. H. *Human ecology*. New York: Ronald Press, 1950.

HELM, J. The ecological approach in anthropology. *American Journal of Sociology*, 1962, *67*, 630-639.

HOLLINGSHEAD, A. B., & REDLICH, F. C. *Social class and mental illness*. New York: John Wiley, 1958.

HYDE, R. W., & KINGSLEY, L. V. Studies in medical sociology I: The relation of mental disorders to the community socio-economic level. *New England Journal of Medicine*, 1944, *231*, 534-548.

JACO, E. *The social epidemiology of mental disorders*. New York: Russell Sage Foundation, 1960.

JENKINS, R. L., & BROWN, A. W. The geographical distribution of mental deficiency in the Chicago area. *Proceedings of the American Association for the Study of Mental Deficiency*, 1935, 291-307.

LANGNER, T. S., & MICHAEL, S. G. *Life stress and mental health: The midtown Manhattan study*, Vol. 2. New York: Free Press, 1963.

LATNER, J. *The gestalt therapy book*. New York: Julian Press, 1973.

LEVY, L., & ROWITZ, L. *The ecology of mental disorder*. New York: Behavioral Publications, 1973.

LORENZ, K. *On aggression*. New York: Bantam, 1967.

MARAIS, E. *The soul of the ape*. New York: Atheneum, 1969.

MEAD, M. (Ed.). *Cooperation and competition among primitive peoples*. Boston: Beacon Press, 1961.

MELLAND, F. *In witch-bound Africa: An account of the primitive Kaonde tribe and their beliefs*. London: Seeley Service, 1923.

MERCER, J. *Labeling the mentally retarded, clinical and social system perspectives on mental retardation*. Berkeley: University of California Press, 1973.

ODUM, E. *Ecology*. New York: Holt, Rinehart & Winston, 1963.

PARK, R., BURGESS, E., & McKENZIE, D. The spatial pattern and moral order. In *The City*. Chicago, Ill.: University of Chicago Press, 1925.

PARSONS, W. *Gestalt approaches to counseling*. New York: Holt, Rinehart & Winston, 1975.

PERLS, F. *The Gestalt approach and eyewitness to therapy*. New York: Bantam, 1976.

PETRAS, J. W., & CURTIS, J. E. Critique and comment: The current literature on social class and mental disease in America: Critique and bibliography. *Behavioral Science*, 1968, *13*, 383-397.

PIETZNER, C. *Aspects of creative education*. Aberdeen: Published for the Camphill Movement, Aberdeen University Press, 1966.

PURSGLOVE, P. *Recognition in Gestalt therapy*. New York: Funk & Wagnalls, 1968.

ROGERS, E. Man, ecology, and the control of disease. *Public Health Reports*, 1962, 77, 9.

SCHROEDER, C. Mental disorders in cities. *American Journal of Sociology*, 1942, *48*, 40-47.

SEARS, P. B. *Charles Darwin: The naturalist as a cultural force*. New York: Scribner's, 1950.

SELLS, S. B. Ecology and the science of psychology. *Multivariate Behavioral Research*, 1966, 131-44.

SHAW, C. R., & McKAY, H. D. Report on the causes of crime. National Commission on Law Observance and Enforcement. Washington, D.C.: U.S. Government Printing Office, 1931.

SIGERIST, H. E. The value of health to a city: Two lectures delivered in 1973 by Max von Pettenkofer. Baltimore, Md.: Johns Hopkins, 1941.

SMITH, E. *The growing edges of therapy.* New York: Bruner/Mazel, 1976.

SPECK, R., & ATTNEAVE, E. *Family networks: A new approach to family problems.* New York: Vintage Books, 1974.

SROLE, L., et al. *Mental health in the metropolis: The midtown Manhattan study,* Vol 1. New York: McGraw-Hill, 1962.

SZASZ, T. *The myth of mental illness.* New York: Harper & Row, 1974.

TINBERGEN, N. *Social behavior in animals.* London: Methuen, 1953.

TINBERGEN, N. *The hering gull's world: A study of the social behavior of birds.* New York: Basic Books, 1960.

TURNER, C. *Sane asylum.* San Francisco, Cal.: San Francisco Book Co., 1976.

VANIER, J. *Eruption to hope.* Toronto: Griffin House, 1971.

WEBSTER, H. *Taboo: A sociological study.* Stanford, Cal.: Stanford University Press, 1942.

WOOD, M. M. *The stranger: A study in social relationships.* New York: Columbia University Press, 1934.

YABLONSKY, L. *Synanon: The tunnel back.* Baltimore, Md.: Penguin Books, 1972.

CHAPTER NINE

Counter-Theoretical Views and Approaches

Introduction

The behavioral sciences such as psychology and education have taken great pains to divorce themselves from their historical origins in such "unscientific" concerns as metaphysics and philosophy. Professional prestige, status, and recognition in the human service professions are the rewards of scholarly endeavor. Research methodology is designed to be as "objective" as possible with all variables under close scrutiny, if not under direct control, by the investigator. The "scientific method" has been erected as a standard against which professional contributions are measured and judged as worthwhile or as dilatory. The theories developed to

This chapter was written by Spencer Gibbons, Assistant Professor, Graduate School of Education, Rutgers, The State University of New Jersey and Michael L. Tracy, Associate Professor, School of Education, Indiana University.

explain the phenomenon of emotional disturbance in children, like those identifying other psychological concepts, differ in content but share a common perspective in their attempts at explanation. All view their purpose as the formulation of law-like generalizations concerning behavior that transcends individual differences. They attempt to identify behavior patterns held in common by groups. These generalized relationships are then used for the purpose of prediction. Data are gathered, correlative inferences are made, and interventions are then formulated. Because of this common viewpoint and process, the various formal theories of emotional disturbance, as summarized by Rhodes and Tracy (1972), are much more congruent with each other than initial perusal might indicate. All view man as a creature of predictable behavior and one sometimes afflicted by a pathological state called "disturbance." The theories differ only in their identification of the etiology and the formulation of interventions.

Few theoreticians are so bold as to assert that their theory is the only explanation for behavior. Most acknowledge the legitimacy and even utility of explanations other than their own. The past two decades, however, have witnessed the emergence of a new perspective in the behavioral sciences that stands in basic disagreement with the "established" theories of psychology—not only in the respectably competitive areas of etiology and intervention, but also in the basic philosophy or view of man and his behavior that it represents.

This new phenomenon or movement has been given various titles: humanism, neo-humanism, humanistic psychology, counter-culture, radical therapy, counter-theory, and radical education, among others. Though the ideas, individuals and groups associated with these labels focus upon a wide variety of concerns and often disagree among themselves about methods of achieving change, all would seem to reject the concept that theory can be used as a predictor of human behavior. Instead of concentrating their energies upon "laws of behavior" for predictive purposes, most counter-theorists focus upon the existential experiences of each individual. They perceive each individual as continually bringing his/her own unique set of past experiences to bear upon an ever-changing setting with its own unique phenomenological and environmental characteristics.

Man and his behavior are studied by counter-theorists operating under a different value system than professionals have used in the past. Counter-theorists recognize the "hidden agendas" and biased results that are silent partners of "objective science." Hardison (1972) points out:

In spite of the trappings of objectivity in which we like to drape our psychological, educational, social and artistic theories, the knowledge they have to offer is always indeterminate in the sense of being relative to the values behind them. When we ask for objective solutions to social or artistic problems, we are asking for brain surgery with a monkey wrench. (p. xx)

Most writers of counter-theory would agree that diversity or variety in behavior is a desirable end rather than a contaminating variable. Man is studied as the unique creation with choice, rather than as Homo sapiens whose behavior is as reliably predicted as that of any other animal if all contingencies are identified. Behavior, in counter-theoretical terms, is studied, not to devise remediation or therapy for those perceived as a standard deviation from the mean, but rather for the purpose of promoting diversity, for "celebrating deviance," and for facilitating exercise of choice by each individual concerning his own behavior.

Given their differences in the content or goals for the behavioral sciences, the writers of counter-theory would also reject the process models of theory—i.e., deductive, predictive, and heuristic. Most would argue for a synthetic rather than an analytic approach to understanding behavior, a molar approach rather than a molecular one. The traditional logical-positivistic approach would be supplanted by the legitimization of phenomenological or subjective experience. Theories concerning emotional disturbance would no longer be limited by the bonds of a "scientific logic," which has never been shown to be applicable to human behavior. Behavioral interventions would be freed from the covert value system embodied in a process utilizing a "norm" as the final logical authority. Perhaps this trend could be characterized in an oversimplified manner by the statement that feelings and the senses— their role in perception and motivation—are becoming a great deal more valid in the behavioral sciences. Also apparent in the movement is the belief that a great deal of what is labeled as "emotional disturbance" may be an adaptive response to an unhealthy environment. Perhaps the social context, rather than the individual should be examined.

EVOLUTION OF COUNTER-THEORY

Reacting to the overwhelming and pervasive effect of institutions within our society, two radical movements are developing alternative means of dealing with the process of socialization and the phenomenon of deviance in children. Their efforts demonstrate a deep commitment to existential thought. The first of these groups are neohumanists (Goodman, 1960; Kohl, 1967; Perls, 1969) who seek to reform and redirect the professional child-servers to provide more appropriate services within the context of existing institutions. The second group rejects the concept of reform and redirection and seeks the destruction or radical reorganization of present institutions—a revolution in child service. This chapter will present primarily the views of the latter group, although both factions avow a common "radical thought."

Although the "writers of revolution" diverge in many directions, they share a common broad philosophical position based upon a mixture of Marxian insight into the development of man and an existential view of the alienation of individuals. Contrary to the position of most of behavioral science, existentialism sees time as a determinant of human behavior. Each man's experience is uniquely his own and cannot be separated from its context of time and setting (Greene, 1966). The existential goal of socialization is growth and adaptation through the optimal use of an individual's experience (Macquarrie, 1955).

The marriage of Marxism and existentialism in revolutionary thought may be seen as a reaction to contemporary political philosophy. However, the roots of the movement can be traced to the nineteenth century. Institutional functions in society arose to augment the Industrial Revolution. The concept of more efficient use of resources through the specialization of tasks is based on the well-articulated rational position of Kant (Wright, 1941; Turner, 1967). His deification of the human mind is seen as the core characteristic of the then emerging and now dominant middle class in Western culture. His assumption of total rationality denies the existences of solutions to problems outside the realm of logic. His concept of individual freedom frees man of obligation to their fellowman so long as they can logically justify their own behavior. A way of life characterized by rugged individualism, both economic and philosophic, ensured the maintenance and extension of a classed society and the colonial structure that supported it.

230

The idea that anything may be thought moral as long as it can be justified before the "bar of reason" led liberal-capitalist thinkers of the nineteenth century (Gilson, Langan & Maurer, 1962) to reject all institutional philosophy beyond the limits of their own bourgeois system. Man is morally bound to avoid influencing his fellow man and he is not responsible for the behavior of his fellow man. One man's losses are justifiably the gains of another. The exploitation "veiled in religious and political illusions" is replaced with an overt economic and political exploitation justified by individual freedom. The manufacturer replaces the feudal lord as slave-master; but the masses remain the slaves, alienated from the social and economic power base.

In response to the system of laissez faire rugged individualism, the Marxist philosophy of the classless state developed (Aptheker, 1965). The intent of this philosophy was to assure the lower classes of social justice. The classless state rejects the economic domination of one group by another. The dominant middle-class manufacturer is replaced by a representative of the workers who is accountable to them through the government. While this change does eliminate domination by a minority, it does nothing to avoid the alienation that the individual worker feels as a result of industrialization.

In summary, the individualistic laissez faire economic system supports the growth and development of an industrialized society. This type of society, however, allows evils to be perpetrated on the lower classes: (1) domination, and (2) alienation. The historical Marxist philosophy deals with the danger of domination but in its pure form ignores the evils of alienation.

Contemporary Marxist philosophy has been extended to deal with the issue of alienation of the worker. A blend of Marxist political thought and existential philosophy focuses on this problem (Odajnyk, 1965). The goal is the provision of a system of social justice in which the individual can assure himself of a personally satisfying existence. A major problem is the tendency for societal institutions to insulate the individual from himself. If the individual determines who he is on the basis of his membership in one or more institutional structures (e.g., student, doctor, factory worker), to that extent he becomes personally alienated. This process is complicated by the institutional tendency to become specialized and impersonal. It is this alienation caused by institutions in combination with the perceived domination of the masses by a "power elite" (the identity of whom varies with radical viewpoint) that pervades most of the writing identified as counter-theoretical.

The alienation process occurs in all societal institutions whether economic, political, religious, medical, or educational. In any industrialized society, whether capitalist or Marxist, institutions are set up that generate professional roles within themselves. People employed by these institutions no longer are addressed as persons but are recognized only by role (for example, Dr., Father, Judge). The professionals in these institutions have merged their own personal identification so completely with their role in the institution that they are no longer seen as accountable outside their institution. To maintain this autonomy, the professionals insulate themselves from those whom they serve by labeling them as clients or patients rather than as consumers of a service. By such labeling and through specialization, the professional roles insure the maintenance of the status quo. Both ascribed roles, that of professional and that of client, alienate the individuals who fill them. The roles artificially discourage opportunities for intimacy and personal identification. Thus, depersonalization and alienation allow the individual to project the responsibility for his own behavior onto the role, thus eliminating any personal accountability. This process is beautifully described by Jay Haley in his hilarious essay "The Art of Psychoanalysis" (Haley, 1969). Aside from creating numerous personal problems, this process recreates the pattern of domination that socialism sought to redress.

The educational institution has reflected these political and economic philosophies more than it has shaped them. The personal alienation that occurred as man's behavior fell more and more under the aegis of specialized institutions was compounded as the school emerged as a principal instrument of socialization. The school was made the mold from which emerged masses of students with "appropriate" skills. Furthermore, the process of education and teacher-pupil interactions were heavily tainted with evils of domination and alienation (Hickerson, 1966).

POINTS OF CONTENTION WITH CURRENT INSTITUTIONS

Counter-theory is a reaction to the growth and subsequent dehumanizing effect of service-oriented institutions that serve children. To understand the nature of counter-theory, its reactions and the alternatives it presents, it is necessary first to examine the character of the institutions it opposes.

Society has set up institutional systems to share the responsibility for socialization and dealing with deviance. These systems have been categorized by Rhodes and Gibbins (1972) as (1) legal, (2) medical, (3) educational, (4) social-welfare, and (5) religious. Each institution has a characteristic modus operandi, historically and philosophically congruent to the purpose of the institution. The methodology of the legal-correctional institution could be identified as coercion; the educational institution uses training; the medical institution, prescription; social-welfare settings, assistance; and the religious institution, exhortation. All these institutions direct a specific service at their target population and may be ranked in the order given from most to least controlling. It might be noted that in the past, services were limited to the polar modes of coercion and exhortation. Through evolution and revision, the intermediate modes of prescribing, training, and helping have been institutionalized. All changes, however, have merely established new points on the same continuum of service. Since institutional behavior is internally controlled and institutions are notoriously hard to change, the establishment of entirely new institutions to assume newly discovered tasks is inevitable.

Traditionally, the primary institutional response to deviance in behavior has been to exclude the individual from the mainstream of the population (Szasz, 1970; Trippe, 1966). Professional groups are appointed to set criteria for readmission. These criteria require that the deviant individual internalize societal norms before reentering the community. This process has been called into question. Several institutional studies (Cumming & Cumming, 1968; Goffman, 1961; Dunn, 1968) have shown the futility of procedures in which the criteria for exclusion and readmission are defined and in which programming efforts are based on these criteria.

Counter-theorists reject the entire continuum of institutional service (Pearl & Riessman, 1965; Szasz, 1970; Tracy, 1971). One of the objections is the nature of the helper-recipient contract. Such a contract is based on the assumption that the one who administers the service (teaching, therapy, rehabilitation, and so on) is superior to the recipient. Thus, the contract relegates the recipient of service to an inferior status. The power to prescribe and administer "treatment" is assumed by the professional. The recipient of the service is, in effect, powerless and actively contributes little to the therapeutic program. The implicit contract increases the helplessness and the dependency of the recipient (Haley, 1969)

A second objection of counter-theorists centers upon the self-perpetuation of societal institutions. In order to assure survival and growth of professional interests and institutions, self-perpetuating mechanisms stimulate the identification and labeling of increasing numbers of youngsters as deviant (Cohen, 1966; Matza, 1969; Mercer, 1970). Many children are repeatedly labeled by various institutions. This seemingly endless string of labels does nothing for the child, since few relevant program recommendations are made. But the labeling process is vital to the social institution, for without a target population the institution cannot maintain itself.

Counter-theory objects also to the concept of normality, a term without valid definition. There can be no standard, no "grand mean," of human behavior. Normality is a hypothetical construct. One can no more expect to find a "normal" person than find a tangible "ego" or "id." There are no natural divisions or discrete units of behavior. When such units are generated they are of a statistical nature, a method used for making generalizations about group characteristics rather than a diagnosis for an individual. The categorization, and the labels based on it, are usually arbitrary and therefore rather meaningless in attempting to deal with specific problems of an individual. The assumption of the existence of normality is more frightening, since it is the purpose of institutions to assimilate and readjust deviant behavior to this vague model.

The revolutionary position rejects the subordination of people to any categorization scheme. The validity of the scheme itself must be examined (Scheff, 1966; Szasz, 1970; Mercer, 1965, 1973). To the extent that individuals internalize labels, to the extent that they "put on," wear, and identify their inner selves with a set of categorical objectives given them by an exterior force, they are alienated. They tend to act in accordance with the labels, to play the appropriate roles. Children who are once labeled "disturbed" are treated as though they are disturbed. Such children have no recourse but to play the role of the disturbed. Thus these individuals are not seen as integrated, but rather as sets of labels acting out sets of roles that match the adjectives. The implications for the maintenance of racism through institutional structures is apparent (Kozol, 1967; Herndon, 1971; Thomas, 1971).

Alienation can be overcome only by a personalization of the individual, which revolutionary thought insists is impossible within an institutional structure. Thus, the philosophy of personalism is necessarily revolutionary in a society organized into institutions.

Counter-Theory and the Educational Institution

"Mass education is a child of a mechanical age. It grew up along with the production line. It reached maturity just at that historical moment when Western civilization had attained its final extreme of fragmentation and specialization, and had mastered the linear technique of stamping out products in the mass," writes Marshall McLuhan (1962). As McLuhan's analogy suggests, the educational institution bears a striking resemblance to the production line. It provides highly fragmented and specialized services. Its sanction by society to categorize children by means of a vast labeling process gives it a rationale for existence while expanding its powers. The child is described not as an integrated whole, but as a diverse set of labels and adjectives.

The implication of the analogy is that mass education has manufactured "mass men." Utilizing the concept of normality as a master die, it impresses, shapes, and manipulates children into a mold of standardized behavior. In such a system, there is little room for deviance.

Writers of counter-theory speak directly to educators in their criticism of the enforced child socialization patterns and the institution's role in human alienation. The writers have diverse backgrounds and opinions but agree in their condemnation of the status quo. In this chapter, no attempt was made to represent *all* viewpoints or perspectives which may fall under the ample umbrella of "counter-theory." Nor was there an attempt to seek reconciliation or agreement between writers where none exists. Instead, these writers sampled the writings of the counter-theorists, particularly those concerned with education. The underlying tenets of counter-theory are discussed and a general historical perspective given. Among those reviewed are writers who advocate the abolition of institutions and also those concerned with the "process" of education apart from the institutional structure. All disagree with some of the basic assumptions made by traditional educational institutions:

1. Counter-theorists oppose the notion that education provides a means of distributing a quantifiable set of knowledge or skills

which must be mastered by each successive generation (Bestor, 1955).

2. The traditional role of the active, knowledge-filled teacher dispensing predetermined gems of "truth" to passive or resistant students brings, from counter-theory, not only complaints of pedagogical irrelevance, but also shouts of slavery and exploitation (Silberman, 1970; Farber, 1969; Ayres, 1968; Wasserman, 1974).

3. The concept of literacy and the value system implied by it is questioned by the literature of counter-theory. Literacy is often viewed as a political device for propagandizing a population (Friere, 1972; Illich, 1971; Reimer, 1971; Levine & Havighurst, 1971).

4. Many writers are concerned with the dangers of all institutions and particularly the personal destruction brought about by the institution of the school. Some writers would abolish the institution; others would reform it. However, most attempt to describe innovative structures and processes which would lead to a new form of interpersonal "community" revolving about the educational process (Gartner, Greer, & Riesman, 1973).

Counter-Theory and Schooling

The school demonstrates all the evils of institutional structure. Counter-theorists object, first of all, to its basic assumption of the value of normality. It is the normalcy standard, the great American mean, that gives rise to many of the ills seen in American education. Without a mean, there can be no comparison of students and hence no deviation. The normality assumption provides an implicit sanction for racism (Crow, 1969; Kagan, 1969). If the institution can define a standard of performance and behavior, it can establish the differentness of ghetto behavior from that of the model. The deviance is then accounted for by genetic differentiation, or more explicitly, racial "inferiority" (Jensen, 1969).

The categorization scheme on which the school system is predicated demands the classification of children on the basis of various aspects of learning and behavior. One example is unit grading; children are assigned to a grade on the basis of age; then discrete units of learning and behavior are deemed appropriate for that grade. The expected performance at any level is arbitrary. No two children in the first grade could possibly share equivalent learning experiences. To expect all children to master the same quantum of knowledge in an arbitrary time interval is an absurdity. Yet this standardization persists.

The notion of successive "grades" is also based on the notion of a closed linear set of knowledge. It assumes that students cannot understand concept C until they have mastered concepts A and B. Knowledge, as presented by the school curriculum, is hierarchical in nature. Fourth graders cannot read a sixth grade book because, of course, they have not yet read the fifth grade text. A hierarchical body of knowledge provides another basis for sorting and classifying students that bears little resemblance to their learning experiences.

Children are also sorted on the basis of physical characteristics, intelligence, and behavior, thus fostering the growth of special education. Within classification schemes based on intelligence and behavior, there is a proliferation of categories. Counter-theorists reject the proliferation of categories and the concomitant fragmentation of the school in the resulting overspecialization. Such fragmentation and its resulting alienation may be seen, however, as only symptoms underlying a basic flaw within our educational model—the subservience of the individual to the institution. Individuals are seen as parts of an institutional structure rather than as valued and unique components of a dynamic group. This distinction of defining a group by summing its component individuals or defining individuals by their role in an institution is not simply an exercise in semantics. Most of us are too aware of the number of instances confronting us daily in which institutional needs take precedence over the needs of those served by the institution. Unionization, professionalization, and civil service protect the rights and serve the interests of the staff, but, unfortunately, those served by an institution have no union.

Educational Enterprise and the Concept of Community

The protests of counter-theorists, whether demand for the abolition of institutions or plans for modifying present structures, may be viewed as striving toward a redefinition of community, in the sense of a structure for interpersonal relationships. No longer content with the types of relationships created by present institutional forms, writers of counter-theory advocate that the educational institution be eliminated or changed at all levels to promote a different type of educational process involving radically different forms of interpersonal relationships. The definition of the community varies with different writers. Some are concerned with the role of education at a national and international level while others speak of the interaction of a teacher and a child. The following definition of community by the writers of this chapter may be used to describe the dimension along which the literature of counter-theory has been sampled: "Community is defined as the dynamic balance of mutually satisfactory reciprocal roles in a setting designed to achieve human potential." The reciprocal roles may involve several nations, or nations and the governed, or a teacher and a student. It is the process, content, and structure of the interaction that is the concern of counter-theorists.

The term community connotes interdependence with individual integrity and respect. Though cooperation and mutual benefit is stressed, most writers emphasize the importance of the individual and his right to authority over his existence. To all of these writers, the contemporary institution of the school is incompatible with the fostering of such community.

Community Within the Classroom

Most criticism of present classroom structure and process stems from the "achievement orientation" impressed on the school during the "Sputnik competition" of the 1950s. Governmental influence in the form of funds from the National Education Defense Act greatly emphasized the school's function as a producer of a product. Great emphasis was put upon academic study, competition, and glorification of intellect. The few nonacademic goals acknowledged by educators, such as physical and mental health, social learnings, and extracurricular interests, were labeled as "frills" and "luxuries" (Conant, 1961; Silberman, 1970). Labels also proliferated within the classroom. In order to accomplish the competitive and intellectual goals of the school, children were sorted and categorized as to their academic aptitude. Special education mushroomed, and classes for the educably retarded, socially maladjusted, emotionally disturbed, slow learners, and other such ambiguously derived categories became the "dumping grounds" for children falling from the academic sieve (Trippe, 1966; Dunn, 1968; Ginsburg, 1972).

This sudden preoccupation with academics facilitated and augmented the work of such cognitive psychologists as Bruner

(1966) and Piaget (1963). Their theories, however, were widely misunderstood and misused. Their constructs of stages of growth were used as rigid categorical systems into which children were pigeon-holed, and growth was seen as following a linear pattern. The concept of individual differences espoused by cognitive theorists was deemphasized in the drive to bring all children to a "golden mean" of behavior and performance. To defend this system and its goals, means were devised to segregate the children who for some reason could not keep up in the classroom. The segregated classrooms were then provided with a watered down curriculum to occupy the children until they could legally be excused from school. "Progressive" schools devised materials which, when presented to the deviant child, attempted to remediate his disability or reprogram the child to fit back into the system (McCarthy & McCarthy, 1969; Peter, 1965).

The ineffectiveness of such linear programming that provided no viable alternatives was demonstrated by a physicist, Jerrold Zacharias (1968), whose case for an individualized curriculum is based upon the scientifically oriented discovery method. Zacharias asserts that the child must be an active, inquiring participant in the acquisition of knowledge. The teacher's role, through the selection and presentation of materials, is to aid the child in his own unique method of discovering scientific facts, laws, and so forth. The academically oriented goal had not really changed for Zacharias, but the nondirective methodology reestablished the importance of individual differences, created fewer "deviants," and gave the child a more active role in the learning process.

The content process and goals of the curriculum are the targets of writers advocating the inclusion of materials and methods concerning affect or emotion in the school's program. Leonard's *Education and Ecstasy* (1968) and Jones's *Fantasy and Feeling in Education* (1968) are both attempts to rehumanize the curriculum. Jones (1968) attempted to demonstrate that education without affect produced a learner devoid of internal motivation. The introduction of affect into the curriculum by stressing interpersonal relations and by fostering a sense of interdependence or community is seen as facilitating the learning process (Greer & Rubinstein, 1972; Schultz, Heuchert, & Stampf, 1973; Glasser, 1969).

This "pseudo-dichotomy" between the cognitive and affective goals of the schools is related to the contention of Cleaver (1968) that black men are aware of their bodies and not their minds while the opposite holds true for white men. Cleaver's prescription for world community rests on the assumption that by coming together black and white may help one another to integrate mind and body into a fully functioning being.

A combination of the emphasis upon affective development, community, and upon the active, exploratory participation of the child in the learning process is found in current practices in British Infant and Junior School programs. Based upon the Plowden Report (Central Advisory Committee, 1967) and described in glowing terms by American Joseph Featherstone (1967), the *Infant School* idea has been a model for radical American "free schools," as well as for innovative programming in public schools (Graubard, 1972; Gross & Gross, 1969). The environment is structured around an activity center, in which children are free to explore many interests. Provision is made for many activities of an affective nature, such as drama, art, and music. Group problem-solving activities such as those of Randolph (1967) are introduced as a means of achieving a learning community. Unfortunately, the structure of these Infant Schools is not easily imposed upon the American public schools, since the British schools tend to serve children from the working class who are not expected to achieve academically. Few studies have adequately described the success of such schools in preparing children for higher education.

Nevertheless, new approaches to classrooms are proliferating, most in reaction to the absence of affective content or child participation in the traditional classroom. Two surveys of the American educational scene have been conducted in the recent past. Gross and Gross (1969) reviewed the "radical" education literature on the assumption that though radical, these approaches were the vanguard of more generalized change, Silberman (1970) conducted the most prestigious and comprehensive study to date of the American educational system and concluded that the concerns voiced by the educational "radicals" and the alternatives they offer are valid and viable. Silberman also supports the radical contention that contemporary schooling is devastating not only to the child labeled as deviant (where the adversive effects of the system are blatant and obvious), but also to the normal child, where damaging effects are not always so easily detected.

An anecdotal description of the futility and frustration of the traditional elementary classroom is given by Holt (1964) in his personal journal, *How Children Fail*. Both the content and the pedagogy of the classroom fall under attack as Holt illustrates mechanisms for insuring failure in the classroom. A follow-up effort, *How Children Learn* (Holt, 1969), is an attempt to go beyond criticism and offer alternatives for classroom practice as does William Glasser in *Schools without Failure* (1969). Most of these alternatives focus upon removing the artificial barriers separating adult and child in the learning situation. Holt places the burden of change upon the teacher, since most of his suggestions modify the teacher role. The teacher becomes more a designer of a learning setting rather than a dispenser of knowledge. However, few if any suggestions are offered for a "support system" to aid the teacher in the redefinition of role. Holt has had great insight into the problems of the learner, but unless the total system is prepared to support a change in approach, no lasting change will occur. Holt attacks this problem in his book, *Freedom and Beyond* (1972), suggesting that the current equation of education and schooling is destructive. This theme is continued within the context of the family as an institution in Holt's examination of the rights of children in *Escape From Childhood* (1974).

The relationship of teacher and pupil is also the interest of Jonathan Kozol (1967) in his vivid descriptions of life in an urban ghetto school. He illustrates the cleavage between the culture of the dominating white, middle-class faculty and administration and that of the dominated black and Puerto Rican students. The school is depicted as destroying the lives of children as it denigrates their ethnic culture. Ghetto children are labeled as inferior if they show resistance to being pressed into a middle-class mold. The documentation of the dehumanization that occurs when attempts are made by teachers to enculturate children is no more chilling than the descriptions of teacher alienation when an attempt is made to teach these children in a nontraditional manner. Kozol finds no alternative but to close the schools or permit the domination of children.

Kohl (1967) in his analysis of this dilemma offers a possible alternative in the establishment of community between teacher and children of disparate cultures. Kohl's experience in a ghetto school led him to create a classroom atmosphere that would be instructive both to teacher and to children, one in which both cultures meet and learn from one another. He details some of his proposed methodology in *Reading, How To* (1973) which, along with Holt's *What Do I Do Monday?* (1970), contributes practical activities to the theoretical orientation. Kohl, too, may be adjudged a failure since he eventually left the classroom. He did, however, make several significant contributions toward the goal of educational change. He demonstrated the futility of attempting to implement a valueless, "culture fair" curriculum in a school setting composed of persons from conflicting cultures.

In a classroom the values of the dominant culture are found in the organization of the building, the curriculum, and the roles assumed by participants. Kohl suggests that it is the adult's responsibility to explain the cultural biases to the children and to assist them in an almost "sociopathic" pseudoadaptation to them. Kohl builds his curriculum on this compromise, using the thesis of Margaret Mead (1970) that the responsibility of one generation to the next is to teach the process of growth, but not to dictate the content of it. Kohl attempts to implement the process of education using the content which children bring with them. Though this approach moves beyond traditional classroom goals, one must question the necessity for compromising conflicting value systems.

The creation of community, despite cultural differences, is portrayed by Hentoff (1966) in his description of Elliot Shapiro's attempt to humanize and revitalize a ghetto school. This account is different from most in that the change agent is a school administrator rather than a teacher. Administrators and teachers play a prominent role in Herb Grossman's account of a psychodynamically oriented classroom for incorrigibles, *Nine Rotten, Lousy Kids* (1972).

A change of pace occurs with James Herndon's books (Herndon, 1966; 1971) since he espouses no theoretically oriented criticism, nor does he delineate a viable alternative. Any generalities or conclusions must be those of the reader. The author describes the successes and failures of a teacher working in a system of which he thoroughly disapproves. Such books, though not often cited in reviews of the literature, may finally spark the changes needed to make classrooms into true communities.

Community in a School

The arguments of some writers are directed toward the general school complex or total curriculum rather than at specific classroom structure. Paul Goodman, for example, represents the extreme in criticism of the nature of the system. He is particularly concerned with issues relating to fundamental teacher-student relationships. His writings concentrate upon what is wrong with the system of schooling and few alternatives are offered (Goodman, 1964). Goodman admits that his criticisms demand changes that cannot be instituted, but defends his position as one of philosophy—the burden of change implementation not falling upon his shoulders.

A reorganization of the school and its curriculum is advocated by Fantini and Weinstein (1968). Falling under the rubric of "humanistic education," their program efforts attempt to achieve a proper balance in cognitive and affective education. Their emphasis is on the establishment of a curriculum relevant to student growth needs and one which offers choice and student participation. Their curriculum, designed to make real "contact" with the student at a basic need level, is based on an idea similar to that of Sylvia Ashton-Warner's "organic reading" approach (Ashton-Warner, 1967; 1972). The "contact curriculum" is designed to help the student answer the questions and fulfill the needs which he, the learner, feels most relevant. This curriculum involves the learner as an active participant in its formulation and execution.

Such learner participation is labeled as "subversive" to the system by Postman and Weingartner (1969), and they wholeheartedly support the concept. The critical condition in achieving change in the educational system, according to Postman and Weingartner, is that students have the responsibility for reform.

Recently, "reform community" schools have been established with the goal of implementing reform outside of the established school system. One of the most cited efforts was the Ann Arbor Community School (Ayres, 1968). The school was based upon the felt need for children to have an arena in which they could experiment and experience success and failure, without the usual adult-imposed consequences. Many cultures provide for such natural and spontaneous activity free from adult domination, but the American culture appears schizophrenic in its approach-avoidance attitude toward childhood freedom. (Friedenburg [1962] has documented the curious American phenomenon of the glorification and simultaneous elimination of adolescence.) The Ann Arbor Community School in attempting to meet this need for total freedom and total acceptance was eventually closed because of criticism involving the lack of consequences for behavior (Ayres, 1968). The Ann Arbor experience was only one of many, however, which are rapidly developing across the country as an alternative for people disenchanted with public schools.

A whole new literature has begun to develop as these radical schools set up communication linkages in the form of newsletters and journals. One of the foremost of such efforts is *This Magazine Is About Schools*, a quarterly offering articles by radical educators, poems and writings by children, antiwar, antiestablishment literature, and classified advertisements. It is the official organ of an experimental school in Toronto, a center for "new school" activity. The *New Schools Exchange* in California serves a similar function with a newsletter format and less emphasis upon articles.

"Freedom schools" (O'Gorman, 1970) have been established in storefronts in urban areas where ghetto children do not succeed in public schools. These schools report a great deal of success in teaching basic skills by accepting the value system of the recipient culture and formulating goals congruent with demands of that culture.

A children's community in a ghetto area is described by George Dennison (1969) in his account of the First Street School. Here are documented the triumphs and problems of the first year of a radical school as seen by the director-teacher. Composed of a few dedicated teachers and serving those children rejected as "unteachable" by the public and parochial schools, the First Street School utilized the principles of student participation in curriculum formulation and execution, extensive field trips, and an informal teacher-learner relationship. The account might well serve as a handbook for others initiating such an effort.

Expanding the Learning Community Beyond a School

The participation of children in curriculum design and the emphasis upon relevance to the learner, is leading radical educators more and more outside the walls of a school setting. Though "field trips" as an enrichment activity are found in even the most rigid and orthodox public school classroom, the concept of shared, firsthand learning "on location" as a major part of the curriculum is a keystone of most new school efforts. Some efforts seem to aim toward an almost apprenticeship approach to education.

The Philadelphia Public Schools had an experimental high school program which has been described as a model of open education on a secondary level (Greenberg & Roush, 1970). The

Parkway Program and its "school without walls" concept placed students in the community in various apprenticeship roles. Small group discussions were held in various storefronts and art and music were enjoyed at municipal institutions. This program attempted to utilize all aspects of the city that have something to offer students—whether it was a job skill or more academic or artistic pursuits. The Parkway School derived its name from the fact that most of its resources in the form of industry, business, and service institutions lay along the Philadelphia Parkway.

Though subjected to the criticisms of "tokenism" by radicals and to cries of irrelevance by some educators decrying visits to the Philadelphia Museum of Art by the illiterate, the effort may provide a glimpse of a new approach to secondary education. Perhaps the criticisms raised reflect the American culture's ambivalence in granting freedom and license on one hand while simultaneously constricting growth on the other. Critics seem to say that the students should have the freedom to choose, but only those things deemed "best for them."

Should education become the arena wherein cultural expectations and personal goals confront each other and are negotiated? Brazilian educator, Paulo Friere (1972) has answered in the affirmative, while the Brazilian government responded in the negative to his largely successful campaign to erase illiteracy by using the entire community as the learning setting. Friere argues that schools should take the teaching of values and the promotion of self-growth out of the philosophical realm and put them into a political one. To Friere, controlled schooling is an antieducational vehicle for the control of the masses. Dominant groups maintain control through the schooling process. This contention is in agreement with the statement by McLuhan that a minimal level of literacy is necessary before successful domination of tribal cultures is achieved (McLuhan, 1962). Friere believes that the educational establishment fosters the manipulation of the masses by an elite oligarchy through the content and process of its teaching. Literacy is purposely kept at animal levels for political purposes. Too ignorant or too educated a populace is dangerous to govern.

Planned illiteracy is only one method of control that the school imposes on those who pass through its doors. Its system of categorization for deviance, the content of its courses, and the relationship established between teacher and pupil all may have great political significance. The mandate for the use of these devices is given the school by the literate oligarchy. For this reason, Illich

(1971) maintains that all attempts at change within the educational system are doomed to being co-opted by the educational source of power. Illich insists that instead of attempting to achieve a more open or egalitarian educational system, one should, instead, "de-school" society. This can be achieved by removing all forms of institutionalized education. By removing the vestiges of imposed curriculum and values, the individual would then be freed to learn. The criteria for learning may then be shifted from a normative or parametric standard to one based upon the individual's achievement in terms of self-growth. The learning community expanded to the individual and his culture may then provide the primary goal as a celebration of awareness (Illich, 1971).

COUNTER-CULTURE ALTERNATIVES

The protests of the counter culture might be summarized as dealing with three types of recommendations:

1. A new advocacy for difference;
2. A search for new socialization patterns;
3. A reformation of the educational institution.

Advocacy for Difference

Marcuse (1964) has taken a position advocating deviance in the individual. He rejects tolerance of deviance, since "tolerance" implies that deviance is not a desirable thing, but a necessary evil. At present, tolerance of deviance is limited by characteristics established by the socializing institutions that see themselves as responsible for man's behavior. Each institution has its own definition of "correct" behavior and cannot tolerate behavior that is beyond its particular definition. For example, in some school systems, children who do not conform to the behavior norms are required to be removed from regular classrooms. Furthermore, each institution feels responsible for only a subset of behaviors that are limited by time parameters (a school's responsibility is only for the duration of the school day) or situational parameters (a hospital clinic is not responsible for aftercare).

Man's tolerance for difference is also limited by the nature of the socialization process itself. As Montesquieu points out, man most primitive is not in fact most desirable. As man takes on, in addition to his animal nature, the components of thinking and rationality, he becomes a more "purified being." Rousseau points out that when man enters into complex human relationships, the evils of society, specifically domination and alienation, get in the way of his function (Archer, 1964). Traditionally, man puts limits on his relationships in order that his ability to deal with difference is not taxed. Man usually imposes a qualitative limit; that is, he extrudes certain types of behavior and the persons who indulge in them. Deviants are categorized and excluded.

An alternative to "tolerance" of deviance is to advocate difference as a right of citizenship. This position is in direct conflict with institutional tolerance of deviance. As institutions develop, the right to individual difference becomes more obscure. Durkheim (1933) described the specialization that occurs as a result of the phenomenon of division of labor. It may be seen as a contract situation, in which the individual gives up certain rights and responsibilities when he participates in a representative democracy or in a mental health institution or in an education institution. The individual personally contributes to a form of institutional domination, and sets up the conditions leading to alienation.

On the other hand, the advocate for difference places the responsibility for behavior upon the individual. It is not possible to exclude an individual on the basis of his behavior. When a community of men becomes complex beyond its ability to advocate for difference, some criteria for exclusion becomes necessary. However, those individuals who advocate for difference do not support arbitrary qualitative exclusion of the individual. Instead, they suggest an egalitarian cut-off point, beyond which the size of the community is no longer viable. Rather than using a complicated rationale for excluding individuals, one then excludes a person because there is no room. Each basic human group consists of a limited number of individuals, all of whom are part of a mutual feedback system. Individual responsibility within the group is for providing behavioral feedback to one another. The call is for a community which, although limited in size, advocates for difference, one in which the only criterion for membership is humanity. Means of obtaining this type of society are now developing.

Alternative Socialization Patterns

The second component of counter culture is the search for an alternative means of socialization outside of the institutional setting. While some of these proposals seem to replace the existing institution with another one, such as substituting a day care center for home child rearing, many writers do indeed advocate the abolition of institutions. The school has come under particular attack as an outmoded form of socialization maintained to foster the domination of the masses by an intellectual and economic oligarchy. The institution of the church has probably been the site of the greatest such erosion (Cox, 1965) and the decline in influence of the home has been well documented (Mead, 1970). Counter-theorists maintain that these signs of institutional atrophy are not omens of ill fortune as usually purported, but rather are health signs of a society throwing off the yoke of institutional oppression for a new freedom for the individual. The way, however, is not an easy one. Often one risks even self-esteem in attempting assault upon institutions. One documentary of such a struggle, *Half the House* (Kohl, 1974), offers much in a realistic approach to change.

Reformation of the Educational Institution

The third component proposed by revolutionaries involves the reconstituting of the teaching-learning contract. The nature of the present teaching-learning contract delineates the entire responsibility for learning with the institution. The school system determines the substance and nature of that learning; the student is only a passive recipient of that learning. The student shares no responsibility for his/her learning, and hence, no accountability. If the learning fails, the institution can be blamed.

But counter-theorists hope to revise this contract such that both teacher and student share equal responsibility for the outcome. To achieve this, the student must be a full participant in the learning process. The student must be able to determine his or her own needs, interests, and resources and negotiate these with the system to produce an outcome for which he or she is fully accountable. The student shares equal partnership with the teacher in this contract. The teacher becomes a resource and facilitator in the learning process. The teacher can help students to determine their needs and resources, not determine them for them. This gives autonomy to both teacher and students. And it is the only way in which both students and teacher can act as truly free agents in a contract of mutual consent and responsibility.

This restructuring of the teacher-student contract has already begun in the newly found emphasis upon due process found in recent special education legislation and litigation. The 1976 Education of the Handicapped Act (PL 94-142) is very specific in giving the parents or child, where appropriate, authority in approving the individual educational plan. An appeal and hearing procedure is outlined for use by the parents if they are in disagreement with the representatives of the school.

This legislation would seem to speak to the core of the counter-theoretical concern that individuals become dominated by the institutions erected to serve them. Such laws are beginning to recognize that individuals should not be required to surrender constitutional rights such as equal protection and due process in order to be served by an institution.

In-roads for the rights of individuals are also being made within other institutions. There is a growing and exciting literature detailing the rediscovery of the individual within institutional structures as laws and judicial procedures reaffirm the worth of the individual in our mental health facilities (Ennis, 1972; President's Committee on Mental Retardation, 1975), in the judicial system itself (Tidyman, 1974), and in the schools (Kirp, Kuriloff, & Buss, 1975).

Some Final Thoughts

Philosophically, man's ultimate goal may be seen as self-actualization or realization of potential. This process involves, among other things, the establishment of a functional relationship between mind and mind, in the case of human relationships. In seeking to better explain and predict behavior, science has utilized various analytic techniques which have polarized, dichotomized, and molecularized behavior, but with the promise of "effective interventions" always just out of grasp.

No analytic attempt has been successful in developing really effective intervention procedures. The analytic process may advance scientific discovery, but it should not be used to generate models for the delivery of mental health services. While it leads to the development of diagnostic models, it generates few, if any, treatment models.

Analytic processes can prove frustrating to the behavioral scientist. The more information he uncovers, the more distant becomes the solution, because more variables and more problems are uncovered. Though most of the "professional" establishments have much to gain from the proliferation of variables and the resultant professional specialization, the outcome for delivery of services is disastrous.

Special education is a case in point. The diagnostic methodologies are extremely well developed, but few effective and proven treatment programs have been defined. Diagnostic categories continue to undergo a process mitosis. What were first "problem children" were divided into "retarded" and "disturbed" children. These are now divided into the *learning disabled* (subdivided into perceptually handicapped, learning disordered, brain-injured, and so forth), the *disadvantaged*, the *educationally handicapped*, ad infinitum.

Counter-theorists reject the analytic mode in generation of descriptive facts and intervention strategies. They describe mind-body unity instead of mind-body separation, not in the individual but in the culture. Delivery of services is an overriding concern, and synthetic processes are more appropriate conceptual modes. Service delivery is seen as a process wherein known configurations of resources are functionally combined. Counter-theorists seek new ways of rerelating such phenomena as mind and body, self and society, or biophysical and sociological conceptualizations of deviance.

The body of literature generated by counter-theorists about the mind (psyche or social self) and body (biologic, "natural" self) relationship is extensive. Instead of reducing each element into its component parts, attempts are made to relate these two basic elements holistically.

The quest for the reunified man takes many forms. All aspects of current culture are under scrutiny. If we listen, perhaps counter-theory, if not providing answers, will at least lead us to begin asking relevant questions. Perhaps counter-theory's greatest contribution can be a reordering of priorities and a renewed sense of awe at the endless varieties and forms of human behavior. Perhaps appreciation for differences can supplant our culture's current obsession with remediation and prescription.

References

Aptheker, H. (Ed.) *Marxism and alienation.* New York: Humanities Press, 1965.

Archer, R. L. (Ed.) *Jean-Jacques Rousseau: His educational theories,* selected from *Emile, Julie, and other writings*. Woodbury, New York: Barron's Educational Series, 1964.

ASHTON-WARNER, S. *Teacher*. New York: Simon & Schuster, 1967.

ASHTON-WARNER, S. *Spearpoint*. New York: Vintage, 1972.

AYRES, B. Travelling with children and travelling on. *This Magazine is About Schools*, 1968, *2*(4), 111-131.

BEREITER, C., & ENGELMAN, S. *Teaching disadvantaged children in the preschool*. Englewood Cliffs, N.J.: Prentice-Hall, 1968.

BESTOR, A. *Restoration of learning*. New York: Knopf, 1955.

BRUNER, J. *Studies in cognitive growth*. New York: John Wiley, 1966.

CENTRAL ADVISORY COUNCIL ON EDUCATION. *Children and their primary schools*. London: H.M.S.O., 1967.

CLEAVER, E. *Soul on ice*. New York: McGraw-Hill, 1968.

COHEN, A. *Deviance and social control*. Englewood Cliffs, N.J.: Prentice-Hall, 1966.

CONANT, J. *Slums and suburbs: A commentary on schools in the metropolitan area*. New York: McGraw-Hill, 1961.

COX, H. *Secular city*. New York: Macmillan, 1965.

CROW, J. Genetic theories and influences: Comments on the value of diversity. *Harvard Educational Review*, 1969, *39*, 301-309.

CUMMING, J., & CUMMING, E. On the stigma of mental illness. In S. Spitzer & N. Denizin, (Eds.), *The mental patient: Studies in the sociology of deviance*. New York: McGraw-Hill, 1968.

DENNISON, G. *The lives of children: The story of the First Street School*. New York: Random House, 1969.

DUNN, L. Special education for the mildly retarded—is much of it justifiable? *Exceptional Children*, 1968, *35*(1), 5-20.

DURKHEIM, E. *The division of labor in society*. (G. Simpson, trans.) Glencoe, Ill.: Free Press, 1933.

ENNIS, G. *Prisoners of psychiatry*. New York: Harcourt Brace Jovanovich, 1972.

FANTINI, M., & WEINSTEIN, G. *Disadvantaged: Challenge to education*. New York: Harper & Row, 1968.

FARBER, J. *Student as nigger*. New York: Contact, 1969.

FEATHERSTONE, J. The primary revolution in Britain. *The New Republic*, 1967, August 19, September 2, September 9.

FRIEDENBERG, E. *The vanishing adolescent*. New York: Dell, 1962.

FRIERE, P. *Pedagogy of the oppressed*. New York: Herter and Herter, 1972.

GARTNER, A., GREER, C., & RIESSMAN, F. (Eds.). *After deschooling, what?* New York: Harper & Row, 1973.

GILSON, E., LANGAN, T., & MAURER, A. *Recent philosophy: Hegel to the present*. New York: Random House, 1962.

GINSBURG, H. *The myth of the deprived child*. Englewood Cliffs, N.J.: Prentice-Hall, 1972.

GLASSER, W. *Schools without failure*. New York: Harper & Row, 1969.

GODDARD, H. *Juvenile delinquency*. New York: Dodd, Mead & Co., 1921.

GOFFMAN, E. *Asylums*. New York: Anchor Books, 1961.

GOODMAN, P. *Growing up absurd*. New York: Random House, 1960.

GOODMAN, P. *Compulsory miseducation: Community of scholars*. New York: Vintage, 1964.

GRAUBARD, A. *Free the Children: Radical reform and the free school movement*. New York: Random House, 1972.

GREENBERG, J., & ROUSH, R. A visit to the school without walls: Two impressions. *Phi Delta Kappan*, 1970, *51*, 480–484.

GREENE, N. H. *Jean Paul Sartre: The existentialist ethic*. Ann Arbor: The University of Michigan Press, 1966.

GREER, M., & RUBINSTEIN, B. *Will the real teacher please stand up? A primer in humanistic education*. Pacific Palisades, California: Goodyear Publishing, 1972.

GROSS, B., & GROSS, R. *Radical school reform*. New York: Simon & Schuster, 1969.

GROSSMAN, H. *Nine rotten, lousy kids*. New York: Holt, Rinehart & Winston, 1972.

HALEY, J. *The power tactics of Jesus Christ and other essays*. New York: Avon, 1969.

HARDISON, O. *Toward freedom and dignity*. Baltimore, Md.: Johns Hopkins University Press, 1972.

HENTOFF, N. *Our children are dying*. New York: Viking, 1966.

HERNDON, J. *Way it spozed to be*. New York: Simon & Schuster, 1966.

HERNDON, J. *How to survive in your native land*. New York: Simon & Schuster, 1971.

HICKERSON, N. *Education for alienation*. Englewood Cliffs, N.J.: Prentice-Hall, 1966.

HOLT, J. *How children fail*. New York: Pitman, 1964.

HOLT, J. *How children learn*. New York: Pitman, 1969.

HOLT, J. *What do I do Monday?* New York: Dutton, 1970.

HOLT, J. *Freedom and beyond*. New York: Dutton, 1972.

HOLT, J. *Escape from childhood*. New York: Ballantine, 1974.

ILLICH, I. *Deschooling society*. New York: Harper & Row, 1971.

JENSEN, A. How much can we boost IQ and scholastic achievement? *Harvard Educational Review*, 1969, *39*, 1-123.

JONES, R. *Fantasy and feeling in education*. New York: New York University Press, 1968.

KAGAN, J. Inadequate evidence and illogical conclusions. *Harvard Educational Review*, 1969, *39*, 274-277.

KIRP, D., KURILOFF, P., & BUSS, W. Legal mandates and organizational change. In N. Hobbs (Ed.), *Issues in the classification of children*, Vol. 2. San Francisco: Jossey-Bass, 1975.

KOHL, H. *Thirty-six children*. New York: World Publications, 1967.

KOHL, H. *Reading, how to*. New York: Dutton, 1973.

KOHL, H. *Half the house*. New York: Dutton, 1974.

KOZOL, H. *Death at an early age: The destruction of the hearts and minds of Negro children in the Boston Public Schools*. New York: Houghton Mifflin, 1967.

KOZOL, J. *The night is dark and I am far from home*. New York: Houghton Mifflin, 1975.

LEONARD, G. B. *Education and ecstasy*. New York: Dell, 1968.

LEVINE, D., & HAVIGHURST, R. *Farewell to schools?* Worthington, Ohio: Charles Jones Publishing, 1971.

MACQUARRIE, J. *An existentialist theology: A comparison of Heidegger and Bultmann*. New York: Macmillan, 1955.

MARCUSE, H. *One dimensional man*. Boston: Beacon, 1964.

MATZA, D. *Becoming a deviant*. Englewood Cliffs, N.J.: Prentice-Hall, 1969.

MCCARTHY, J. J., & MCCARTHY, J. F. *Learning disabilities*. New York: Allyn & Bacon, 1969.

MCLUHAN, H. M. *The Gutenberg galaxy: The making of typographic man*. Toronto: University of Toronto Press, 1962.

MEAD, M. *Culture and commitment.* New York: Natural History, 1970.

MERCER, J. Social system perspective and clinical perspective: Frames of reference for understanding career patterns of persons labeled as mentally retarded. *Social Problems,* 1965, *13*, 18-34.

MERCER, J. Sociological perspectives on mild mental retardation. In H. Haywood, *Social-cultural aspects of retardation.* New York: Appleton-Century-Crofts, 1970.

MERCER, J. *Labeling the mentally retarded.* Berkeley: University of California Press, 1973.

ODAJNYK, W. *Marxism and existentialism.* Garden City, N.Y.: Doubleday, 1965.

O'GORMAN, N. *The storefront.* New York: Harper & Row, 1970.

PEARL, A., & REISSMAN, F. *New careers for the poor.* Glencoe, Ill.: Free Press, 1965.

PERLS, F. S. *Ego, hunger and aggression: The beginning of Gestalt therapy.* New York: Vintage, 1969.

PETER, L. J. *Prescriptive teaching.* New York: McGraw-Hill, 1965.

PIAGET, J. *Origins of intelligence in children.* New York: Norton, 1963.

POSTMAN, N., & WEINGARTNER, C. *Teaching as a subversive activity.* New York: Dell, 1969.

PRESIDENT'S COMMITTEE ON MENTAL RETARDATION, *Mental Retardation and the Law.* Washington, D.C.: U.S. Department of Health, Education and Welfare, September, 1975.

RANDOLPH, N. *Self-enhancing education.* Palo Alto, Cal.: Sanford Press, 1967.

REIMER, E. *School is dead.* Garden City, N.Y.: Doubleday, 1971.

RHODES, W. C., & GIBBINS, S. Community programming for the behaviorally deviant child. In H. Quay and G. Weary, *Psychopathological disorders in children.* New York: John Wiley, 1972.

RHODES, W., & TRACY, M. (Eds.). *A study of child variance. Volume I: Conceptual models.* Ann Arbor: University of Michigan Press, 1972.

SCHEFF, T. *Being mentally ill: A sociological theory.* Chicago, Ill.: Aldine, 1966.

SCHULTZ, E., HEUCHERT, C., & STAMPF, S. *Pain and joy in school.* Champaign, Ill.: Research Press, 1973.

SILBERMAN, C. E. *Crisis in the classroom.* New York: Random House, 1970.

SZASZ, T. *The manufacture of madness.* New York: Harper & Row, 1970.

THOMAS, C. Child advocacy: A model for social facilitation. In J. Cohen, *Confrontation and change.* Proceedings of the Second Annual Spring Conference, Institute for the Study of Mental Retardation and Related Disabilities, Ann Arbor, Michigan, 1971.

TIDYMAN, E. *Dummy.* New York: Bantam, 1974.

TRACY, M. L. Designing a community advocacy program. In J. Cohen, *Confrontation and change.* Proceedings of the Second Annual Spring Conference, Institute for the Study of Mental Retardation and Related Disabilities, Ann Arbor, Michigan, 1971.

TRIPPE, M. G. Stigma and schooling. *High School Journal,* 1966, *49,* 241-247.

TURNER, M. B. *Philosophy and the science of behavior.* New York: Appleton-Century-Crofts, 1967.

WASSERMAN, M. (Ed.) *Demystifying school.* New York: Praeger, 1974.

WRIGHT, W. K. *A history of modern philosophy.* New York: Macmillan, 1941.

ZACHARIAS, J. A portmanteau proposal. Paper given to Tri-University Project in Elementary Education, New Orleans, February 1-3, 1968 (mimeo).

Existential Views and Approaches

Many existential thinkers (e.g., Rank, 1941, 1945; Becker, 1973; Foucault, 1973, 1975; Zweig, 1970), in order to grasp deviance, move to the phenomenological ground. It is in the cultural experience of "normalcy" that certain existential states are authenticated and inauthenticated. Ruth Benedict's phenomenological studies of culture (1961) were an existential view of state-experiences of cultures. She showed that there are common existential states across cultures, but that these states are experienced in different ways in different cultures. Although they are common ways of being in the world, they are experienced differently in different cultures. That which is experienced as authentic in one culture may be experienced as inauthentic in another. The ground of existence is experience. Therefore, all of these states are experienced by individuals participating in the culture. It is *how* they are experienced that gives the existence meaning. Any state can be experienced as either authentic or inauthentic and, therefore, allowed *to be or not to be* in the particular world inhabited in common by a particular group.

From the point of view of the above writers, our normalcy is a general neurosis taught to civilized man to protect him from devastating realizations about himself. Once learned, he uses this neurosis to conceal from himself his own state of human frailty. He uses it to conceal from himself the limits of his individual mental apparatus, the relative stupidity that cannot outwit the vicissitudes of life that overtake all of us, such as the loss of social respect, loss of job, loss of love, loss of money, of health, of physical wholeness, of our very life. He uses the reified abstract "normality" to conceal from himself his own individual madness, his general irrationality, the psychoses revealed in his night dreams and his day dreams, his paranoia toward his love, toward his neighbor, toward his boss, the secret perversions down in the recesses of his mind that he savors but quakes that they may be disclosed. He uses the public myth of normality to conceal from himself his own disabilities, those crippled parts of his body or his psyche that we all possess, but do not acknowledge to ourselves or others. Normality is a modern totem through which we claim kinship with the mythically unblemished and invincible ones, and cover from ourselves our own vulnerability in a world that is not ours and which will go on without us after we are gone. It makes us feel safe.

In sum, normality is a mass cultural neurosis contracted by individuals with group support to conceal the knowledge of their mental and physical limitations, their private madness, and their personal disabilities. It is a shared illusion, taught by the culture and maintained by means of a set of hiding places into which each individual burrows to screen himself from view. As long as the individual presents these niches as himself, he is relatively safe from disclosure. As long as his identity is confused with his work, family, church, neighborhood, reference group, etc., he will not have to face his individuality and his relative helplessness, nor will we have to face him or ourselves as individuals. He will not have to face the inadequacy of the group to shield him, protect him, or console him.

There is unspoken agreement, a folklore, if you will, which says that this assumed identity is normality. As long as everyone pretends they cannot see through to the individual, these outer shells work as an adequate cover. Let us conspire together. You do not catch a glimpse of me, and I do not catch a glimpse of you. Let us agree that we will not look very carefully behind the screens. Pretend they do not let us see who the other is; and in this way we will not have to face the mental limitations, madness, and disabilities that make each of us so vulnerable to the world. We will not have to face our own aloneness and defenselessness and can bury ourselves in the protective cover of the continuing herd. This is our normality.

Anyone, who, because of his own natural exigencies, stands out behind these screens, becomes *it*, the one observed, the different one. This can be a simple man, who fails to don his social masks; or the anguished man who feels suffocated and rips off the masks; or the jaded, playful man, who drops his mask sardonically and raises a finger to the conspiratorial world—these are the ones we must tag quickly. We've got to rush them back into the game, or push them far away from us so we cannot see they are not wearing masks. We must strive with might and main and all the social resources at our disposal to get them into job, school, church, family—all those covering places we use ourselves—or we may look into the mirror of their faces and reveal ourselves. For, when our vulnerability is starkly revealed, we face stupidity, madness, and disability.

The Modern Ship of Fools

Becker in his final, recent Pulitzer-winning book *Denial of Death*, written when he was dying, declared:

We can say that the essence of normality is the refusal of reality. Or, putting it another way, normality is neurosis and vice-versa. We call a man "neurotic" when his lie begins to show damaging effects on him or on people around him. (p. 178)

Essentially, what Becker is saying is that the person or group, who categorizes himself or themselves as normal, are not aware of their lie. He agrees with Otto Rank that what we call neurosis represents the point at which a person begins to realize that his "normality" is an illusion, and, in coming to that realization, this insight causes so much anguish that he acts, thinks, and relates in ways that begin to show damaging effects on him and others. Michael Foucault quotes Pascal in saying, "Men are so necessarily mad, that not to be mad is another form of madness" (p. ix). Foucault also quotes Dostoevsky, as saying, in his *Diary of a Writer*, "It is not by confining one's neighbor that one is convinced of his own sanity" (p. ix).

Foucault's book points out that madness bursts upon the landscape of Western civilization at the end of the Middle Ages, after the middle of the fifteenth century, and that this classic event coincided with the receding of leprosy in that area of the world. Whereas in the first half of the fifteenth century the mask of death was the macabre motif of literature, art, science, and iconography, the latter half of the fifteenth century saw madness sweep like wildfire across the literary, scientific, artistic, and iconographic imaginations of Western civilization. In that brief century the obsession with death gave way to a civilization-wide neurosis, or morbid preoccupation with madness.

The emptied Lazar houses, the leper houses, suddenly were filled with madmen and madwomen; colonies of lepers banished to the spaces outside the city gates gave way to the ascendancy of images of the mad; and the *Ship of Fools*, pictured so vividly in the literature, iconography, and art of the classic age, was reflected in the actual ships upon which fools were set adrift on waterways that connected European towns. Although both crew and passengers were called fools or madmen, the inhabitants of these floating exiles actually included thieves, pestilence carriers, debauchers, and others who lacked a functional place in the communities out of which they had been driven. All were included in the magic ambience of madness, encircled by the "normal" paranoia of the closely knit communities that could not incorporate these "individuals" whose lives were solitary and unfitted to the "ideal" order of feudalism and townism.

According to Paul Zweig, in his study of subversive individualism, *The Heresy of Self Love* (1970), during that period in history

The individual was by nature a suspicious character—the nuances exist in some uses of the French word, "individu". He was banished into exile, which was even thought to be a spiritual death, for life without a prepared function was an absurdity. Madmen, lepers, thieves were made to wander from town to town; or, as on the nefs des fous (Ships of Fools) were floated aimlessly down rivers, belonging to no place or people! (p. 66)

Zweig feels that during this era the rights of community had come to be inviolable. The community formed an organic whole in which the lowest niches of rank and precedence were integrally linked to the highest and most auspicious niches. Anyone who fell outside of this knitted unity was, by nature, without a place in the whole, and, therefore, located in the placeless space of the ships of fools.

According to Foucault, until the end of the fifteenth century, man broke through his illusion of immortality and invulnerability only in the icons of pestilence and war, whose hidden referent was death. He distanced his own vulnerability and mortality through abstract references to death—in statues, in paintings, in literature, and even in more concrete, but still distancing mechanisms, the exile structures of the Lazar house. As an individual, he defended himself against death by picturing death as a threatening potential, rather than an imminent reality. However, by the end of the fifteenth century, both outer and inner events took away the haunting imminence of death, which had been represented in the scourge of leprosy. Now that the threat of immediate death had receded, he had to create a new motif in which to pour his terror, his existential anxiety. This motif, madness or Man's folly, rather than man's death, became the scapula that warded off the evils that befell everyone. He could bear the intransigencies of life by epitomizing them as folly and by going a step beyond his literary and artistic representation of these truths about himself. He gave them flesh—another man's flesh—the follies of the "individu." He then cast this flesh adrift on the nefs des fous.

Man could overcome his folly—those mad, meaningless things that happened to him from outside or inside—by acts of reason, by rationality. If he was smart enough, if he was rational enough, he could be safe. The live, fleshed representations of folly out there kept reminding and warning him to be sharp and alert, or else he would also be shipped out on nefs des fous.

Before the middle of the fifteenth century and a little beyond, it was, "look alive lest you be dead." After the fifteenth century it was, "look alive lest you fall into folly." That flesh out there, on those ships, beyond those walls, that is madness. It doesn't dwell within. It is neither within me, nor around me, in my functional spaces. Instead it dwells out there, outside of me, in those arid, functionless spaces which we—the scared "us"—have relegated to them—the spoiled "other," brought down by fate, and now, beyond the pale. Those are the unknitted ones, the ones without a place. They carry my burden for me, drifting off and away, taking it with them.

There was, nevertheless, a double allegiance in the "us," the citizens of the banishing towns. That part of them buried deep beneath the life of their differences from the fools was the hidden identity with the plight of fools. In the dim recesses of their being, those who continued to exist within the sacred circle of community, were, beyond their mask or reason, resonating to their banished counterparts.

According to Zweig, these exiled "individuals" continued to exercise a strange fascination for those they left behind.

Like *les socières*, they were thought to converse with the suppressed pagan gods, who had a great though underground influence on the people, as Michelet has pointed out. . . . But more than that, the solitaries and the "fools," because of their very indigence, recalled the prestigious image of Christ, the great exile. (p. 66)

And so, the fools not only mediated between the non-fools and the suppressed pagan gods, but also between those still fitted tight and safe within community and the Christian God-figures. The rejected individuals were somehow equated with the self-chosen anchorites, the desert saints of that time who also dwelled outside community, outside the town walls, and without institutional ties. Zweig points out that these desert saints were revered by the people because of their extreme asceticism and their rejection of all social bonds, and because they scorned the institutional church, which the people had come to see as their oppressor.

This gesture of the fifteenth-century Western communities, whereby the town vomited out of itself the individuals it construed as alien, indigestible, or spoiled matter, thereby purifying and saving itself, is certainly not a unique psychic phenomenon in the regularities of communities. Nor is the schizophrenic attitude of alienation-dissociation, of reverence-terror, displayed toward the extruded symbols, a unique collective response. The public expulsion of evil in the form of a human proxy is a psychological principle of community functioning. The proxy is always simultaneously maligned and worshiped as the carrier of the evilness and divinity of the community.

Scapegoating

In one of the great books of all times, Sir James Frazier's *Golden Bough*, the writer says:

In the foregoing chapter the primitive principle of the transference of ills to another person, animal, or thing was explained and illustrated. But similar means have been adopted to free a whole community from diverse evils that afflict it. Such attempts to dismiss at once the accumulated sorrows of a people are by no means rare or exceptional; on the contrary they have been made in many lands, and from being occasional they tend to become periodic and annual. (p. 633)

Frazier says that it requires some effort on our part to realize the frame of mind that prompts these attempts. He either did not know about, or did not make the connections between the more ancient examples that he presents of collective transference of diverse collective ills to another person and the phenomenon of nefs des fous at the end of the Middle Ages. He does document the universality of the community process very thoroughly by showing that in all parts of the world and all forms of culture the phenomenon has existed. The public expulsion of evil is a pattern of many colors, many threads, but always the same pattern. The evils expelled are disease, misfortune, affliction, the breaking of taboos, and threats of all kinds, real or imagined.

In fact, the very symbol of water and ships represented in the nefs des fous is universal. Frazier reports, "The vehicle which conveys the demons may be of various kinds. The common one is a little ship or boat."

In the East Indian Islands of Timor-laut a small boat containing the image of a man and provisioned for a long voyage is allowed to drift away with wind and tide. As it is being launched the people chant: "O sickness, go away from here; turn back; what do you do here in this poor land?" (p. 453).

On the island of Ceram, when a whole village suffers from sickness a small ship is constructed and filled with foods, tobacco, etc.; and when it is launched, a man calls out to the sicknesses, "O all ye sicknesses, ye small poxes, agues, measles, etc., who have visited us so long and wasted us so sorely, but who now cease to plague us, we have made a ship ready for you," etc. He then tells the sickness to sail away to another land far from here.

Often the vehicle that carries away the collected demons or ills of the whole community is an animal or scapegoat. As Frazier documents over and over again, the scapegoat upon whom the sins of the people are periodically laid may also be a human being. Here are a few examples. At Onitsha on the Niger, two human beings were sacrificed annually to take away the sins of the land. Everyone who had, during that year, grossly sinned, such as incendiarism, theft, adultery, witch-craft, etc., were taxed. This money was used to buy two sickly persons "to be offered as a sacrifice for all the abominable crimes—one for the land and one for the river" (p. 650). In spite of the vigilance of the British government, the same practice was secretly carried out by many tribes in the delta of the Niger. Among the Yoruba of West Africa, a sacrificial victim was chosen from a town or city to be sacrificed for the well-being of his government. The people would rush out of their houses to touch him and transfer onto him their sin, guilt, trouble and death (p. 660). In Siam it was the custom on one day of the year to select a woman who was physically broken down by debauchery, carry her through the streets, where the populace pelted her with mud and dirt, and then she was thrown on a dunghill outside the ramparts of the city.

Frazier gives numerous examples of this practice. To bring the ritual closer to home, the witch fever that wracked the New England towns in the eighteenth century had many elements of these phenomena. As a matter of fact, one of the ways in which towns in colonial America rid themselves of the dependent insane was by transporting these undesirables to a distant town at night. The practice of "warning out" strangers to a settlement was quite common.

It does seem strange that these practices, so reminiscent of the nefs des fous, should be carried over into America. According to our own mythological, or true history, the whole United States was founded as a vast "Ship of Fools," a newly discovered open territory into which Europe and Russia could empty out the recalcitrants and undesirables that they could not digest. We were founded as a nation of misfits, recalcitrants, or rebels, depending upon how you want to look at it. A large portion of our forefathers, according to popular conception, were driven out, or opted out, of communities in the old world. From this point of view, we built a nation upon deviants or abnormals, people who had been without a niche, or who had occupied uncomfortable niches, in their sending community.

Nevertheless, what seemed to occur, and apparently what always occurs in the inevitable tension between individual and community, is that when the spaces were filled and people regularized their commerce, their relations, and their practices, a communal illusion began to assert itself, the illusion of "we" and "they." The "we" was not of "them." They were different from "us."

As late as 1921, as we saw in the chapter on psychohistorical views, H. H. Goddard, a famous psychologist, warned America against differences.

There are two million people in the United States who, because of their weak minds or their diseased minds, are making our country a dangerous place to live in. The two million is increasing both by heredity and training. We are breeding defectives, we are making criminals. (p. iv)

Today, we do not talk about weak minds and diseased minds. Instead we talk about mental retardation and mental illness; we talk about "abnormality." We have built vast scientific fortifications as prevention and protection against "abnormality." Certainly much of what has been done is out of compassion. We do have strong elements of compassion in all of our research and service delivery campaigns. But what else might motivate these vast public efforts, and what sort of eco-static process are we professionals engaged in? Where does the discovery of new disabilities in our populations end? In our diagnosing and healing role, what sort of symbol do we represent to the public? As a matter of fact, who is that nebulous public, as distinguished from our clients? Is it the great army of "normals," that faceless, indistinguishable mass?

If we listen to Ernest Becker's voice from his new made grave, "normality" is an illusion, it is a vast identification myth, a false abstraction that binds all those who claim kinship with "normality" into a passenger list for the modern nefs des fous. The need to be normal is so great that one almost willingly adopts the group self-delusions that are erected to hold death at bay, to transfer to a few others our own helplessness, our disability in face of universal odds, our own craziness that caused us to design concentration camps, nuclear weaponry, body-counts, or the more simple and individual craziness of our personal night dreams, our personal persecution of the ones we love most, etc.

Becker seems to shift back and forth in discussing the neurosis of normality and just plain neurosis. He seems almost to contradict himself over and over. And yet, how could it be otherwise? As Becker himself says:

But we can also see at once that there is no line between normal and neurotic, as we all lie [the lie he is talking about is the refusal of reality] and are all bound in some ways by the lies. Neurosis is, then, something we all share; it is universal. (pp. 178-179)

The Disease of Perfection

Today, the need to be "normal" is overwhelming, so overwhelming that we are increasingly alert to signs of "abnormality." Once having discovered a flaw, we immediately sound the alarm and set our forces of protection into motion. But protection of whom? This is the confusion. Protection of "them"? Of "us"?

The neurosis grows and spreads, fastening its hold upon us all, forcing us to face our own illusions. An epoch is passing, another is beginning. The veil of accepted reality that stands between us and the world is being brutally torn away. We are being forced back upon our resources and are doomed to create our own realities. The danse macabre begins its measured beat again. Its rhythm grows wilder and wilder as the specter of death grows stronger daily. We are once again under the shadow, and this time it is not an impersonal and impassioned doom ruled by external fate. This time man has fashioned his own death. This time death comes directly from the brilliance of his rational mind. It comes out of the intelligence which he so passionately enshrines in his cathedrals of education. It is the same intelligence to which he pays homage in his clinics, institutions, and treatment centers.

The madness of his sanity, the stupidity of brilliance has split the atom and has rent asunder his illusory world. Suddenly we are naked, thrown back upon our lonely selves. Now we are forced to stand upon the only ground left to us—the immediacy of our own personal experience and our own interpretation of that experience.

In *Will Therapy and Truth and Reality*, Otto Rank (1945) said:

While the average well-adjusted man can make the reality that is generally accepted as truth into his own truth, the searcher after truth seeks and finds his own truth which he wants to make general—that is real. (p. 251)

A few short years ago, the average, well-adjusted man had a generally accepted reality which he could borrow as his own truth. Now each individual is being forced to seek and find *his* truth, not out of choice, but out of the force of external exigencies against which there is no buffer. The anguish of man today is that former truths are now his lies. He has been catapulted away from his illusions with brutal violence. As he is hurled into the spaces of his own experience, he clutches desperately at a few shreds of illusion remaining to him—his own normality.

In a deeper sense, to be normal is to be safe—safe from death, disability, and folly, safe from all the properties of those *not normal* ones. Let them take all those properties we disclaim and carry them away from us on the twentieth century nefs des fous (our institutions, clinics, treatment centers, special classes, etc.). It is they who bear the burden of our abnormality. As long as they are out there, just beyond our reach, we are safe. They are our safety. They take away our abnormality, and we are made normal.

There is a sense of desperation in our ever increasing concern with deviance and disability. We are obsessed with it, just as we are obsessed with normality. Like the Island of Ceram, when a whole village suffers from sickness, we construct our ships, our programs, projects, and so forth, and as they are launched the people chant, "Oh all ye sickness, ye small poxes, agues, retardation, mental illness, learning and developmental disabilities, who have visited us so long and wasted us so sorely, but who now cease to plague us, we have made our ships ready for you. Float away from us."

Otto Rank said that the neurotic was the normal made aware. The neurotic was on a way-station between normality and creativity. Creativity was the process of seeking and finding one's own truth and trying to make it real. For Becker, normality is neurosis, a state of "being" in which one lives out universal lies without awareness of the lies. The neurotic, as we know him, is the individual who has discovered the lies and cannot live with the discovery, but he will not do anything else. He is caught at the beginning of a journey which he will not take. He is in pain, suspended between illusion and life. Thus, normal and neurotic are conditions of incompleteness, of unrealized potential, of disability, or delayed development. Both are illusions of normality; one is without awareness of the illusion; the other is aware, but desperately trying to patch the old illusions into a workable oblivion. Neither voluntarily suspends the illusion; both are being forced by the circumstances of our modern lives to relinquish these claims.

A recognition of sorts is beginning to appear in cultural reflections of ourselves. Our movies, our literature, our modern iconography are revealing the depth of ourselves. Strange antiheroes appear upon our screens, our stages, in our books, and our art. In the darkness of a theatre we acknowledge ourselves in the kinky characters looking down at us and acting out our abnormal normality. We laugh and cry and clap and cheer and recognize ourselves without our masks. We break through to the multiple dimensions of our truer nature in those new portrayals of ourselves. We acknowledge their deviance and our own and make a celebration of the fact.

But in the daily market place of our lives we continue to hide. We conceal ourselves behind our work, our rituals, and our customs. We ask our professionals—our teachers and care-givers to help us maintain our delusions a little longer. We ask them to search out and find the ones who do not fit. Help them become like us. Normalize them. Perhaps in normalizing them we can normalize ourselves.

For at one level, we know this is lunacy and we are living it out. But, like Rank's neurotic we are caught—unable to move, unable to take that first step away from the common reality with which we deluded ourselves so long. That first step is a lonely step. It is a step without illusions, without the comfort of normality. That pulls the world from under us. That puts us out beyond our depths, without a ship to float on except the ship of fools.

That journey we will not take. We will not move onto that ship away from the comfort and body warmth of the physical masses. Although we speak a different language and are intensely aware of the delusions, we involve ourselves in their lunacy, knowing that the ones we point to are no more foolish, disabled, or stupid than we are. We know that we can comfort and console the extruded ones, give them hope and help, ease their loneliness and sorrow.

But let us not delude ourselves and identify our fate with the illusion of normality. Let us not borrow the false reality that goes with the illusion. Nor should we lend ourselves to the endless anguish and despair of the enlightened neurotic. For this is a fruitless and empty course. Let us make our peace with the deluded ones, as well as the extruded ones. Let us love them both and, if possible, give them peace out of our own peace. And for a handful at least, leave the charted path and blaze a way in the wilderness; for on the other side of enlightened neurosis is creativity. Creativity is our hope, our answer, our new enlightenment. To quote Otto Rank again, "The searcher after truth seeks and finds his own truth—and then makes it general—that is, real" (1945, p. 251).

He fashions a new reality, a reality in which normal and abnormal are without meaning—a new reality without a ship of fools.

The Illusion of Reason

From this perspective our major moral problem in caring for others is what has happened to those who dedicate their life to caring. They have almost exclusively identified themselves with "science" and reason, and have subjected themselves to years of training to learn to control their immediate sentience of others through that reason. They make an equation between professional caring and reason. They put what we call "reason" between themselves and those who are clients and students. They identify reasoning about others as their major tool and extrareasoning apprehension of others as suspect.

Perhaps we have come to a time in history when we should begin to question our solidarity with Western civilization's definition of reason and its derivative, social "science," and examine their cost to us and those with whom we have a helping covenant. In his book *Psychology and Madness*, Michel Foucault (1973) has said:

Renaissance culture put its values to the test and engaged them in combat in a way that was more ironic than tragic. Reason, too, recognized itself as being duplicated and dispossessed of itself: it thought itself wise, and it was mad; it thought it knew and it knew nothing; it thought itself righteous and it was insane: knowledge led one to the shades and the forbidden world, when one thought one was being led by the eternal light. (p. 77)

To paraphrase Foucault we might say that our social "science" training, which emphasizes the ideology of reason as the path to helping others

is more ironic than tragic. Our professional union with "reason" thought itself wise, and it was mad; it thought it knew and it knew nothing; it thought itself righteous and it was insane: Our knowledge has led us to the shades and the forbidden world, when we thought we were being led by the eternal light.

Our denial of modes of apprehending others and their world outside the boundaries of reason and psychology has estranged us from them and from ourselves. The medium is the message. The mental medium we use conveys our message to our care-receiving counterparts, our so-called retarded others, our so-called irrational others. They cannot come to us openly with their unconcealed selves when we limit our approach to them to our "unnatural" reason. This limitation conveys to them a denial of their right to exist as they are. By inference we are saying, "I will be logical with you nonlogical people, I will be intelligent with you nonintelligent people. I will be reasonable with you irrational people. I will grasp you only with my reasonable mind and teach you to be like me in my reasonableness." The message is clear: "I will not accept your existence as it is."

"Come," we say, "this is a reasonable world we live in; and you too must reason like the rest of us. This is your price of admission to society. This is the identity bracelet that will save you from being locked up. I will offer myself to you only if you come to me on these acceptable grounds of existence."

This rite of reason, which surrounds everything we do, drives them further away from us and into their own shades, drives them away from the world we offer them. We cannot say, "*Be in the world* as you are." They have no way of knowing, as we seem to have no way of knowing, that the world we offer them is probably mad, not reasonable, when we put it to the test of the criteria of reason provided us by our culture and our profession. This lie of reason denies the extrareasoning ways used by all persons in responding to, and acting upon, their world. It denies the extrareasoning motivations, and rationalizations surrounding our actions, decisions, or convictions.

There is a play within a play where we act out sanity and logic and reasonableness and thus deceive ourselves, like an audience within the play watching reasonable men do reasonable things. But the holocaust of Nazi Germany, of Hiroshima, of Mai Lai, of Watergate, is the outer play—the real play. And the outer play is made of the same stuff as those neighbors whom we take as clients and try to convince of their differences. We convey to them that they are insane and we are not. They are stupid and we are not.

But that is because we professionals may have been taken in by the play within the play and have become actors acting out our assigned parts. Our part in the play is good works through reason and rational knowledge. We are the "scientist"-professionals.

As long as we are mainly that, we separate ourselves from them. We lie both to ourselves and to them about who we are and who they are. We lie to them about their differences from us. There is no real difference. We do not say that we, the great mass, are only more socially malleable, more capable of acting then they. We do not say, "this is a charade we're in, this inner play, and if you knew that, there would be no need to be alone, shut off from the rest of us crazies, us stupids. And if we then locked you up you would know we are only trying to prove the reality of this inner play, the play about our sanity and wisdom."

What is this "reason" we worship so blindly? Where did it come from? What does it do for us? It first gave us the illusion of mastery of the world. It has flourished vigorously and prolifically since the "Enlightenment." It promised to lead us to the eternal light and therefore we built temples to it, our universities and schools.

The successful French Revolutionaries, immediately after their victories, dedicated the Madeline as a Temple of Reason—a temple, ironically, which was to commemorate and celebrate Napoleon's Grand Armée. Shortly after its construction that temple became a religious shrine, but in the first full flush of victory those men and women of the French Revolution offered their own temple to their own fraternity of heroic reasonableness. And then, in a very reasonable fashion, they began the bloody execution of each other in the midst of their reasonable chaos, until Napoleon forced his ego-maniacal rule upon them.

The Language of Reason

The language of reason is the kind of thinking men are capable of, the kind of brilliance that, under the exigencies of having to kill each other more efficiently in World War II, developed the ultimate destructive weapon, the atomic bomb.

This may sound like a polemic against reason, but it is not that. It is a call for the acceptance of what exists. What we call "reason" is a conventional wisdom, a general consensus, if you will, of what reason is. It is a long forgotten agreement among men that we will exclude from the category "reason" all processes through which we receive knowledge about the world and wisdom about life around us, which are not subject to cognition and logic. It is a tyranny of a particular mind set, a particular limited group of mental structures over all other sentient apprehension of the world. The terms sentient and apprehend are used here for a particular purpose. Sentient is defined as "(1) Having sense perception; conscious; (2) Experiencing feeling or sensation. The mind." Apprehend is defined, "to grasp mentally; understand."

There are ways of understanding, of having sense perception, of feeling or sensation, of consciousness of things that are not included in the limited boundaries we allow to "reason." The *New Heritage Dictionary* definition of reason is "The basis or motive for an action, decision, or conviction."

Isn't this definition a contradiction to the prevailing ideology of "reason"? Doesn't that ideology see reason as divorced from motivation, divorced from justification? Does it not see reason as something purer than that, something undiluted by irrational impulses, drives, biases, etc.?

As far back as 1941 Otto Rank wrote in *Beyond Psychology*,

My main thesis which was derived from a crisis in psychology appears quite applicable to our present general bewilderment, inasmuch as it lays bare the irrational roots of human behavior which psychology tries to explain rationally in order to make it intelligible, that is, acceptable. When I first realized that people, though they may think and talk rationally—and even behave so—yet live irrationally, I thought that "beyond" individual psychology simply meant social or collective psychology until I discovered that this too is generally conceived of in the same rational terms.... (p. 11) Thus, what we need is an irrational language with a new vocabulary.... (pp. 12-13) For the most part what we call "irrational" is just natural; but our "rationale" has become so unnatural that we see everything natural as irrational. (pp. 14-15)

He then goes on to say something very important for those of us who work with variant children.

Hence our psychology as the climax of man's self-rationalization is inadequate to explain change because it can only justify the type representing the existing social order of which it is an expression. (p. 15)

This was said more than thirty-five years ago, but in spite of its profound implications it has not been heard by those who find themselves in the business of "justifying the 'type' representing the existing social order." We have been justifiers of the social order. We have been sleepwalkers, unaware of what we are doing. Unknowingly, we have been justifying the unnatural, man-made order surrounding us by elevating the representative type in that existing social order to the pinnacle position of normal man, ideal man; and we have judged as inadequate those extruded from the social mainstream, because they do not fit this standard. We have judged them against the model man, and the model man is an unnatural man, a myth.

One of the characteristics mythified in this representative type was "reason." Above all, the ideal against which we judged all others was the appearance of reason. We did not look inside the heads of the living, breathing models of the social ideal. We judged them by surface appearances and accepted, at face value, their normality, or their appearance of such.

The Tyranny of Reason

Ruth Benedict's study of cultures (1961) helps us understand how certain human patterns are authenticated and others are inauthenticated. If she is correct in saying that the authenticated ones move more and more toward exaggeration, then there are profound implications for our choice of a particular state of reason. We would understand why Rank should say that our rationale has become so unnatural that we see everything natural as irrational.

This kind of thinking puts "scientist"-professionals in quite a difficult position. They find themselves in a reversed field. The standards for normal or ideal social members now come under serious suspicion. This is very disconcerting. If the model now becomes the unnatural, then what is the basis for calling our labeled fellows unnatural or abnormal?

If we are, as Rank says, only justifying the type representing the existing social order, then aren't our professional practices a form of tyranny? If Rank is right and we see everything natural as irrational, then those we have made exceptional are the natural ones. If Ruth Benedict is right about culture exaggerating the characteristics of the chosen type, then we can begin to suspect that what psychology calls rational has really become unnatural. As a matter of fact, to prevent the cultural requirements for human types from distorting what is natural in human being, we badly need our intractable ones, those who for one reason or another are not malleable and cannot be molded to the requirements and expectations of culture. They are our saving grace. They prevent culture from suffocating humans. If their condition is rooted in the genes, then we badly need their gene pool to keep from becoming totally unnatural.

What is being suggested, in phenomenological language, is that we should welcome variant children. Rather than spend so much time looking for cures for them we should spend more time accommodating to them. They are a precious natural resource which we should use as a standard against which to measure the extent of unnaturalness we are nurturing in the plastic ones. It should help us counter the extremes of pathological normality we are fostering.

It is probably not by accident that the limited measuring instrument we call intelligence tests should have been developed in France. It was there that the tyranny of the ideology of reason, so narrowly conceived, became a governing ideology for Western civilization. This instrument, which education has adopted so fervently, has given a technological dimension to that narrow band of human sentience and wisdom acceptable as reason. Ask a psychologist what intelligence is and his hard, circular answer is, "what the intelligence test measures." Is that reasonable?

The School of Reason

For over half a century education has tightened its noose of acceptability over a gradually diminishing group of normal educables. With the help of the human "sciences" educators have arrayed their resources against unchosen qualities outside the iron band called reason, which walls out all human processes outside its ideological confines.

Educators have always talked about serving the whole child; however, they would accept as whole only the child who functioned well within the narrow confines they marked off as reason. Furthermore, the vast territories of receptivity to the inflow of the world outside these confines were declared off limits for these children as long as they operated in the territory of school. It is not only that these children were not encouraged to use these capacities for knowledge about the world, but they were actively discouraged from using them. The wholeness of other children, who lacked this specialized talent for learning through cognition, was discarded. The school ignored all of their other capacities for growth and development and simply declared them ineducable.

This means that much human material was discarded as low-grade or marred when put to this ideological test of educability. The population that was chosen by education through a set of increasingly finer screens represented a relatively limited range of natural traits and capacities in human beings. Intelligence and achievement, as displayed in cognitive processes, was the sine-qua-non of reasonableness; and, therefore, educability. Those who did not pass the intelligence test of reasonableness were discarded. Likewise, those who could not engage the exclusive curriculum of cognition, were declared ineducable—at least until we could find ways around this educationally-declared handicap for that individual child.

Unless the student could be brought back into reason; that is unless he or she could be exclusively cognitive while in the classroom, education was not possible. It was not so long ago (perhaps fifteen years) that both educators and superintendents of mental hospitals assured us that there was no point to classrooms in mental hospitals. When the child was "cured," and only then, he or she could be educated. Reasonableness and nonreasonableness were mutually exclusive human qualities.

In such statements and behaviors the professional community totally denied and repressed the existence of the rational and irrational mixture within *themselves*. They repressed the fact that a major part of their lives was as irrational as the condition of even those children who were captives in mental hospitals. Our dreams are the most striking example of this.

Over time, the kind of process that Ruth Benedict says operates in all cultures to develop an extreme form of the chosen type had happened in the narrowing, increased selectivity of schools. Together with the social "science" practitioners they had ruled out more and more students who were not eligible for rational education. The schools, then, became the breeder pens for the chosen reasoning mind, and the place where society very early made its choice of rejectees. It was an effective way to select and discard for later social membership.

Social "science" practitioners cooperated in this process of successively narrowing the definition. Both students and teachers, over a period of two or three generations, began to be exposed to a more and more restrictive range of the general population. The images of normality in their own minds also became more and more limited because they were exposed to a nonrepresentative sample of the population. Special classes and exclusions ruled out the others.

Now, with PL 94-142: Education of the Handicapped Act, 1976, we are faced with the readmission of what Goddard called weak minds and diseased minds into the classroom, i.e., minds that function outside the tight ideological band called reason. It is certainly not a mandate to teach anything that does not fall into this narrow scope. It merely mandates that we cannot exclude those characteristics of functioning minds we call irrational. This does present a dilemma, because essentially ours is a cognitive curriculum. It is difficult enough to present this curriculum to the most reasonable or rational among us even with all of the psychological knowledge available to back us up in this endeavor. What are we going to do now that it is mandated that unreasonable people be integrated into the educational mainstream? We know how difficult it is to teach rational and cognitive knowledge. We know that behavior modification, perceptual training, megavitamin and nutritional therapy, and even psychotherapy have their limitations. How can we make them rational in order to involve them in our curriculum, or how can we find ways to teach them the same curriculum that gets around their rational limitations? We do not ask serious questions about the curriculum of reason. Nor do we ask questions about the reasonableness of our criteria of educableness. Most important we do not ask questions about our rational images of human beings.

There has been a gradual, dawning realization of the craziness of man. Our picture of man as a reasoning and reasonable animal has been so flagrantly violated in the last forty to fifty years that we are reeling from total disorientation. We have lost our identity. We feel that we have gone insane, that the world is insane. We do not believe what has happened to us since these momentous experiences fall into that vast uncharted wasteland that is off limits to reason. All of these irrational things are unreasonable, and therefore we cannot deal with them.

This is a lonely awareness. Each of us faces it separately and questions our own reason; because after all, the national media uses the language of reason when it talks about body counts, about the inevitability of nuclear reactor plants going awry and wiping us out, of the social security funds running out, of killings at Attica, of groups of youth taking over the city, etc. We feel mad because we feel the schizophrenic split between what we experience and the language of reason used by society to make irrational things appear reasonable. It is the language of the Mad Hatter which seems to make sense, but actually makes no sense at all.

We need to invent a new irrational language to talk about irrational things. The time has come to reclaim ourselves in those students we have ruled out. They are the true representatives of all that we are, and not just the unrepresentative outcasts of what our society says we are. "Science" has not and cannot rule them out of existence in the way it pretends to have done. The rational language of "science" cannot give us information about them because they do not fit a rational language. They are indeterminate humans in the determinate spotlight of "science."

Implications for Intervention

If one adopts this existential perspective the obvious action implications are advocacy. We look at abused children who are "called out of their name," that is, called something other than their own name—learning disabled, schizophrenic, retarded, etc. They are abused in the same sense that we have come to recognize family child abuse; only, in this case, the "family" is a much larger unit than the biological family. Through the abusing process the child's "being" is destroyed. He experiences his own existence as inauthentic. The child pays the price of the family's existential agony.

He also absorbs the inauthentic states of the larger family. Since these states are not allowed to "be" in the world, they must have clandestine existence somewhere. Through the alchemy of reclamation in the "other," the child becomes the continuous receptacle of disembodied inauthentic states that have been "thrown out" upon him by the bearers. Thus, these existential states are experienced as alien to the existence of the projector and the receptacle child "itself" is experienced as the alienated possessor of the disowned state.

In order to understand the more general process and to understand how to advocate for the inauthenticated child, let us look at the way it works in a biological family unit. The dynamics of child abuse are clear and recognizable here, because the family is a small, microscopic unit that we can grasp and understand. Over and over again such children are referred to psychological and psychiatric clinics by the abusing parents or by others because of their "difference." They are referred for "learning disability," "emotional disturbance," "social maladjustment," "retardation," "behavior problem," "brain damage," and so on. It is only through subtle cues that you begin to encounter the child-abuse aspect of the case. Usually, you do locate the differences the parents or the schools point out to you. However, by the time you see the child, the interaction between the parents' brutalization and the subtle cues the child originally gave out to cause the parents to fix him upon the cross of their existential anguish, is totally obscured. Of course we expect that a brutalized child does have learning difficulties, a battered child is brain damaged, a sexually, physically, or emotionally abused child is disturbed. What else could one expect? When we look closely at the situation, whatever else we find, the child is the family hostage, the sacrificial lamb, the family scapegoat.

We are beginning to take both an ethical and compassionate stand against child abuse in biological families. In the exaggerated cases of child abuse we are beginning to see very clearly the part the family plays in the problem, and although we deal with the existential anguish of the other family members, we advocate for the child.

Those who have professional responsibility for such children must take the next courageous step. They must recognize special children for what they are. They are the victims of social child abuse. Therefore, the professional must stand against this abuse and help authenticate the child's state, whatever it is, and insist that he or she be allowed *to be in the world*, in the same measure and to the same degree that authenticated states, called "normality," are allowed to be in the world. The child's existence in his or her own state must not be violated either by withholding rights and privileges accorded others, or by denying authenticity through enforced change procedures.

This calls for changes in the experience which professionals have of such children. Professional experiencing of the child usually mimics public experiencing of the child as inauthentic unless he or she changes. This new perspective calls for the professionals to reexperience and authenticate for themselves those parts which they have aliented as inauthentic. It is only in being with and identifying with those parts of the self that the professional enters into communion with the inauthenticated child.

The advocacy role of the professional also encompasses teaching the child to experience the authenticity of his or her state of being, and to recognize the projections of others upon that being.

At the same time it requires intervention in the world to allow the child to be just as he or she is and to teach the child to impose the same demands upon the surrounding world.

References

BECKER, E. *The denial of death*. New York: Free Press, 1973.

BENEDICT, R. *Patterns of culture*. Boston: Houghton Mifflin, 1961.

FOUCAULT, M. *Madness and civilization; a history of insanity in the age of reason*. Translated from the French by Richard Howard. New York: Vintage Books, 1973.

LORENZ, K. *On aggression*. New York: Bantam Books, 1967.

RANK, OTTO. *Will therapy and truth and reality*. New York: Knopf, 1945.

RANK, OTTO. *Beyond psychology*. New York: Dover Publications, 1941.

VANIER, J. *Eruption to hope*. Toronto: Griffin House, 1971.

YABLONSKY, L. *Synanon: The tunnel back*. Baltimore: Penguin Books, 1972.

ZWEIG, P. *The heresey of self-love: A study of subversive individualism*. New York: Harper & Row, Harper Colophon Books, 1970.

Index

279